D1539107

JOHN LOGAN:
THE COLLECTED POEMS

JOHN LOGAN:

BOOKS AND CHAPBOOKS 1955–1989

POETRY

Cycle for Mother Cabrini, 1955.

Ghosts of the Heart: New Poems, 1960.

Spring of the Thief: Poems 1960–1962, 1963.

The Zigzag Walk: Poems 1963–1968, 1969.

Cycle for Mother Cabrini, revised edition, 1972.

The Anonymous Lover: New Poems, 1973.

Poem in Progress (Chapbook), 1975.

John Logan: Poems / Aaron Siskind: Photographs (Chapbook), 1976.

The Bridge of Change (Pamphlet), 1978.

Only The Dreamer Can Change The Dream: Selected Poems, 1981.

The Bridge of Change: Poems 1974–1980, 1981.

The Transformation: Poems January to March 1981 (Chapbook), 1983.

John Logan: The Collected Poems, 1989.

FICTION AND CRITICISM

The House That Jack Built; or A Portrait of the Artist as a Sad Sensualist, 1974.

A Ballet for the Ear: Interviews, Essays, and Reviews, 1983.

The House That Jack Built, revised, trade edition, 1985.

JOHN LOGAN:
THE COLLECTED POEMS

BOA EDITIONS, LTD. · *BROCKPORT, NEW YORK* · *1989*

ISBN 0-918526-64-7 (Cloth)   First Edition
                                                                LC #: 88-71552

The following poems, previously collected in *Only the Dreamer Can Change the Dream: Selected Poems*, copyright © 1981 by John Logan, are reprinted with the permission of The Ecco Press. All rights reserved:

from *Cycle for Mother Cabrini*: "Pagan Saturday," "A Dialogue with La Mettrie," "The Death of Southwell" and "Cycle for Mother Cabrini."

from *Spring of the Thief*: "Monologues of the Son of Saul," "To a Young Poet Who Fled," "The Thirty-three Ring Circus," "On Reading Camus in Early March," "Song on the Dread of a Chill Spring," "Lament in Spring," "Lines on His Birthday," "Tale of a Later Leander," "On a Photograph by Aaron Siskind," "Eight Poems on Portraits of the Foot," "Spring of the Thief" and "Whistling Wings."

Grateful acknowledgment is made to the editors of the following publications in which many of the poems in this volume (or earlier versions of them) originally appeared:

Accent, The American Poetry Review, Antaeus, Audience, Beyond the Square, Big Table, Boundary 2, The Brockport Review, Buff, Cafe Solo, Chelsea Review, Chicago Choice, Chicago Review, Choice, The Commonweal, The Critic, Evergreen Review, The Fair, Field, The Fifties, Gallery Series One, The Georgia Review, The Greenfield Review, The Hawaii Review, The Hudson Review, Indian P.E.N. (Bombay), *The Iowa Review, Ironwood, Jeopardy, Journal of Creative Behavior, Kayak, The Kenyon Review* (First Series), *The Kenyon Review* (Second Series), *Lillabulero, The Literary Review, The Massachusetts Review, Memphis State Review, The Minnesota Review, Modern Poetry Studies, Mouth, Mutiny, The Nation, New Letters, New World Writing, The New Yorker, The New York Quarterly, New Mexico Quarterly, New University Thought, The North American Review, Northern Review* (Montreal), *The Northwest Review, The Ohio Review, The Ontario Review, Our Original Sins, Panjandrum, The Paris Review, Partisan Review, Poetry, Poetry Dial, Poetry Flash, Poetry Northwest, Poetry Now, Prarie Schooner, Quarterly Review of Literature, Rapport, Revista Mexicana de Literatura* (Mexico City), *Salmagundi, The Seattle Review, The Sewanee Review, The Sixties, Sonora Review, The Southern Review, The Spokesman, Statements, The Sullivan Slough Review, Tar River Poetry, The Texas Quarterly, Toothpaste, Voyages* and *West Hills Review*.

The following poems from *The Bridge of Change: Poems 1974–1980*, "Poem in Progress" and "The Bridge of Change," were originally issued as chapbooks: *Poem in Progress*, San Francisco: Dryad Press, 1975; *The Bridge of Change*, Brockport, NY: BOA Editions, Ltd., 1978.

The following poems from *The Zigzag Walk: Poems 1963–1968* and *The Anonymous Lover: New Poems*, "On a Photograph by Aaron Siskind," "Eight Poems on Portraits of the Foot," "A Suite of Six Pieces for Siskind" and "Three Poems on Aaron Siskind's Photographs," were also collected in the chapbook: *Aaron Siskind: Photographs/John Logan: Poems*, Rochester, NY: Visual Studies Workshop Press, 1976.

The following poems from *Manhattan Movements: Poems 1981–1987*, "Gallery Walk," "Avocado," "February Awakening," "The Piano Scholar," "The Transformation" and "A Visit to Bill Merwin at His Hawaiian Home," were originally collected in the chapbook, *The Transformation: Poems January to March 1981*, San Francisco: Pancake Press, 1983.

Publications by BOA Editions, Ltd., a not-for-profit corporation under section 501(c)(3) of the United States Internal Revenue Service Code, are made possible in part with the assistance of grants from the Literature Program of the New York State Council on the Arts and the Literature Program of the National Endowment for the Arts, a Federal Agency, as well as with the assistance of grants and donations from private individuals, corporations and foundations.

Cover photograph by Aaron Siskind.

Photograph of John Logan by Christopher Felver.

BOA logo by Mirko.

Designed and typeset by Visual Studies Workshop, Rochester, New York.

BOA Editions, Ltd.
A. Poulin, Jr., President
92 Park Avenue
Brockport, New York 14420

CONTENTS

SPRING OF THE THIEF: Poems 1960–1962

THE ZIGZAG WALK: Poems 1963–1968

THE ANONYMOUS LOVER: New Poems (1973)

THE BRIDGE OF CHANGE: Poems 1974–1979

MANHATTAN MOVEMENTS: Poems 1981–1987

PREFATORY NOTE

While editing the poems for this volume of John Logan's *Collected Poems*, we have kept as much as possible to the last printed versions of the poems. In most cases, these are the versions that appear in *Only the Dreamer Can Change the Dream: Selected Poems* (New York: The Ecco Press, 1981) and *The Bridge of Change: Poems 1974-1980* (Brockport, NY: BOA Editions, Ltd., 1981). However, the need to bring the full text into consistency has required our having to make a few, small technical changes (in spelling, punctuation, and the like) and to restore a line in "New York Scene: May 1958" that was inadvertently dropped in Logan's *Selected Poems*. Moreover, for all of *Cycle for Mother Cabrini*, we relied entirely on the text in the revised edition (Berkeley: Cloud Marauder Press, 1972); and for the order of the sections in "A Suite of Six Pieces for Siskind," originally collected in *Spring of the Thief* (1963), we relied on the revised order in *John Logan: Poems/Aaron Siskind: Photographs* (Rochester, NY: Visual Studies Workshop, 1976).

The poems that make up the final section of this volume offered a somewhat greater challenge. The manuscript versions of some poems in *Manhattan Movements*, which John Logan was still working on at the time of his death, occasionally differ from the magazine versions of the poems, and it is clear that many of the differences are either later revisions by Logan himself or changes suggested by the editors of magazines. Decisions had to be made as to which were the best readings (or combinations of readings), and we hope that in all cases we have made decisions that preserve the level, authenticity and strength of Logan's characteristic poetry. (Thus, we also have not included one poem from the manuscript, "Tribute to Isabella Gardner" [1982], although it had been published in a journal, because we believed that it was not consistent with the level of Logan's usual work.)

In order to make this volume as comprehensive as possible, we have included four poems which were not part of the original manuscript version of *Manhattan Movements*. "Homage to John the Baptist," "Spring Revelations," "My Daughter's Wedding" and "Letter to My Son" are from a folder in which John Logan kept poems to circulate among friends for their reactions and to rework (although "My Daughter's Wedding" [1982] also had been published in a journal). Limited to the kinds of choices available to us, we believe the texts included in this book are faithful to Logan's spirit and style in his later poetry, including his increasing reliance on a combination of isolated and paratactic, though rich and resonating, phrases and longer breathing units, as well as on the dominant variation of eight, ten, and thirteen syllable lines. (In keeping with his wish that this book be a volume of his "collected" rather than of his "complete" poems, we have left out those poems which John Logan decided were not to be part of his earlier collections.)

Given our professional association and friendship with John Logan that spanned more than two decades and included a wide variety of totally frank and detailed suggestions for a number of the poems he wrote during those years and shared with us for our comments, we are confident that he would have welcomed our editorial judgment in the preparation of this book for publication. In naming us to execute this and possibly subsequent volumes of his work, we are sure he understood that we would not be any less venturesome or responsible than he knew us to be. It is with this confidence, tempered and strengthened by our sustained high regard for his work, that we offer the present volume of John Logan's collected poems.

—Jerome Mazzaro

—A. Poulin, Jr.

*Well, I am still a traveler and I don't know where
I live. If my home is here, inside my breast,
light it up! And I will invite you in as my first guest.*

CYCLE FOR MOTHER CABRINI

(1955)

to Guenevere

CYCLE FOR MOTHER CABRINI

1   A Chance Visit to Her Bones

I thank God Mother Cabrini's
Body is subject to laws
Of decay. To me it is
A disservice when flesh

Will not fall from bones
As God for His glory
Sometimes allows. I say this
For flesh is my failing:

That it shall fall is my
Salvation. That it shall not
Conquer is my blind hope.
That it shall rise again

Commanding, is my fear.
That it shall rise changed
Is my faith. I think
I can love this saint

Who built high schools
And whose bones I came upon
Today. I laugh a little
At the wax mask that smiles

Surely through her box of glass:
Artificial faces cannot
Frighten one who remembers
No face is real for long.

Blessed Mother Cabrini
Lives here her saint's life,
I said, she sees me all;
I only see her face

Mask, and see her habit
Given form by bones
Which carried about her flesh,
Gone now. The bones will rise

To carry changed flesh
And I may walk—I
Might walk with her!
Whom I seek to pray to

Some, and strain
To love. Moisten me
With dust from her bones.
I see their shape—help me

Love them help think of
Breast white doves that rise
Over earth-smelling fields
Their wings tremble for her

Birth, as I wait: mine
Is a dry waiting.
Her mask stares, she
Stirs—ah

Her bones move *me*!

2 Recollection

i.

I found your bones that lay
Off the highschool hallway
And drummed them with my need;
They rang and rose and hurried

Me. I bought and set
Your picture in my wallet
And chose a cheap ring,
A piece of junk but something

Your sisters sell; to me
Its feel and pull heavy
On my fingerbone wore
In for a time the terror

Of your delicate flesh, the scant
Weight within the fragrant
Bones that it seemed turned
To me as to the bright and the unburned.

ii.

Blessed Mother I know
You met me once in Chicago.
I didn't go there
To hunt for saints (or anywhere):

You bowed and smiled at me
Out of a film biography.
I don't know why I went
Except perhaps for amusement

And rest; your skill is hid
Behind a sweet and lurid
Piety O queen
Of a Holy wood unseen—

Your eyes and art sent
A deep tiredness apparent
To me as an expected thing
But (until I knew) unsettling

Because of breathlessness
And a hot and blood shocked duress
At my ribs, that sickened me,
And turned the colors of the city.

iii.

Long years Mother had gone
Before I met you in Tryon
Park although you knew me
At Chicago and eternally.

One time in New York again
Under the wicked regimen
Of grace, I thought to come
To your girls' kingdom

To the middy world of your tomb
By text, principal, and schoolroom.
You know I did not go;
I went another place though:

Can I say what you did
Those days I invalid
At church, ambiguous at its door
Was tried by my confessor;

Without luster hair
Sprouts at arm's root bitter
Sediment upon the flesh dead
The nail slides from folded

Skin, so shall I be
Till Christ reafford the luxury
By which bodies sing
And souls have their breathing;

Sweet virgin it was you
That left the gay retinue
To cry me grace at its head
Till I like your bones was not dead.

iv.

Saint who overlaps
Our lives who knows the mishaps
Of our times the flaws
Of men no longer outlaws

Even; who knows our schools
Our stores our gods and business rules;
Saw charts rise and fall
In your chromium hospital—

You helped shape our city
And the city in the sky:
Now help me shape your beauty
In this scarred and remade eye.

3   Mother Cabrini Crosses the Andes

i.

The tiny saint got the best mule
Though an opera singer was in the party,
And St. Joseph the muleteer was gentle
And helped a lot; providentially,

For the soundest beast leads
And she had never ridden and was jittery—
Tried to guide! Though she learned
Early to be passive to the sea.

Small and weightless as she was
She could have risen to the saddle
Or St. Joseph would have tossed her
Humbly, could she have put

Her foot into his hand
But she could not, ascending
Rather from upon a chair
And set off cowled in furs

"Like a monk" (her saving comment)
Or Xavier in the mountains of the orient.

ii.

And the air in the high Andes
Was thin and lucid as milk
Or fire, or as violets she sailed
In boats in Lombardy,

A child afraid of the water
But sick for the fire and milk
Of the sea's wake and for the souls
That flashed like fish

For the souls that love like milk
And like fire, for the spring soul
That bursts quiet as a violet
And swings upon its thin

Stem to flame at the sun,
Ridiculous as a nun.

       iii.

Had she known the pressure
Here will bleed the skin
Or that the muleteers would be
Too busy to say the Rosary,
That she would fail to jump her mule a-

Cross a crevasse, would fall
Into St. Joseph's arms and
Faint in the snow bank that flanks
The rim (the heights of her cheeks
More pale more glowing than crystal
Vanishing on her habit—eyes

As they opened as soft as furs),
Or had she somehow discovered
She and Mother Chiara
Would spend the evening in a bar
Beside the pampas' edge: she

Would lead the pilgrimage again
Over the high Andes,
Forego the closed cabin,
The turn around the horn; would climb,
Would rest the party at the Cumbre
Again draw breath and for a moment again

Would turn away forever.

     iv.

Air shivered in the Andes
As full of color as blood
Or bells, or ice the saboteurs
Left on Lytle Street
When angered by the sick and alien

They opened her mansion pipes;
Yet what was this to her
Who dynamites hearts: rivets,
Quarries, shapes bricks, and built
In Chicago two hospitals
Besides the one they chilled awhile

And burned a little bit.
But they kicked the sisters out
Of Nicaragua—the schoolgirls no trash
These, necks blue as Andes
Snow and thin as moons: hair

Black as the bird-live valleys;
The saint was away on business—
New Orleans orphanage or the villa
Or the novitiate at old Manresa
On the Hudson. (Or perhaps the hotel
In Seattle.) There was trouble in France

Since the archbishop was on the Riviera,
And the priests turned her a cold
Parisian shoulder, but she moved in
At a gilt estate where the sisters
Had to put up sheets over the many mirrors.

Whether they went on their continents
Or ours the austere skirts
Were strangest brushing by the summer-house
In Rio the intemperate flower parts:
Though here the black was closest
To the holy red that flowed her into God

In Chicago, upon her martyrdom.
She should have died in Lombardy
Safe from a saint's life and the traveler's
Malady that chilled her and brightened
Her gown, like a bell she jangled in her room
Where she rocked and, died, in a wicker chair.

v.

A good mule like God's will and the sea
Does not mind those who disagree
And bore her safely
So that, the stars at easy
Height again, the party
Rested.

But the pampas at night are a sky
Where masses alive and unknown
Are relieved by constellations of bone.

vi.

High cold keen the Cumbre air
As the light from the stone and shattering stars

But there is nowhere mountain air
So cold or keen or bright or
Thin as is Francesca's wrist
Humming hyaline
Along the risen limb.

PAGAN SATURDAY

Hiking out to Ratcliff
School we took our shoes off
In the field of stubble
Where the graveyard ends; we ran
Shouting thru the stalks

Of pain that grow tipped
And colorful as grain.
We swarmed the woods and looked
For fun and fuel and packed enough
To pile and build to a roar

A very satisfying fire.
We set our mouths on hopes
Of stolen corn and raided
An easy field behind a barn;
And burst the milky kernels

On our thumbs. Letting
The fire at one side turn
To ash we buried our yellow
Catch inside its wraps of husk
And later, ate in heights

Of joy the cindered ears.
Then racing along the rim
Of Indian Gully sudden
As fear light as laughter I felt
A creature flare with beauty

At the back of my eye;
I knew my limbs and body
Sang on me sometimes—
But this was brighter than my arms.
Coming back we played

Some rapid hide-and-seek
Among the graves; I hid
Awhile and searched the stone
Face for Mother; and ran on
Into the pointed groves of pine.

GRANDFATHER'S RAILROAD

I think my grandfather knew
I'd never seen a Negro
Before I thought I saw

The shallow trough that cut
The field he showed me real
As a railroad, and reached

North for Kemling Store.
I could have seen the bright
And keen two rails where they hid

Grow so thin I could have
Run, vanishing where they did.
My grandfather told me

The old underground railroad
Wound thru Montgomery
County; he pointed a fine

Haired finger and led
Across the dust-lit land
The believed Negroes — gold

Lithe and wild as the wind
Burned wheatfield.
My grandfather didn't see

My pickaninny doll had three
Pigtails she shook like
Ribboned wings on wires

From the train windows, and fires
Shivered in our captor's eyes
Who cares! the cars of great

Black men roar past
Shadowing the field like clouds
Or giants that seem to slow

And stride as lean as trees
Against the north sky.

A DIALOGUE WITH LA METTRIE

Since thought visibly develops with our organs, why should not the matter of which they are composed be susceptible of remorse also, when once it has acquired, with time, the faculty of feeling?
　　　　　　　—La Mettrie, *Man a Machine* (Leyden, 1748)

Where does one look
To purify the remark of an ancient
Cynic? I am afraid not
To the eighteenth century
And the mechanist La Mettrie;
If he is one, for here
The ambiguity

Begins. Let me explain.
The ancient has us build on
Supposed Plato's supposed
Definition, Man is two-legged
And without any feathers: add,
To tell him from the plucked bird,
His nails are flat.

Now this idea of the dog
Diogenes shook me. But,
Let me say, no more so
Than the mind of La Mettrie.
I think we are not mushrooms
Swollen for a day, nor even
"Flowers bordering a ditch."

And I want a violent leap
Beyond the dog. Do not
Tell me from him as you mark
The ape by his more intelligent

Face. For once there was
A blurred and giddy light
In my enormous eyes.

A few more wheels a few
More springs than in,
Say, your better animal?
And with a closer heart
To fill the brain with blood
And start the delicate moral
Hum in the anxious matter.

Suppose I agree the soul is
An engine, admit Descartes
And the rest never *saw*
Their pair of things—never,
As you say, counted them;
Then here's the ambiguity,
And a further problem:

You say you find an inner
Force in bodies, and watch
The smallest fiber turn
Upon an inner rule.
Now I don't see that this
Is such a clear machine!
In fact I think I wish it were.

For I have weighed
Your evidence: I don't forget
Your newly dead
And opened criminal
Whose still hot heart
Beats like the muscles in the face
Of the severed head.

I don't forget you say
The flesh of bats
Palpitates in death,
And even more of snakes,
That never sweat. "Why then
Do men boast moral
Acts, that hang on these?"

Besides injected warm
Water animates the heart;
The hearts of frogs move
If put in the sun or if the heart
Is placed upon a hot
Table or a stone. If it stops,
It may be poked or bathed.

And Harvey noted this
In toads. (The great physician,
I could add, once
Professionally cut a toad
A burnt witch had kept
For her familiar,
And found it puffed with milk.)

A piece of a pigeon's heart,
Lord Boyle has shown, beats
As the whole one did.
It is these same motions
Twist along the eel,
In spiders or in the tiny
Hands sliced from moles.

And last, Bacon of Verulam
Has in his *Book of Spears*
The case of a traitor caught

And opened alive: his heart
In a pan of boiling water
Leaped several times
To a perpendicular

Height of two feet.
Let us then conclude
Boldly! Man is a machine.
And there is no other thing
Underneath. Except I believe
Ambiguity, with its hope
Or its ancient agony;

For to what do we look
To purify his remarks, or purge
His animal images? What
Piece in us may be cut free
Of the grieved matter of La Mettrie,
That underneath a temporal reeling
Took on this arch of feeling.

MONOLOGUE FOR THE GOOD FRIDAY CHRIST

The good Friday crowd went
In queues to kiss the crux
Fidelis; soon shall each
Have back to the least
Joy and red cent
What he gave up for Lent.

But christ what do we do
That hate pain and can't
Pray and are not able
Not to sin; that stay
Contrite, until night: did you
Not die for us too?

That will not move to welcome,
Or like The Baptist, leap
And so live; or cannot feed
Upon the quick and lean
Locust, are not at home
With the eyed and austere honeycomb?

Are not the nails sweet
The wood that held thy weight
And what other tree ever put
Such leaf or flower or root
But why am I here in my seat
By my sins and your defeat—

I shall read psalms and wait,
But why can I not kiss
The crucifix my lips
Are dry my tongue sticks
In my jaw oh come great
God as the early and the late.

Rains come bind the thorn
From my soul the raged light
Lions from my flesh my sweets
Hold from the dog's hand let
My afflictions be not torn
On the turned spear of the unicorn:

God, God do not die
This afternoon, we but
Enact: but Christ rise
And before Easter light
In us new fire and spring
The cold, burned root of the old!

Our holy master has died;
We kneel and touch lips to our pride.

PROLOGUE AND QUESTIONS
FOR ST. AUGUSTINE
On His Sixteenth Centenary

Adhuc vivunt in memoria mea, de qua multa locutus sum, talium rerum imagines, quas ibi consuetudo mea fixit; it occursantur mihi vigilanti....
—S. Augustini, *Confessionum* X. xxx.

Austin you write all
Our lives and Petrarch
Was sensible to keep you
All his later years
Beside his heart; I too

Have loved this book
Over any other
Have held it in my hand
Long times: have been its author.
But saint I would take hold

Of you with my mind's hand.
Here I only reach and
Catch at you as mind
At memory
Or memory at us.

1

You know them saint tell me
Is it incidental
That Botticelli who left
The best sketch of hell
We have also gave us

Your best picture?
Or that Dante who sent the
Count to read you to find out
What Paradise is about, showed
Hell to Sandro: and began

With an image from your Seventh Book —
The wood, the impassable road,
And animals square in the way?
My guess is he knew you
Would be good for Hell too.

2

In Botticelli's portrait
Do you in your red and yellow
And white Bishop's robe
Care for the solar globe?
And do you hint a saint's

Use of instruments?
Or have you meant by your
Ornamented mitre
And ecstatic frown to say
They should stay with the geometric

Texts in the background? Saint years
Later you were not sure
Whether it was sin to make
Mistakes, later than the garden
Agony and the book —

Voice and child and the fig tree;
And were not sure when souls
Enter bodies, later than
The dialogue Te Deum in Milan,
Retreat and long discussion

At the villa. Surely these
Ambiguities
Are hell at least for lesser
Men: Should we hate
These myths of Mithridates?

And whom shall we go see;
Faustus, Manichee? Or shall we
Watch the shows of Bishop
Ambrose. Or no, read us
Victorinus. Which great

Book next? What debate,
Essay or Poet's Prize?
What woman. Which idea. Place?
What other fruit of what
Tree; and do I dare

To eat another pear?
Your mind hung in the hell
Of minds the tor-
Tured and tumescent
Intellect, unrested:

3

It was a hell of hearts
You spoke of when you lost
Your sweet bedfellow;
The blood's old noise, and in
The loins their ancient sorrowing;

The will that freely will
Choose what alters it,
And goes without us,
Like parts that move themselves,
Or you worm that worked

In Eden. The brass knobs
On doors twist easily
Spring back
And I lift bread to mouth
Without trouble, at the corner

Turn right sin is like this
Why sin is natural as blue is
But drags at joints
Unnaturally
Dries membranes with sand

Is most clinging most cold most
Crabbed of all the casual
Things. And you lost your mother
Just as you learned rejoicing
And before you studied

How not to grieve: your brilliant
Bastard Adeodatus
Died too. Oh in Botticelli's
Picture you watch heaven
And in your Book Ten you

Did but god you kept
A memory of hell.
Is not Lethe best
Of the streams of heaven,
Not most whispered

With the slow blowing
Lotuses of the stars? I have
Felt this rain and it was
Cool in my neck's root;
Saint, is our forgetting

The *least* of the memories of heaven?

LAMENT FOR MISENUS

...atque illi Misenum in litore sicco,
ut venere, vident indigna morte peremptum,
Misenum Aeoliden, quo non praestantior alter
aere ciere viros Martemque accendere cantu.
—P. Vergili Maronis, *Aeneid VI*

By the cold shore we came on
Aeolus' son who lay
Young *ai* who lay
Ruined by his smashed
And slivering horn and spear.
He was Hector's friend and fought
By him; we loved him first
As one to move and fire us
On this bended horn.

It may be he was young
And mad and sounded gods
To combat over the sea;
It may be Triton heard
His echoing horn in caves
Of stone or tombs and pale abandoned
Shells, and challenged him.
But Triton's is a rounder
Horn of the howling sea:

Ai here lies Aeolus' son
Come bury him in the wood;
How use this rock for sorrow
These dried stars' arms this
Rigid face of the fish?˘
Axe now strike the ilex! Pitch
Trees fall quivering
Ashes cleave and the giant
Rowan trees roll from the hill!

We build his pyre with resined
Wood and the long firing
Oak that's interwove
With mourning boughs, and place
The funeral cypress. And last
Arrange on top the towering altar
His radiant arms,
That catch the glint of flames
Underneath the brazen kettles.

These limbs are cold to wash
With water from the fire. This oil
Anoints more durably than tears
This oil anoints more
Durably than tears.
Now lay him on the bier with purple
Clothes beside his coat;
And now this last melancholy
Office tops his pyre.

We turn our eyes aside to
Fix the funeral torch;
The incense burns, the gifts
And meats and chalices of olive oil.
At last the altar ashes
Fall and flames burn out; we pour
Much wine on the red embers.
And here the priest collects
The bones in a bronzed cask,

And walking round us thrice
Sprinkles us with white
Water as with dew he shook
From a branch of the lucky olive;
And says our farewell word.
We bury him, his spear his
Oar and his remembered horn

Beneath a snowy peak,
A massed a blue and airy

Tomb for Aeolus' son.

in memoriam F.C.M.
killed with his father
in a plane crash
17 December 1954

A PATHOLOGICAL CASE IN PLINY

Hirto corde gigni quosdam homines proditur, neque alios fortioris esse industriae,
sicut Aristomenen Messenium qui trecentos occidit Lacedaemonios…
—Plinii, *Naturalis Historia XI.* IXX.

The guards sleep they breathe uneven
Conversation with the
Trees the sharp cicadas
And knots of pine the flames
Have stirred to talk: their light

Shows him rolling in his bonds
As if he dragged his bones
Again beyond a tall
And ghosted mist of blood;
He took three hundred lives

And will not give his own for capture
Even. The smell of searing
Hemp and flesh startles
As the scream of birds—
Should wake the guards of men

Or dead. The fire flares and frames
A running giant his wrists
Caught between his thighs;
A burned and awkward god.
Once he tried the foxes'

Paths out of the shattered quarry.
No way now. One may
Kill his hundreds; still
No way. How can he live
Without his heart. Throw him

To the ground and prepare knives!
Do they by their hate
Or wonder break the breast
He shut to fear? Mock
Or pray as they cut flesh

Crush ribs and lay all open
To the alien chill of air?
No scream tears
From him; the tiny veins
Along his eyelid swell

And pools of sweat gather at its corners.
But they do not see his
Slowly swinging eyes.
They watch his heart; its brown
Hair is whorled and dry.

A SHORT LIFE OF THE HERMIT

The storms are on us, the sailing
Nearly over; you know
The restlessness of the post.
Thus I set down very briefly
What I can
As one who was his friend
As one who poured the lucid
Water over the black or gold
And austere fingers of his hand.

He sprang of highborn parents
Well-to-do. He never
Took to school; in fact
Consistently despised
Your ancient learning. He found
The touch of other children
Also inessential.
He stayed at home and lived, we may
Suppose, by hidden violence.

He lacked a business sense
Or loyalties, and sold
For gifts the good and fertile
Land his fathers kept.
At first he saved a bit
To meet a maiden sister's
Need for funds, until
Impatient at a Sunday text
He took the sister to the nuns.

He forgot his home
And friends and by the narrow
Wisdom of the bee, found
Many holy souls
Zealous for what is good

And began to practice some
Ascetics near the town,
Fighting with his fellows gently
Over the higher things.

The devil with his customary
Care began to try
The joys of villages and taught
The weakness of the body and the strength
Of time. And failed and tried
The things at the navel of the
Belly and came at night
And dared to take a woman's breast
Trembling by his bed.

Although he wept to find
The coals of lust he kept
His mind upon the greater
Heats of hell and sharper
Tremblings of the worm,
And by the holy force
Incarnate in the blood
He fought and beat the agile old
Intelligence of lust.

He worked and ate but once
A day his salt and bread
And drank his water and slept
On a rush mat. He locked
Himself in a tomb. The devils
Lashed and left him dead.
A friend who brought his bread
Bore him to the church and prayed.
He woke and cried for his grave.

Too weak to stand he lay
And sang in his tomb. The devils
Burst the walls in guise
Of animals and goaded

Him. The bull with its horn
The lion its furious eye
The snake its fork and the scorpion,
Young in the holes in its back. They scatter
At light from the roof's crack.

In twenty years his friends
Returned and smashed the tomb;
And he came forth a god
Out of his shrine—white
With spirit and lean with the sacred
Mystery, his body graced
With the rapid games of imps
And the lack of the bloods in meat. Air
In the tomb was thin and sweet.

He told the crowd "The devils
Crash and rumble as boys
Or thieves, are tall as roofs
And heavy. Their mouths are black
Their eyes are dead as the agate
Dawn. Their stony paws
Click on the eggs of souls.
But at the whispered name they shriek,
Vanishing with a cast of heat.

"And all your devils lie;
They're full of psalms and echoes
And rouse to pray and take
The look of a monk. They boom
Or hiss and prance about.
If no one sees, they gnash
Or wail and seem to fall
Into a melancholy fit
Like an angry child.

"At times they prophesy,
Say, a flood or guests.
But what business of theirs
Is this? No one wonders

That they fly ahead.
But if they claim angelic
Sight, they lie! The little-
Known bird in your pure
Soul has a keener eye."

Once he made a basket
Out of stems of reed
And felt a gentle tugging
In his hand; and met
A giant with the withered
Face of birds and long
And whitened arms of men,
Which at the secret name snapped
Into sticks of reed.

And once he felt his ghost
Stand aside, saw it
Climb the lower hills of air
To meet the fallen Lord
Whose morning beauty still
Shivers in the brightness there,
And flings its protean hands
Of light. His soul fought and turned
And stood again in him.

But grieved by fame and many friends
He fled into the upper hills
Of Thebaid. He loved the inner
Mountain best and came out once
To raise some vegetables for guests,
Or counsel, or dispute with Greeks,
Or drive the Arians with sticks,
Or get the Emperor's note. He died
Old and left the skin of a goat.

after Athanasius;
and after a painting by Morris Graves

THE DEATH OF SOUTHWELL
A Verse Melodrama with Homilies on Light and Sin

I never did take so weighty a man, if he be rightly used.
—Richard Topcliffe, *Letter to the Queen*, 6 July, 1592.

Cold dawn Harrow-On-The-Hill.
The unquiet curtain is too
White this hour, the candles
Too drawn their flames rest-
Less ruddying the cup
Of thin breads with its thin
Hands not yet bodied
In the dawn: the priest's face
Floats like cloth fair
For sacrifice, watch! his vestments
Are gaudy as dawn light grows.

Topcliffe's horses shake
The steam of gray morning; men
Grow sad with cold.
The house is sketched well-marked
Where mass is said. What argument?
The traitor's vested. Take him.
Cloak his colors! These horses
Scream. Now load his books,
His papist images; and this
Damned altar furniture
That burnishes with sun!

Westminster six o'clock
Topcliffe binds him hangs
His hands to pull the gentle
Wrists with weight of flesh.
God its bulk on these thin bones!
Down from the altar to be tall's
A curse. How real these heavy

Limbs! Is death a stretching
That makes flesh more slight;
A thinning of the blooded brain?
And emptying of eyes.

Fainting breaks these days
And nights by the wall. Toes
Touch sometimes. Won't
Say priests or people or place
Of meeting or color of his horse
That might be seen by houses.
Fainting breaks it. Look!
Here's fire! The child flames
In white and wintered places!
The paper lit to his face
He vomits blood, and wakes:

"Your fire is angular as pain and keen
As stone that killed the haunted Stephen.
Still its corners cannot hide
Its numbers or its god. Why look these gentle
Fires gesture to their home. They're tongues
Of doves are leaves and many-colored prongs
Of bush. How can a Child of Light
Forget His every perfect gift
Of art or ken! Well then! Our Christ
Is our Prometheus: His steep
And formal angle keeps our flame!"

No mass how is a man
A priest, without its folk.
Why, when you come for cauliflower
Take away his blessing from his tower.
A poet and no ink? Let him read,
His Bernard's here; his Bible: the lilies
Business, foxes light
And blood of grapes the seven
Porches on the graying pool.

But he writes with pins only tallies
Of his sins and the pious name of Christ.

This priest that hath a boyish
Look's a man most lewd
And dangerous! Keep him closed
Three years lonely in his cell.
(Perhaps Arundel's dog shall
Visit him to seek the blessing
Lions gain that with
Their paws have digged the graves
Of saints.) And now at sword's
Point drive the traitor
Forward to the bar for trial.

He knew he'd hang, and the rest.
He was always very white of face.
What falconry he had he
Put in poems. Uneasy in disguise.
No champion. In fact quite
Unfavorably compares to Campion.
A slight man, a poet pulled
Into the common prose of crowds
And guts. The comic Cinna screams.
Ignatius offers English wheat
The lion's head shall thrash for bread.

He speaks from his cart at Tyburn:
"When you are free of the whale's
Belly you cannot hope
To sit with Jonas in the shadow,
Except some envious worm
Gnaw apart the ivy's
Root. And should you move
From thorn or briar to the sweet
Odored cedar, your worm,
That cannot breed in you shall gnar
About and snap his teeth.

"Your proper devil all his imps
And instruments shall feed
Like storks upon the venomous
And evil acts of men.
And shall rejoice, if we
Amend, at men's calamity.
The delighted ravens fly
To the smelling corpse, but won't
Hunt the sound body;
So the wicked flock and stick
About us if we stink with sin,

"But if the healing soul
Slough from it this wanted
Flesh, it will abandon too
These hundred melancholy loves.
In winter when the vine is bare
Let the devils lie:
They shall be struck in April
When the flower starts, and at
The wild scent of virtue
Die like snakes
Beneath the blossom of the lime."

HANGMAN SITS IN TYBURN TREE
PREACHER SAYS HIS HOMILY
NOW HIS CART IS PULLED EMPTY
HANGMAN HANGED HIM AWKWARDLY
LOOK THE PREACHER'S HAND IS FREE
BLESSES HANGMAN BLESSES ME
HERE'S A FRIEND TO PULL THE KNEE
GHOST NOW LEAVES HIS YOUNG BODY
THIS POET SAINT WAS THIRTY-THREE
THE HANGMAN MOANS IN TYBURN TREE
NOW UNBLESS HANGMAN, UNBLESS ME.

GHOSTS OF THE HEART

NEW POEMS (1960)

---

to all the family, friends, and students who put up with me during the four-year period (1955-59) in which these poems were written

Contradictions—there is a really sharp hair shirt! There is a penance which has made saints and which everyone can practice.   —*Francis Xavier Cabrini*

In reality we are the juxtaposition of infinite, blurred selves.   —*Luigi Pirandello*

I am a frigate full of a thousand souls.   —*Herman Melville*

We walk through ourselves meeting robbers, ghosts, giants, old men, young men, wives, widows, brothers-in-love. But always meeting ourselves.   —*James Joyce*

I

THE LIVES OF THE POET

to Wallace Fowlie

So much the worse for the wood that finds it's a violin.
And to hell with the heedless...

Christ, éternel voleur des énergies.   —Rimbaud

1

His hour of birth he rolled
From his pillow to the
Floor having hoped a somewhat
Longer trip that day
Than this brief stay
From death. Although he fought
The usual Sunday walk
To church, Frederick and Arthur
Hand in hand, Vitalie
And Isabelle—each with a blue
Umbrella, Madame at her careful space:
Christ and thief to life.

2

He heard her shrill from the porch;
He flew to the farthest points
Of the garden wall and hid
His fists in his eyes
And felt the gate and fruit trees
Breathe, and discerned the envied
Inner lives of the vine.
Her shattering voice
Split the neighborhood games
And ruined the solitude even
In the latrine, where he tried fitful
Kinds of love and flight.

3

He traveled alone in his room
Lying on a canvas piece
Of sail harsh to skin
As salt burst to the novice
Lips or the pitch of deck
Underfoot. He found
The pilgrim roads of song
And played the keys of a book
In his lap; he carved the table's
Edge in the shape of a spinet:
But couldn't stand the braid and
Fat of the township band.

4

One day he left Madame
Waiting in a field;
And ran. "Come beloved soul
We *need* you," wrote Verlaine
(A view not shared at home)—
The boy had grown quite tall,
Sat ill at table; his peasant
Hands were huge and red
His hair and eyes unstyled;
He sneered at the talk and meal
And house and the pregnant wife, and fled
Insolently up to bed.

5

The white of the chair in his room!
The white of the stoned moon
Certain and alone, pearled
And unpassioned in its lights
Unhounded in the silence

Of its round O
Perfect sure voyager!
The white of the furniture the
Glow of the cube and sphere!
The joy and glow of the body
Of the boy in the cold window of his room
White or gold as the moon!

6

He saw in Verlaine a child
Of Sun—burnt by the ancient
Memory, moved on the ancient
Sunwarmed flank: struck
As the great brass bells
At the breasts of the cattle of the sun:
Pierced or wheeled by the sun-
Keen tips of the ancient horns.
But Verlaine, stuck by an ordinary
Arrow, moved with the faith
Of his fathers and made a minor sound
His Place and his Formula found.

7

Some are moved as the gray
Eyed Io by the god
From home and call: are hurried
To the drowsy lengths of the reed
Or the pulse of space to the west
Or east to the lands where huts
Of clay and wattles made
Are raised on wheels; where nomads
Turn with the feel of the goad—
Some have the face of a god
Some have the tooth of a swan, or the laughable
Lust-sad eye of the calf.

8

Always bent to depart (it seemed)
The poet took the Alps on foot
Suffered a stroke in the sun and was helped
By monks; was robbed on his way to Russia.
He caught a cold with a circus troupe
In the north. At last he joined the Dutch
And sailed to Java. He left and lived
With native tribes till he signed on His Majesty's
Ship. He hired on a farm in Egypt
And plundered a wreck in Suez and worked
As foreman in a quarry. He smuggled guns and slaves
And lost a leg in Harari.

9

He went home when hurt
And so his mother won
In the end. After the Verlaine
Melodrama he came,
His arm in a sling, and wrote
Une Saison en Enfer
In the barn (she heard him groan
And rave like some Saint
Anthony in his cave). She won
Too when he gave up his life
Of rigorous debauch and tried to help
Swell the family stock.

10

Madame and Isabelle together
Might be heard to cheer
When he thought of raising a child
An engineer. He gave up Verlaine
And the love of a native wench

And the gentle servant boy
Of Aden. Those fierce women
Nurse the men home
From the humid wars. They alone
Walked with him to his tomb
After Mass, they and he and the black trees
Shadowless in the rain-wet grass.

11

He tried in the bird the rule
Of the snow, the peculiar luck
Of flutes: so much the worse
For the boy who flies his home
And god and verse, for the brass
That wakes a horn. The weight
Of the gold about his waist
Shall make him sick. The horizon's
Shift of blue is a change
In the man. And the verse will clutch
And cast. And the apter alchemies
Of God make one change last.

After Fowlie and Aeschylus
and after a remark of Maritain's on Wilde.

A CENTURY PIECE FOR POOR HEINE (1800–1856)

to Paul Carroll

Give up these everlasting complaints about love; show these poets how to use a whip.

—Marx

My forefathers were not the hunters. They were the hunted. —Heine

Heine's mother was a monster
Who had him trained
In business, war and law;
In the first she failed the best:
At work in his uncle's office
He turned a book of Ovid's
Into Yiddish. And Harry's memories
Don't even mention the family's
Chill and scare at the chance
Of a fortune from a millionaire. But a grown
Heine fainted and wept
If an uncle failed to provide;
And there was no money in the house when he died:

2

Except what he got from mother.
Syphilis brought
Its slow and fictional death—
Still he never would tell
His folks how sick he was of sex.
He wrote her frequently
To give no cause for alarm
Dictating because of a paralyzed
Arm, into the willing
And ready ear of some

Lady fair, reporting
For today, criticizing his wife
And telling the details of nearly-married life.

3

He called his mother a dear old
"Pussy cat";
His wife was a "wild cat";
She was the stupid Cath-
Olic opposite of the Jewish
Other—and cared even less
For his verse, being unable
To read and listening little.
Which is worse. Their need for love
So shocked him, he ran away
To a princess friend—like his sister
A rather crystalline dolly
Charitable toward sexual folly.

4

Two weeks after his mother
I mean his wife
And he were married, having harried
Each other for a number of years,
He put himself in a fight
With a man he got a cuckold;
He chose the absolute pistol,
But found he was only shot
In the thigh—and his own weapon
Of course went high.
So he went to visit his mom
After years of exile from home
Because of politics he put in a pome.

5

He left his mother I mean
His other at home

With her nervous bird and her
Shrieking tantrums—or else
He left the bird with the wife,
Et cetera—he wrote her a letter a
Day like a scolding parent
Afraid she'd become a Paris
Whore as he hoped she would
(And as he was) but she stayed
Till death, tho she shattered a glass
In her teeth, and all the rest—
Such as throwing a fish in the face of a guest.

6

As soon as he left himself
To the needs of a wife
He was shook to find in the face
In the mirror the eyes of his father
When his flesh had started to fade:
He began to be blind, and gave in
To a kind of paralysis that made him
Lift the lid of his eye
By hand to see his wife.
At the end, cones of opium,
Burned on his spine, helped him
To dream of a younger father
Doing his hair in a snow of powder;

7

He tried to kiss his father's
Hand but his pink
Finger was stiff as sticks
And suddenly all of him shifts—
A glorious tree of frost!
Unburdened of the sullied flesh.
His father died before him

Leaving him free to be
The Jew—he had fled their flight
To that of the protestant fake
Exacted in Christian states,
But pain had him lucid (or afraid)
Till the ancient covenant with God was made.

8

But his tough old mother stayed on
And he never became
The husband; he took to his marriage
Couch interesting women,
Remaining a curious virgin.
In the last years of his life
He wept at the pain of lust
Stirred in his tree-like limbs
Already dry. And he left
Framing with paralyzed lips
One more note to his mother.
Only the ambiguous Dumas cried
At the holy rite they danced when he died.

9

His soft old flesh slipped
Inside its great
Trunk with a sound he held
Too long inside his skull.
God absolve his mother,
His wife and him: after all
As Heine said, thrusting
Again that Freudian wit
He showed to prove to friends
And self his sanity had not
Come to the fate of potency—
"It is God's business to have mercy."

10

There is no need to forgive
His saintly poems
As there is for the work of another,
To whose New York park
The marble Lorelei fled—
Banned with the books of her maker—
To mock and lure at him
And us from a Catholic plot
Like a baptized, voluptuous mother
Powerful over the figure
Of the frantic Harry, and over the
Three mother-fishes:
Melancholy, an idol of the Hebrew Smart,

And one with the mended, broken arm of Art.

After Antonina Valentin
and after a memorial to Heine in Kilmer Park.

ON THE DEATH OF
THE POET'S MOTHER
THIRTY-THREE YEARS LATER

to Isabella Gardner

The tongue fits to the teeth and the palate by Number, pouring forth letters and words.
—St. Augustine

Years ago I came to the conclusion that poetry too is nothing but an oral outlet.
—A.A. Brill, M.D.

1

My mother died because
I lived or so
I always chose to believe.
At any rate I nursed
At a violent teat with the boys
Of the bronzed picture. In my
Memories of taste I find
Bits of the tart hairs
Of an Irish dog that hangs
Its red arch over me; I'm not
So sure of that beast
That it has stole as much from me
As I shall suck from it.

It had an eye of milky
Glass with a very
Reddened spot that sent
Threads or streams of red
About the eye's globe
And this eye moved
Among the long red hairs
At the skull of the dog as it
Leaped in the childhood grass,
As it springs in the childhood

Trace, as it arched and pulled
And arched and pulled the sheath of its livid
Tongue through the wisps of its breath.

July began with the Fourth
And the moon in a box
Like a flaming house in the grass
At the edge of the fair with the frames
Of the fireworks there, but next
It floats, like a carnival balloon
That drops out weights of men,
And turns the festival tips
Of the sparklers hot: fear
Shot up in a kite when it burned
My throat white—like an eye
My friend once cooked in his head, as he mixed
Carnivals of fluids in a shed.

Yet I was not so scared
Or scarred I could not
Scream and climb to find
My aunt to cry for help
High in the mounts of bleachers:
I saw a face and told it
All my needs, but my hot
Throat beat with fright
As a strange mother bent
From the stands—her flanks were blood
In the moon and festive light
As she heard my plea of hurt and
Saw my burnt neck twitch,

Arched over me a God-like Bitch.

2

Don't think I took this dog
Too quick for mother:

I looked for another in the book
Of art where I found the Latin
Kids at the dugs of the wolf,
But most of the stone women
Wore no clothes and some of them
(With help from a borrower's pen)
Showed the genitals of men.
I looked for her in girls
At games and aunts who said
Her face was mine—so I tried to catch
Her in some epicene line.

I guess I looked the most
In father's wife
Whose hair was Welsh and red
Who rocked me once so ten-
Derly on her lap
As I could not lace my boot
Today I remember that—
The boy and his mother and his shoe
His wrists so thin and his hands
Fit so wrong around
The square boot-thong the work
They did or sometimes would not do
Made him weep for them.

I looked in Palgrave's book
She left, and I looked
Through her pearled glass.
But did she read the verse?
And where in that still
Unpretentious town
Did turn the brass wheel
To clear the glass? How many times
I tried the German names!
And felt the foolery of gems:
Pearls like "Braes of Yarrow"
Let new Palgraves gather (and let

Me help my mother, if after

These aids she had no other).

3

I watched at last for her
Among our sacred
Stones, for I was grown
Before I found her tomb.
Today I point to that:
It's there my heavy mother
Rots. Remember!—
Of all the grades the last
Before the next is beautiful,
The lines of ribs, the grace
Of skulls, exquisite levers
Of her limbs; the next is spirit,
Musical with numbers of the flesh:

The formula of eyes'
Ellipse, the thrust
In the gentle eye's lash,·
The figures of the listening
Fingers' nerves and of the
Fetal logarithm curves,
Of hidden colors of the guts,
Of buffered tensions of the blood
"Figured in the drift of stars,"
And pale Ameba's gestures.
Self forcing numbers
Enticed into her hyaline tips,
That stop in earth—and smell to Christ.

She suffers there the natural turns;
Her nests on nests of flesh
Are spelt to that irrational end,
The surd and faithful Change. And stays
To gain the faultless stuff reversed

From the numbers' trace at the Lasting Trump.
So here my mother lies. I do not
Resurrect again her restless
Ghost out of my grievous memory:
She waits the quiet hunt of saints.
Or the ignorance of citizens of hell.
And here is laid her orphan child with his
Imperfect poems and ardors, slim as sparklers.

February, 1956

After a definition of Xenocrates
and a poem of Richard Eberhart
and after lines of Eliot and Alejandro Carrion

ACHILLES AND THE KING
A Verse Re-telling

1

The terrible wrath I say
Bore to Greece
Every kind of sorrow
And sent to hell the souls
Of fighting men leaving them
Food for birds and dogs
Through some will of the Gods
Who brought Achilles and the King
Together over the matter at
First of the Priest's daughter.

2

The Priest came to the beached
Ships of the Greeks
With prize of gold and the powerful
Staff of the God Apollo
Who sends or holds off evil;
He prayed for the luck of Greece
At war with Troy so long,
For a fast return home,
And asked in his stead his daughter's
Freedom from the King's bed.

3

But this King of Men
Does not send
Her free: she will grow old
He said a long way
She will grow old a long
Way from her own country
And she shall work her loom

And share my bed; now get
The hell out the King said
And you will keep your skin.

4

The old Priest's heart
Shook as he left
And walked without a word
Or sound alone along
The shores of the moaning sea
(Oh Son of Leto hear me!)
God of the bright bow
If I have burnt you thighs
Of bull and goat now let me weep
Your arrows for my tears!

5

Within their quiver silver
Arrows clanged
At the radiant God's side:
He shot from the holy height
With speed of night and knelt
By ships and rang his silver
Bow; its terrible song
Struck the busy dog
And mules and men, and again many
Fires burned the dead.

6

The arms of the goddess turn
Themselves as white
Smokes of sacrifice
That rise for Greece until
Achilles calls the well
To council, and the seer
Whose gifts have kept the swift

Fleets tells all the guilt
Of overlord and King; now hate
Turns itself toward him:

7

The King's face flares—
You hound of hell
When have you told the good
Or given any aid
But bad or loved any
But your own god damned
Word: you know well
How much I want the girl;
If I give her up to end this death
What shall I have instead?

8

Achilles rose shouting
Most glorious King
Most greedy of men indeed
What shall the lusty Greeks
Give for prize; can you find
A common store of wealth
Out of our pillaged towns?
Give her up and wait; when God
Lets the walls of Troy fall
You shall be triple paid.

9

Achilles you have guts
And you may be
Godly, but here's a wit
You'll find hard to beat.
Do you expect to keep
A girl while I sit and wait?
No you don't! I'll take

Your prize of Aias' or bear
The prize of Odysseus away—for someone
This will be a hard day.

10

Achilles said you wise
Son of a bitch
Whose war is this anyway?
Those mountain shadows and sounds
Of the sea for a long time
Put Troy from me: no Trojan
Spears and men have robbed
Sheep or corn or wives
In lands of mine, and today I could lead
My beaked ships away.

11

Walk out then said the King—
Others honor me;
Take your rage and your men.
Play cock-of-the-walk with them!
I'm sick of your taste for blood
Anyway and your touted bravery
Is some affect of the gods—
You don't scare me and you won't
Forget my strength when it has sent
Your girl weeping from your tent.

12

Achilles trembled and said someday in your
Despair remember what I now swear:
By this staff your men shall reel to the Trojan
God, shall feel his eyes that flame and glint
Along his gold mask to guide his lance
He flings from his glorious arm bringing heavy
Death and the melancholy clang of brass;

He slays from life in his shining limbs as lean
And stripped as the holy staff of Zeus I cut from the hill.
And by these things shall Kings tell Achilles!

13

As for me I no more
Obey the King.
He may take the girl
He gave; of all else
Beside my good black ship
Not a thing, or mark, his dark
Blood will soon be flowing
Down this idled spear.
Achilles and his King now end
Their war of hate full saying.

14

The King puts a fast
Ship to sea—
The daughter of the Priest and twenty
Oarsmen under Odysseus
Captain: her white sail
Swells, the gray god whis-
Pers busily by the stem;
Others bathe them in the salt
And unspoiled sea and twist their prayers
With curls of sacrifice.

15

The horns of the sun-cattle gleam
Along the hill
As Apollo's Priest and daughter
Weep together by the well-
Built altar and the King's
Men rinse their hands
To scatter holy grain

Beautiful as morning
Rain and catch the blood of bulls
And flay their quivering hides

16

And wrap the bits of thigh
In fat the Priest
Shall flame with wine above the hiss
Of prayers, while at the fire's
Edge they plunge their bronzed
Forks and eat the brilliant
Inner parts that hold the God.
At last they feast, and shift
The mixing bowls of wines and sing
Loud to the Archer King.

17

The Priest's daughter home
Achilles' prize
Gone he sat alone
By the gray seas sat
Alone by the black ships
And wept, lifting his arms:
This fastest runner this shortest
Lived Achilles cried
As a child to its mother, eating his heart
For the lost fury of the fight.

After Homer Iliad I *and*
after a terracotta figure
of an Etruscan warrior

THE MONUMENT AND THE SHRINE

1

At focus in the national
Park's ellipse a marker
Draws tight the guys of

Miles, opposite the national
Obelisk with its restless oval
Peoples who shall be

Deeply drawn to its
Austerities: or
For a moment try the mystery

Of the god-like eye, before
Our long climb down past relic
Schoolboy names and states

And one foolish man
Climbs up, his death high
In his elliptic face.

2

A double highway little
Used in early spring
Goes to the end of the land

Where Washington's chandeliers
Are kept, his beds and chairs,
His roped-off relic kitchen

Spits, his pans; his floors
Are worn underneath the dead
Pilgrims' feet; outside

The not-so-visited tomb;
And over the field and fence
His legendary river:

And so I walk although
The day is cold for this;
I eat a thin slice

Of bread and one remarkable
Egg perfectly shaped,
A perfect oriental por-

Celain sheen of white.
Suddenly the lost
Ghosts of his life

Broke from the trees and from the cold
Mud pools where he played
A boy and set as a man

The sand glint of his boot,
The flick of his coat on the weeds;
His wheels click in the single road.

RECOLLECTION ON THE DAY OF A FIRST BOOK

A monstrous fish came up to devour him and Tobias being afraid cried out; and the angel said: take him by the gill and draw him to thee.

—The Book of Tobias

Now let this present act
This book bear some fruit
For it has buried some dead
And only the minor things
Turn ghost or whine
In my dream to wake my wife:
But Tobias when he had buried
Most dead grew most blind—
What does this mean! That his man
Weary of burying fell asleep
Beside his house, where a jealous
Never buried bird
Burnt his eyes with its stinking drops
(And that man was a favorite of God's)?

I know my book is blind
Yet if I ask it speaks
With the knowledge of the dark
Tiresias or the angel Raphael
To tell me I am my own
Enemy: but the angel came back
For Tobias, one of the Seven
From His presence—and when it breathes
The holy lights are terrible
Changing in the faces of its wing!
And beautiful as Raphael's saying
"I come today to heal you,"
And he poured the gall of a fish in his eyes
And peeled their scars like skins of eggs.

Then let this book be a juice
Of a fish that makes me see
And let her love be its heart
Whose smoke as it lies in coals
Exorcizes evils
And makes marriage: my love
And her book are parts of the self-
Same monster—Hippolytus was slain
Who stayed a bachelor! But young
Tobias and his holy wife
Are safe. Yesterday a Roman
Saint sanctifies her spouse;
Now let him watch with ungalled sight
As today Evaristus draws up the marriage rite.

Oct. 26, St. Evaristus
Oct. 25, St. Chrysanthus and Darius
Oct. 24, St. Raphael

NARCISSUS:
VISION AND RETROSPECT

*The Little-known Bird of the Inner Eye. Consciousness
Assuming the Shape of a Heron.*
—Titles of Morris Graves

Et quels événements éntinceler dans l'oeil.　　—Valéry

I taste the bones of my enormous skull.　　—Lorca

Still I kneel in the colorless
Pew, my skull in my hands
One of those arid, usual
Times of the end of prayer,
After the forms I made
Or learned my hope-
Ful and innocent years
(After the easy and
Almost indigenous Aves).

My hands bring to my eyes
Shut in their dying sockets
A grieving touch of pressure:
Why, this starts blue colors!
Whirled parabolas! Tipped
And formal diamonds! A thin
Bronze perimeter of a sun
That shoots its Bernini rays
Into the lids of my eyes.

I meant to try the aid
Of a saint this needful day.
It is long since help,
Will she grudge me a sign?
Why, why not show
Herself among these bright

And baroque shapes (that grow
Huge as my head) and this
Counterchange of pain?

I find a nerve, it crosses
Bones of the nose at the eye's
Corner: Holidays of fire
Swirl in my head awhile!
Until the work of my eyes
Flowing the places of vision
Rests me with its beauty.
Still a mild pain
Recalls my uncalled saint:

I lure her picture to mind
(Opal and green Kandinskys
Skirr in my sight)—first
The great and luminous spheres
Of her eyes assume her face;
Now the cowl, its black
Most fragile edge, its Gothic
Crease at top. I fit,
I attempt to fix, her eye

To one of the quieter discs
I find, I try to catch
A shifting, colored bit
Inside her elliptic coif:
No, her common pious
Image sticks in my brain!
Goes not forward to the eye.
And will these damned optic
Ducts not send what they brought?

I grip my eyes to my skull
Until they can despair

Of her: but now an obscure
Alien pain begins
In the quick of my brain
And grows to travail fold-
Ing and comforting me;
Ah, God, this is no Rex
To rip his sight from his head:

My hand stops. Look!
To my eye an exquisite
Vine of blood! With blossoms
Or roots of white! The retina
Once, without these reds
Or forms, floated from a sheep's
Eye's mass in a laboratory
Glass. I watch in my joy
My eye's desperate sight

∎ ∎ ∎

Of itself. My eyes opened
Full, my view restored,
I forgot to kneel as I left
And forgot the aid and visions
Of saints for a while having seen
Instead unto my closed
Sight by some secret
Of Light a sheer, glistening
Cloistered piece of myself!

EPILOGUE, SONGS OF THE SPOUSES, COMPLAINT OF LOVE

The Bridegroom's Song

How lovely are her feet
And the joints of her jeweled
Thigh. Her belly is a hill
Of wheat with a fault of lilies
Her navel is beautiful with wine
Her breasts are grapes and her teeth
As flocks white from the washing
And in her mouth is a taste of apple.

The Bride's Song

His legs are pillars of marble
At a base of gold
And his golden head is hid
With the ferns of his hair. His eyes
Are washed with milk as doves
At the water and under his tongue
A place of honey! O my love
Is a place of spice beneath my breast.

Tale of Courtship

A wild flower in the weeds
Of fields is my love
Among the loves of the daughters
And so is my beloved
An apple tree an apple
Tree in the woods of sons.
I sit down under his shadow
And his fruit is sweet to my mouth.

Help me with wine O comfort
Me with apples
For I am sick of love.
His hand is under my head
His right hand shall hold me O daughters
By the deer and harts of the field
Do not stir! You do not
Wake my love until he please.

Look, my loved one
Leaps on the mountain!
Like a young deer whose horns
Leap from its head look
My love is like a roe
He waits like a young hart
Beside my window he
Watches through the lattices.

The voice of my loved one:
"Arise my love
My beautiful one and come
For winter is gone the long
Rain past and flowers
Appear in the earth. It is
The time of the birds' singing
And the voice of the turtle is heard in the land.

"It is the time of pruning
For the fig has shown
Its fruit and the flower of the grape
Spills forth its sweet smell.
Rise my love arise
My beautiful one and come
And catch with me the little
Golden fox that plays at the vine.

"My dove in the ledge of rock
In the secret place
Of the stair show me your face
Let your voice come to my ear."
And I to my love (you know
He feeds on the flowers of the field?):
"When the morning breaks and the shad-
Ows turn, come with the deer from its hill."

My heart kept watch in my sleep
Until he spoke:
"My head is full of dew
And my hair of the drops of night
I have put off my coat
I washed the dust from my feet
Now open to my love." And I felt
My hand drop with myrrh at the lock.

The Complaint

My love had gone; tho my soul
Shook to hear him
And my guts moved for his touch.
I cried for him through all
The streets of town till the guards
Found me and tore away my veil,
And still I weep for sons
To tell how I am sick of love.

Epilogue

And others cry for you
Melancholy
Unicorn though your bright pen
Keep you splendid in a field

Of color where ev'ry flower
Bends to you. Over-
Whelmed by violence of scent,
Struck with color, one fails almost

To see where your white
Fur bleeds
Lanced with a formal strength
Strange to such a gentle one,
Such eyes! There is another
Hunt and another gentler
Hunter. There is another
Love and another holier lover.

*After Solomon and after
the Seventh Unicorn Tapestry*

II

PROTEST AFTER A DREAM

So what did old Diogenes find
When he took his lantern in his hand
And looked everywhere for a true man?

You tell me, for I
Am sick of tales
And books; I do not find
Your wide Dantean seas,
Your black, shimmering Alpine
Skies of De Rougemont;
I have not exchanged
For an Easter plain Raskolnikov's
Narrowing cell—Good God
If they cannot make us well, as it looks,
What the hell good are our books?

If Sophocles offered eggs
To a sacred snake
Or led the victor's dance
Naked after Salamis
He did more in this
Than in his poems, for poems
Are dreams and dreams are wants:
Our wants are what we are
And what we are is not
The man we hoped, it seems, so what
The hell good are our dreams?

THE POET SCRATCHES HIS HEAD

to A. R. Ammons

Editorially
We wonder why we
Sit and pull our hair
Reading in our over-
Stuffed chair. Do we
Punish us for some
Crime in our unconscious
Or are we trying to
Equate with some fatherly
Friend of fifty-eight
Who wears less and less
Fur on his emerging pate?

Or maybe we, again,
Just hate our body,
Being Irish and a
Manichee. Or possibly
We feel a nostalgic ruth
For having given up some
Of the manual pleasures of youth?
Perhaps that son of a bitch
Beneath the roots of our scalp
Makes it itch. Anyway
These ravelings of flesh look
Beyond the arts of art to unmesh.

BYRON AT SHELLEY'S BURNING

The brain of Shelley cooks
Inside its smoking case;
The bones and flesh fall off
And show the seed of Shelley's thought.

The wine of Byron fumes
Inside his cup of skull;
The lengthy hair of Percy
Streams on his romantic pyre.

The scissor legs of Byron
Swim where Shelley drowned
In wine romantic seas
Of Italy. And Byron notes

The wine red beauty
In the sheets of flame
Of Shelley, as he sees
The body burn upon the beach.

But Byron's brain could not
Foresee how *he* would die
In Greece, his blood ebbing
Into his eye out of a drunken leech.

LINES AGAINST A LOVED
AMERICAN POET AFTER HEARING
AN IRISH ONE'S NICKNAME

When Munson was in Paris Harold Crane
Sent him twenty bucks for one of Joyce's
Dirty books. What did *Ulysses* do for him
If he could only write while he was young,
Or felt he couldn't stand to face the boy
And woman in the aging man. Oh,
I know he lived an adolescent hell
Hurt by a candy merchant father
Who made his son wheel it in a cart—
A pimp who got a fortune from the itch
For sweets, which is like the itch for love
He didn't give. The dirty bum. The dirty
Father. What can you say? He was a dog.
He had his son's day. In the night the boy
Would stand beside his sleeping mother's bed.
Puzzled. Didn't know what the hell. Who does?
Who does. Still it takes particular heart
Not to eat the fondant of the sea,
That winking merchant attractive to any body.
Easy admirers have lied. A man
Cannot be a poet if he died.
They hold in them the feeling of the living.
I learn little, but he learns less from "Germs
Choice" crying in the wilderness.

NEW YORK SCENE: MAY 1958

It is just getting dark as the rain stops.
He walks slow and looks, though he's late. It's all
Muted. It's like a stage. A tender light
In the street, a freshness. He wonders, a
Funeral?: at uncertain intervals,
Up the block, the corner, small, old women
Walk home with soft lamps, holding them with love
Like children before them in the May night.
A few people move down East 10th Street. They
Do not look at these ladies with their lights
Blowing in the rain-wet airs by the stores,
Their ancient hands guarding their ancient flames.
Three boys race out of the YMCA
At the corner, carrying the brief god-
like gear of the runner. Two jackets hunch
Over two kids. There is high, choked laughter.
The third wears a sweater, black as his head
Lit with the wet. They sprint across the street,
And are gone into a tiny candy shop
Half underneath the walk. A dialogue
As the jackets and sweater cross leaves him
One clean phrase, "tomorrow again." He grins.
He turns, pauses by a store with small tools
Held in half spool boxes in the window,
With beads, clocks, one hand-turned coffee grinder
And way in the back, a wooden Indian.
Now he stops a girl he feels he knows. He
Asks her where he's going, gives an address.
She teaches him, lifting her arm up, rais-
ing a breast inside her poplin raincoat.
He listens carelessly. He wants to see
The long, full hair that gives form to her scarf
Of a wine and golden colored woolen,
Some turns of it loose about her forehead
Like a child, some lengths of it falling at
Her back as she walks away, having smiled.

CONCERT SCENE

to John and Jane Gruen

So he sits down. His host will play for him
And his hostess will come again, with wine.
He has a chance to see the room, to find
The source, defend himself against something
Beautiful, which hit him when he came in
And left him weak. On the baroque fireplace,
Whose stone has the turn of a living arm,
Some lacquer red poppies now are opened
In a copper bowl. Over the mantel
A warm oil against the white paneled wall.
An open coach; a girl and bearded man,
Both young, canter through a summer landscape
Soft with color, their faces full and flushed.
The Brahms on the piano is about
This. To the left a black coffee table
Topped with strips of crossed cane beside a green
Cloth couch. On this top a wicker horn leaks
Out white grapes by a tin of purple-wrapped
Candied nuts, and a thin white porcelain
Cream pitcher with a few, loosely figured
Very bright blue anemones and greens;
At the right of the fireplace a great teak
Desk has a red Chinese plume or feather
In a silver pitcher, then a clear; wine-
glass shaped, tall bowl—full of golden apples.
Still the music is Brahms: golds, blues, and wines
Of the stained glass panels in the far door,
A light behind. The hostess brings a tray
Of sherry and a jar of caviar
In ice, the thousand eggs writhing with light
Beside the lucent lemon slice. She sits
Upon the green or gold cloth couch. She holds
The thin stemmed glass, and now he looks at her,
Shook with the colors or the music or

The wine, Her hair is blue black and drops straight
From the part—directly in the middle
Of her skull—its long, moonwet waterfall.
Her smile is warm for him, lips large without
Paint, gentle eyes hollowed in the high bones
Of her white face. Now he sees above her
A graceful, black iron candelabra
On the white wall, green of its candles spin-
ning in the whorls of shiny surfaced leaves
At the top of a thin plant in the corner,
And in the jagged-necked, blown-glass bottle,
As big as a child, standing on the floor
By the piano. His hostess rises
To sing. (She doesn't know he's trembling.) Her
Voice is too strong. Suddenly the color
Is intense. And he finds no defense.

THE BROTHERS:
TWO SALTIMBANQUES

Two boys stand at the end of the full train
Looking out the back, out the sides, turning
Toward each other. Their arms and shoulders brush
As the train shakes. They've been to the ballpark
Together, and can prove it with the huge
Red and blue scorecards in their hands. A sense
Of repeating in the shapes of the ears,
In the bearing of the clefted, young chins.
The older brother is perhaps fifteen,
The other, twelve? A gold of Indians
In summer faces, the color of their
Like hair, which is cut short, though with more bronze
In the younger. The brows of the older
Are surprisingly rich. And this young man
Is ripe with strength, his long face keen shaped,
Arrogant, rather sad about the eyes,
The face not yet tight. They wear green T-shirts
(Perhaps for some school sports?), their khaki pants
Sagging from the day in the sun. The two
Brothers slowly sway together with the
Motion of the train. The younger works hard
At his great scorecard. Now the older son
Bends to whisper: mixed, uncontrolled higher
And lower laughter runs over the train's
Screams, and raises heads out of newspapers.
Suddenly we strike a curve. The small one
Loses balance, and the other moves to
Steady him, leg and thigh muscles tight a-
gainst the steel weight of cars. They straighten. They
Smile, and the older boy's hand rests awhile
At his brother's side. Now as the train slows
A school of jets wings at the left windows
Tracking flame from the late sun. The boys lean

To the glass and the small one grins, gestur-
ing toward the planes, his long young arm poised,
Giving the lie to awkwardness at twelve
Catching for a passing moment the grace
Of what he felt. Now they move to the front
And get off. I watch them walk the platform
At the station. On the invitation
Of a vendor they buy Coke. They won't look
At the penciled dirty word, with its figure,
On the margin of a sign scorecard red.
They start home together for supper and bed.

THE PICNIC

It is the picnic with Ruth in the spring.
Ruth was third on my list of seven girls
But the first two were gone (Betty) or else
Had someone (Ellen has accepted Doug).
Indian Gully the last day of school;
Girls make the lunches for the boys too.
I wrote a note to Ruth in algebra class
Day before the test. She smiled, and nodded.
We left the cars and walked through the young corn
The shoots green as paint and the leaves like tongues
Trembling. Beyond the fence where we stood
Some wild strawberry flowered by an elm tree
And Jack-in-the-pulpit was olive ripe.
A blackbird fled as I crossed, and showed
A spot of gold or red under its quick wing.
I held the wire for Ruth and watched the whip
Of her long, striped skirt as she followed.
Three freckles blossomed on her thin, white back
Underneath the loop where the blouse buttoned.
We went for our lunch away from the rest,
Stretched in the new grass, our heads close
Over unknown things wrapped up in wax papers.
Ruth tried for the same, I forget what it was,
And our hands were together. She laughed,
And a breeze caught the edge of her little
Collar and the edge of her brown, loose hair
That touched my cheek. I turned my face in-
to the gentle fall. I saw how sweet it smelled.
She didn't move her head or take her hand.
I felt a soft caving in my stomach
As at the top of the highest slide
When I had been a child, but was not afraid,
And did not know why my eyes moved with wet
As I brushed her cheek with my lips and brushed
Her lips with my own lips. She said to me

Jack, Jack, different than I had ever heard,
Because she wasn't calling me, I think,
Or telling me. She used my name to
Talk in another way I wanted to know.
She laughed again and then she took her hand;
I gave her what we both had touched—can't
Remember what it was, and we ate the lunch.
Afterward we walked in the small, cool creek
Our shoes off, her skirt hitched, and she smiling,
My pants rolled, and then we climbed up the high
Side of Indian Gully and looked
Where we had been, our hands together again.
It was then some bright thing came in my eyes,
Starting at the back of them and flowing
Suddenly through my head and down my arms
And stomach and my bare legs that seemed not
To stop in feet, not to feel the red earth
Of the Gully, as though we hung in a
Touch of birds. There was a word in my throat
With the feeling and I knew the first time
What it meant and I said, it's beautiful.
Yes, she said, and I felt the sound and word
In my hand join the sound and word in hers
As in one name said, or in one cupped hand.
We put back on our shoes and socks and we
Sat in the grass awhile crosslegged, under
A blowing tree, not saying anything.
And Ruth played with shells she found in the creek,
As I watched. Her small wrist which was so sweet
To me turned by her breast and the shells dropped
Green, white, blue, easily into her lap,
Passing light through themselves. She gave the pale
Shells to me, and got up and touched her hips
With her light hands, and we walked down slowly
To play the school games with the others.

SHORE SCENE

There were bees about. From the start I thought
The day was apt to hurt. There is a high
Hill of sand behind the sea and the kids
Were dropping from the top of it like schools
Of fish over falls, cracking skulls on skulls.
I knew the holiday was hot. I saw
The August sun teeming in the bodies
Logged along the beach and felt the yearning
In the brightly covered parts turning each
To each. For lunch I bit the olive meat:
A yellow jacket stung me on the tongue.
I knelt to spoon and suck the healing sea…
A little girl was digging up canals
With her toes, her arm hanging in a cast
As white as the belly of a dead fish
Whose dead eye looked at her with me, as she
Opened her grotesque system to the sea…
I walked away; now quietly I heard
A child moaning from a low mound of sand,
Abandoned by his friend. The child was tricked,
Trapped upon his knees in a shallow pit.
(The older ones will say you can get out.)
I dug him up. His legs would not unbend.
I lifted him and held him in my arms
As he wept. Oh I was gnarled as a witch
Or warlock by his naked weight, was slowed
In the sand to a thief's gait. When his strength
Flowed, he ran, and I rested by the sea…
A girl was there. I saw her drop her hair,
Let it fall from the doffed cap to her breasts
Tanned and swollen over wine red woolen.
A boy, his body blackened by the sun,
Rose out of the sand stripping down his limbs
With graceful hands. He took his gear and walked
Toward the girl in the brown hair and wine

And then past me; he brushed her with the soft,
Brilliant monster he lugged into the sea…
By this tide I raised a small cairn of stone
Light and smooth and clean, and cast the shadow
Of a stick in a perfect line along
The sand. My own shadow followed then, until
I felt the cold swirling at the groin.

ON A PRIZE CRUCIFIX
BY A STUDENT SCULPTOR

to Catherine Brunot

The cross of boy with man within is an
Anguished one. The boy who made this curve
Of Christ, the man who made this anxious cross
Of Christ, stripped, inside a classroom case,
Has hung, stripped, inside the college gym.
He knows. He sees the bodies of the boy
Men, beautiful with beauty caught
In him also, with agony, with grace.

His Christ has his turned shape of muscle,
Lean with this leanness of the young
Becoming men; lithe within the brass
Along the hand and limb; bright as skin
In light of campus sun upon the rolled-up
Arm. This Christ's chest heaves with the
Runner's breath, the legs torqued, the tight,
Powered thighs not at rest, as though

They jump in contest. The belly caves beneath
The holy human building of his ribs;
His thin belly feels the touch of hands,
Of lance. His navel buds above his loins
Where lies his genital, secret as a
Boy's breeched, denied, terrible with weight
Of seed and with the supple strength of God.
The student Christ tries for middle thirty:

Ah God, if Christ has not a body as
The student (and the older) artist does,
And all of that, what good is He to us?
The student Christ has lived through being born

And through the awful time of being young,
And not so young, I think. He sees the lasting
Crucifixion in the growing man
Who every passing day lets die a little more

The body of the boy grieved for.

LINES FOR A YOUNG
WANDERER IN MEXICO

This lonely following in the old town
When dark hides the agèd blood drawn up
From the Latin bricks your young feet form on
In the light rain, after many dead men
And women, after small, peasant-shrouded
Children, who burn in the big, Mexican
Suns, and cry with you in these late night times
(But laugh when you do not): this wandering,
I say, is a dancing. Young man you come
Before these live and dead, and dance. Light clothed
And lithe, intent, you dance before them all,
Still, without any songs. The supple chang-
ings of your limbs pass, movement to movement,
With every grace of youth and of distance
From the ancient dead in the audience
Of wanderers. You hold the agony
Both of young and old in the cloak of your
Lean body, which quickens to a spider
Wheeling, fragile, and which quickens to a
Star. I desire to shout my words of praise,
To shout arrogantly over the heads
Of the multitude: See, see his dancing!
It is not the dancing of the harlot,
For it goes up from the midst of us all,
Sudden, and male, and sweet, until we fall
With it into this rain-wet, brick real street.

After James Joyce

ACAPULCO CANYON:
TWO KODACHROMES

to Raymond Roseliep

1

Five young men, canteen
knapsack and bed
roll, loll and stretch
spiked heavy booted
legs lined up at the ledge
their fathers' hats on heads.

The manly blues and reds,
plumes of color,
fade underneath the veils
of heat and sun, and one
profile faints and fails del-
icately as a girl's.

At this light the photo-
graphic look
of each is so detached!
They are novice monks
solemn, poised upon the rim of
Acapulco Canyon.

Or native young at their
initiation:
around the foot a fixed,
measured rope of hemp
like a wreath, about to drop
toward the rock beneath.

2

Five young men no clothes
(mist for vestment)
dip their monks-cut
skulls and rinse and lift
priest or pagan bowls of arms
in Acapulco Canyon

Falls. As though with oils
all along these
walls of streaming stones
the lines of limbs are drawn,
the ceremonial trace of heads
a sweep of birds, a

Paradigm of play,
a mime of clowns:
they sit upon the haunch
in rocks, misogynist,
godlike animals at green
water rituals.

They mock with wigs of moss
and heavy thighs
the hidden siren women
as one half-turns to look
back, over a powerful shoulder,
the ageless fury in his

face matched by his ageless grace.

NUDE KNEELING IN SAND

The girl in the sand
colored hat
of unfinished straw
with its sides of waves
of water weaving
in the winds of her
yellow hair, her eyes
hives of bees, touch-
es her breasts toward her knees.

Like a child she digs
and buries
her thin hands in the
desirable flesh
colored sands, as small
animals or pairs
of birds that wait to
rise and stir scat-
tering streams of amber myrrh.

Out of ecstasy
her bright mouth
opens to the sun
as she lifts herself
to it and rests, with
breasts sweet and full, back
beautifully curved,
arms down, lap and
loins packed with moist, golden coin.

LINES TO CATHERINE

There's not one fact that's certain in
The life of Catherine: as what she suffered
Under Maximin, who wished to try her body
(They say she had surpassing beauty),
Or how she fled from Rome to Araby,
How she stood like Joan before the elder
Enemy or like an adolescent Christ,
Or like the young Rimbaud telling his peers
In poetry what they didn't know,
So uncannily, so boy-brilliant:
So much like a patron to the student
Of philosophy, whó if hé is young,
Will tear and chew upon the bones of truth
Showing teeth, savoring the cut,
Sometimes spitting out the Eucharist of thought;
And when not so young, if he has come again
Lean and starving to the meal of men,
Finds that there is mystery to Catherine:
Something stays with her whether or not
She spent her days still virgin under Maximin
And failed to burst her human heart and bone
Upon that wheel and not some other one.
And because it isn't false
I want to know in what way it is true
That she is buried on old Moses' mountain,
Her slender relics and the laws of women
Mingling with the relics and the laws of men.

LINES TO HIS SON
ON REACHING ADOLESCENCE

I've always thought Polonius a dry
And senile fop, fool to those he didn't love
Though he had given life to them as father—
To his beautiful young boy and beautiful
Young daughter; and loathed Augustine's
Lecherous old man who noticed that his son
Naked at his bath, was growing up
And told his wife a dirty joke. But
I have given my own life to you my son
Remembering my fear, my joy and unbelief
(And my disgust) when I saw you monkey
Blue and blooded, shrouded with the light down
Of the new born, the cord of flesh
That held you to my wife cut free from her
And from my own remote body,
And I could fill you up with epithets
Like Ophelia's father, full of warnings,
For I have learned what we must avoid
And what must choose and how to be of use.
My father never taught me anything
I needed for myself. It's no excuse,
For what he might have said I think
I would refuse, and besides (is it despair
I reach?) I feel we learn too late to teach.
And like Augustine's dad I have watched you bathe
Have seen as my own hair begins to fall
The fair gold beard upon your genital
That soon will flow with seed
And swell with love and pain (I almost add
Again). I cannot say to you whether
In a voice steady or unsteady, ah Christ
Please wait your father isn't ready.
You cannot wait, as he could not.

But for both our sakes I ask you, wrestle
Manfully against the ancient curse of snakes,
The bitter mystery of love, and learn to bear
The burden of the tenderness
That is hid in us. Oh you cannot
Spare yourself the sadness of Hippolytus
Whom the thought of Phaedra
Turned from his beloved horse and bow,
My son, the arrow of my quiver,
The apple of my eye, but you can save your father
The awful agony of Laocoön
Who could not stop the ruin of his son.
And as I can I will help you with my love.
Last I warn you, as Polonius,
Yet not as him, from now on I will not plead
As I have always done, for sons
Against their fathers who have wronged them.
I plead instead for us
Against the sons we hoped we would not hurt.

III

HONOLULU AND BACK

to James Brunot

Ruth had been moved out of her job in an
Hawaiian school for leaving it on Good
Friday to go to church. It was tough to
Get the place for her, but the year the war
Was through you couldn't ship without a job.
Ruth was pregnant and quite ready to rest.
I was sick of greeting an empty house.
In any case we thought we might go back
When school was ended. We celebrated
The loss of the job buying a hot, red
Dress for her and stepping out to dinner.
We had one of those concoctions of wined
Meat sizzling on a stick to be eaten
Piece at a time with salad of lucid
Geometrically beautiful bam-
boo slices. I knew better than order
The oily chicken and rice with chopsticks.
There's an incommensurable ratio
Between a chopstick and a grain of rice,
And a Chinese chicken wants pots of tea.
Later we went to the Honolulu
Art Gallery: we heard a local group
Play quartets and looked at the tropical
Fish mugging in the intermission. Much
Better than the Waikiki movie spot
With its real coconut palms looming up
On either side of a screened Oberon
Or Cary Grant. Somehow I could not get
Used to that, or to the military
Colonies inside of their volcanoes,
The new screams inside Honolulu's zoo,
The powerfully beautiful Pali
View, with land dropping rapidly away

A thousand feet and following in miles
Wide patterns to the sea. I dream of this,
And of another view over downtown
Honolulu from the Heights where I sat
With Ruth in an Hawaiian shade and read
The Oxford Book of Christian Verse. At left
Was a sheer fall and stream and then a great
Field behind King Kamehameha's tomb.
Ruth and I had lain at night in the grass
Behind Kamehameha's bones and his
Relic arms, and saw the planes pass to East:
After a native feast—pig in a pit
At a luau, with raw fish, raw whiskey,
Raw seaweed on the side, and gray, bland poi
Dipped with the hand—a party for a boy
From school. His family presented Ruth
With a brilliant, Chinese-black, lacquered bowl
Full of pineapple, freshly cut with salt,
Barely moist, a most delicate yellow.
Ruth's red laquer dress was paid for after
Several days in those pineapple fields.
Everybody, students and teachers both,
Simply took off to help in the harvest.
There was a pretty dilapidated-
Looking, empty-looking water tower
In the field—it was no barrel of fun
And neither was the job. You don't forget
The terrible heat on the storm helmets
Over the thorn leaves of the pineapples.
They're not so gentle as the mango is
(Or, for a tree, as is the tamarisk).
Once I went on a trip with the school of
Botany at the University.
We left our ten cars and walked off all roads
Slushing through the fields of clay and over
Sluices way up into the lifting hills.
Each one you see of a certain kind of
Tree is a different variety:

Something to do with rain forests, they say.
It didn't stay dry very long that day!
Those trees lose their years for they form no rings
To reckon in this eternal season.
It has no hour. I saw the exciting
Passion flower, that smells of burning flesh,
Taking on the shape and colors of a
Tropical bird, surrealist, absurd.
I loved the trees of sandalwood. They made
The merchants rich; they were carried in ships
To England for incense and then later
Were banned from the island for some reason
Or banned from the Orient or else went
Largely extinct. I forget. Was it burnt
All off in a tropical forest fire?
I am sure the branches of certain trees
Contain so much pitch they will flame for hours
As the naked men, wet skin torchlit, by
The sea's blackened edge, swing out their big, white
Billowing net, and spill its thousand fish.
Evenings on board ship the best part of the
Trip. Clouds catching several lights of sea
And those of the losing sun, and scudding
At times like bunches of scrubbed wool with soft,
Trapped light about the sky. When we arrived
Late at night the island lay like money
In the story on the velvet prince's
Pouch, or like drops of rain upon the tongue
Of a black flower. My god how it rained
On that field trip!... No place in those high spots
To cover up. You know the rain will last
And you have to get back. You single track
So as not to separate and be drowned.
You crush a while in a futile kind of
Trial against a bank, but soon or late:
You agree to soak. Occasionally
I stopped in that wet to collect some moss
For a friend in an Iowa college.

A coed helped. The immodest effect
Of the rain on her particularly
Hit me. I thought her blouse clinging to her
Small breasts well worth remembering. I left
All my moss in our Honolulu house
That last wild day on the island. We went
Because there wasn't any winter there.
We had trouble getting reservations;
But found some on the Matson through a friend
Of mine, a Buddhist, business aide at school.
He had a contact at the ocean line.
The liturgy was done with perfect art
At Convent of the Sacred Heart. The priest
Gave a homily that was to the point,
And the chants of nuns were never human.
On Mayday hundreds of Hawaiian girls
In uniform crowned the Blessed Virgin
While the nuns' house was open, and every
Body sang on the lawn. The convent gate
Gave access to the sisters in their clouds
Of woolen white, a perfect, needle point-
ed bleeding heart under an ageless face.
We talked to one when she was stopped for rest.
She had huge moles with shining hairs on her
Chaucerian countenance. The ancient
Face of sky changed and changed at night. I watched
Figures of ballet slow and settle there
In puffs of powder. We lolled one night late
Outside the music room and heard a Swan
Lake tide and fall by the island rock wall.
One night's noon saw the odd moon flower bloom
Beside the school at Punahou. I thought
Of werewolves' London whines. At school recess
Boys played the ukulele and the girls
Always wore hibiscus in their hair. Those
Boys loved quite young, and all day long they rode
Surf in the summer sun. Waves knock, and gun.
Ruth was far gone in the malaise that gives

Life to men: that last day was mean for her.
She was a little green as we were kissed
In our cabin by friends who gave tear full,
Fragrant leis of ginger and of jasmine.
Strawberry guavas were good or better
Than gooseberries I remembered at home.
I hunted them when I went for lessons
On the piano. The teacher played flute
In the chamber group at the gallery.
There were guavas by the light, quiet spot
Where I got off the late afternoon bus.
Children were way down the block, and the sun
Slanted in the special air. Enough rain
To have it fresh to breathe. I had trouble,
Because of envy, with a sonata
Brahms wrote at twenty. As the ship pulled out
From under the pier's high clock, I thought that
I had not said goodbye to my teacher.
The charming, muscular children still run
For gold in the quick, bright wake of the ship,
Their breech cloths blowing in the waters' air
Like feathers of Hawaiian birds up there
Before the rain. But all the birds were dead
In Bishop's museum. I for my part
Cared more for the Polynesian village
In the court. I liked the snails that became
Extinct when their shells curved into a spi-
ral six feet across and equal angled.
And once a colony of good kids flowed
Past a dusty glass case, all fully dressed.
They took some kind of notes. And now they dove
About the wake and were lost, and now they
Broke again and grinned with lips of shocking
Color I had seen off Diamond Head
From a glass bottomed boat, their teeth like
Stunning shells that have sunned on the sea's steps.
There are certain shapes in the deeper sea
And certain exquisite tones in the dark

There where light never goes. I think these kids
Were bright as those shapes. I am sure they shrieked
In a gaudy English. The gulf grew wide
And Ruth and I had our picture taken
By the rail. Our hair blew to Hawaii.
The flowers around our necks all stayed fresh
In that picture, no more changed than the land
Marking mountain in the background; a bus
In the road at its foot waits for passage
Like a vassal at the palace. I know
How beautiful the sea is on this side
Of that road: many colored marvelous
High poundings, caught a moment before spilling
In that particular light, had held
Me all one Sunday. The picnic sand was
Pointed and wet on the skin of my back.
I took Ruth's hand. We walked on the beach and
Found a stream hid away from there. We crossed
A fence. We felt it wasn't meant for us.
We did not trespass, for there was some spring
Or source to find we thought, and we moved a-
round the side of a lower mountain
Along that stream. At this angle, though not
From the road or beach, above the level
Of the shade, a thin water fall sudden-
ly dropped before us, as colorful tears
The acacia trees cry down from their tops
On the hill. This beauty was unsupposed.
There was no one about! Along the bank
Of the stream small shells lay, passing much light,
Brought in some way out of the bright sea. I
Loved Ruth in this place. Ruth loved me. We found
Our son beside that stream in that now
Alien heaven. We have not told him.
Perhaps he'll come upon it in himself
Someday to make lucid some mystery
About his midwest youth. To look back and
Find that!.... The long unknown wisps of water

Dropped from tropical woods where sandalwood
Smells so sweet and burns so bird bright, and then
Gone in to the masculine sea where im-
mense tunas tremble off the shore and small
Devil fish, a brilliant blue in the sand,
Die with malice and sting the bone white feet.
I ran over the stone, wet beach at night
My first trip around the island past Di-
amond Head. I was alone. I stripped and
left my clothes in the borrowed jeep. That fresh
Nakedness in another world was good.
I fell on the shore out of human breath
And I smelled in that damp sand sandalwood
And faint bits of fish borne from the agèd
East which I was closer to, separate
Only by the long, slow movements of the
Deeper sea that touched my face now and skin
With its own tide, and I felt under my
Shivering chest and belly and under
My Iowa loins, ancient Polyne-
sian grains blown from the sea, the fertile rice
Of a great and furious race. At last
I stood quiet by that fathering sea.
From its iridescent froth a golden
Flying fish winged and rose in front of me
Into a weightless arch, and at the end
Went again into it. The whitening
Wake of our ship spread with the better speed
And I saw in it the arcs of fireworks
At New Year rocketing in the valley
Below as we watched from our window. Ruth
Had been so startled at the lack of snow.
I did not mind there were no fallen leaves.
It was Ruth who missed the season, and I?
I would have missed her had I stayed. Better
A short time, I thought, as the ship moved out;
After all, the trees are not my trees. The
Obscene breadfruit which they say the natives

Used to eat. The exhibitionistic
Hibiscus. The austere eucalyptus
With provoking oil and tattered gray.
The papaya is not right on the west-
ern palate. But the mimosa tree, so
Sensitive it shrinks to the limb at touch
Of its tip, one could feel inside the heart.
I hoped I had forgot the gnarled village-
like, cavernous banyan tree on the lawn
At Kamehameha's Palace, where the
Hundred thousand feathers on official plumes
And hats gather dust: they had been picked
From those fields of birds. Our Buddhist friend
Will not allow us to forget *Ficus*,
The Fig, where Buddha sat at the center
In the world, as its quivering leaves tell.
Perhaps the last sound we heard as the space
To Hawaii grew great was the clapping
Of the Buddhist boards as from the temple
On our hill—waking us at four o'clock,
Clattering from time to time through the day.
One Sunday, waked by that, I walked beyond
The school to a lucent, deep rock-lined pool;
I swam as the boards clacked and the tinny
Cymbals clanged their morning prayers; and I sat
A while, my legs crossed upon the pool's ledge.
I knew I was too narrow for a god.
I thought the tone of Buddhist funeral
Reeds better suited me. Later I looked
At the awesome inside of a temple.
The brass and gold of the great canopy!
The brilliant, occult lights! I found their book
Inside the pew and said a Buddhist act
Of faith and thought about our friend who helped.
He also served the priest and taught holy
Wrestling to the young; an ancient kind of
Champion, a powerful, neckbreaking
Man, a great Chinese who's solid as his
Ancestral wall, and who revered the foods

I would not eat. There was no job to miss
On board the ship, but you could go to Mass.
The trip was terrible for Ruth. We went
First class. She could not eat the likable
Squab under glass. We read Sigrid Undset
Out loud on the deck in the better airs.
Now home, we have our trees and seasons'
Change and our own, unmixed, midwest prayers.

A TRIP TO FOUR OR FIVE TOWNS

to James Wright

1

The gold-colored skin of my Lebanese friends.
Their deep, lightless eyes.
The serene, inner, careful
balance they share. The conjugal
smile of either for either.

2

This bellychilling, shoe soaking, factory-
dug-up-hill smothering Pittsburgh weather!
I wait for a cab in the smart mahogany
lobby of the seminary.
The marble *Pietà* is flanked around
with fake fern. She cherishes her dead son
stretched along her womb he triple crossed.
A small, slippered priest
pads up. Whom do you seek, my son?
Father, I've come in out of the rain.
I seek refuge from the elemental tears,
for my heavy, earthen body runs to grief
and I am apt to drown
in this small and underhanded rain
that drops its dross so delicately
on the hairs of the flowers, my father,
and follows down the veins of leaves
weeping quiet in the wood.

My yellow cab never came,
but I did not confess
beneath the painted Jesus Christ. I left

and never saved myself at all
That night in that late, winter rain.

3

In Washington, was it spring?
I took the plane.
I heard, on either side,
the soft executives, manicured and
fat, fucking this and fucking that.
My heavy second breakfast
lay across my lap.
At port, in the great concourse,
I could not walk to city bus
or cab? or limousine?
I sweat with shock, with havoc
of the hundred kinds of time,
trembling like a man away from home.

At the National Stripshow
where the girls wriggle right
and slow, I find I want to see in
under the sequin stepin.
And in my later dream of the negro girl's room
strong with ancient sweat and with her thick
aroma, I seem to play a melodrama
as her great, red dog barks twice
and I stab it with my pocket knife.

4

In Richmond the azalea banks
burst in rose and purple gullies by the car,
muted in the soft, wet
April twilight. The old estates
were pruned and rolled fresh
with spring, with splendor, touch-
ing the graceful stride of the boy who brings the paper.

5

My friend has a red-headed mother
capable of love in any kind
of weather. I am not sure
what she passes to her daughters
but from her brown eye and from her breast
she passes wit and spunk to her big sons.
And she is small and pleased when they put
their arms around her, having caught her.
They cut the grass naked to the waist.
They cure the handsome skins of chipmunks and of snakes.
And when they wake in their attic room
they climb down the ladder, half
asleep, feeling the rungs' pressure
on their bare feet, shirt tails out,
brown eyes shut. They eat
what she cooks. One shot a gorgeous colored hawk
and posed with it, proud, arms and full wings
spread. And one, at the beach,
balanced on his hands, posed
stripped, in the void of sand,
limbs a rudder in the wind,
amid the lonely, blasted wood.
And two sons run swift roans in the high, summer grass.
Now I would guess
her daughters had at least this same
grace and beauty as their mother,
though I have only seen their picture.
I know she is happy with her three
strong sons about her, for they are not clumsy
(one, calmed, so calmly,
bends a good ear to his guitar)
and they are not dull:
one built a small electric shaft topped with a glowing ball.

6

In New York I got drunk, to tell the truth,
and almost got locked up when a beat
friend with me took a leak in a telephone booth.
(E. E. Cummings on the Paris lawn.
"Reprieve le pisseur Américain!")
At two o'clock he got knocked out
horning in with the girl in the room over him.
Her boy friend was still sober,
and too thin. I saw the blood of a poet
flow on the sidewalk. Oh, if I mock,
it is without heart. I thought
of the torn limbs of Orpheus
scattered in the grass on the hills of Thrace.
Do poets have to have such trouble with the female race?
I do not know. But if they bleed
I lose heart also.
When he reads, ah, when he reads, small but deep voiced,
he reads well: now weeps, now is cynical,
his large, horned eyes very black and tearful.

And when we visited a poet father
we rode to Jersey on a motor scooter.
My tie and tweeds looped in the winds.
I choked in the wake
of the Holland Pipe, and cops,
under glass like carps, eyed us.
That old father was so mellow and generous—
easy to pain,
white, open and at peace, and of good taste,
like his Rutherford house.
And he read, very loud and regal,
sixteen new poems based on paintings by Breughel!

7

The last night out,
before I climbed on the formal
Capital Viscount and was shot home
high, pure and clear,
seemed like the right time
to disappear.

June, 1959

SPRING OF THE THIEF

POEMS 1960–1962

for
C S C
A   E
S   S

The Redemption Has Happened.
The Holy Ghost is in Men.
The Art is to Help Men
Become What They Really Are.

I

MONOLOGUES OF THE SON
OF SAUL

1

Ah, so our first load of honey heavy Christmas trees.
Then the sweet Christ comes again. See, in the high truck bed
the greens spring easy as the thighs of young lovers
while the aromatic golden gum, gift of The Magus,
oozes under the light cover of snow, rising slow
as the milk of the dead. Mothers will survive these rites
of birth, it is said. We prove it by our liturgy.
But I do not believe my own theory, and am cursed
to figure how I was blest at the root of my heart
by a man sitting underneath a flowering tree
in a white shirt open at the throat, dark face lucid,
saying the stories of a father for me. Yet I,
I have thieved my father's treasure. And I cannot pay.
On my naked birthday I brought to bed his amber haired,
shy eyed wife, her face birch white against the linen
loaf or coif of her pillow. Now, Advent, her quilted,
copper coffin glows again with a green, harlot's light
inside my head. Oh I've tried boyishly before to-
day to lay her virgin ghost in this enormous house,
but still I feel her black teeth click and push at the roots
of its dying blood (or apple) colored bush.

2

I did but taste a little of the honey with the
tip of my rod and my eyes were opened, and behold
I must die. May God do so and more my father said
for thou shalt surely die, Jonathan, but the Lord God
sent leaping from the heart of a bush a saving ram,
and so I live. Oh I have not my father's wisdom,
gift of a tender God to strike me blind in the road
and send me wandering, goodly monomaniac,
all one-eyed, over the oceans of Odysseus
(while my wife's fingers bleed as breasts on her unfinished web).
Yet though I have not my father's light I would know
my fault. For I did but taste a little of the honey
with the tip of my rod. Through God my life was knit
to his who killed the giant king with a stalk he ground
into the single, brazen eye: showering his blood
like rays of lucid wine watering the green slips of men.
I loved him as my own soul. I took off my clothes
and gave them to him, even my sword and bow and belt.
See, I have made myself naked for my brother. I
have made myself poor. Later when my jealous father
spoke to him alone at the table and had him play
the melancholy lute in his room, I loved him more
it seemed and took his part before the throne of Saul. Then
suddenly my father saw him enemy and sought
his life, the hot young breath of David, who won his wife
with foreskins of a thousand dead. When my father threw
the javelin at him, he fled. God what was his fault?
We sat at meat. I felt the cold growing in my groin
when my father cried for him, and so I lied for love
till my father called my mother whore and threw the spear
at me! It struck the wall. What was his fault then, or mine,
David's friend, who shot my arrow past the barren shelf
where he hid and turned the wrath of Saul against myself?
Out of a place toward the south my brother rose and

falling to the ground bowed himself thrice. He kissed my face.
We wept together for our human need, praying God
forever be between him and me, and among our springing seed,
for we but tasted honey in the summer wood.

124

3

"Far off the road on the left on a slight rolling hill"
I cannot eat my son in the tower of the barn
black with rain, though I lie on my back and starve to death
in a dirty shirt, sick and pierced in the flank by spears
of bronze straw, where he sits beside, his curious eyes
open in the dark, having twice dressed with rags my sweat-
tossed nakedness as I tore slobbering at my sack.
Christ I wish my sin in the barn had me drunk with wine!
Or that I lay in my chains looked at by gentle guards—
muscled, grizzled, Roman hero stripped and left to starve.
If a brown-eyed woman came to the barn in the long
rain, shivering with wet, child folded at her big breast,
I was too weak to talk. My son told I vomited
his stolen bread six days, even when he chewed and fed
the pap for me. (I know he cried as a child who tried
to keep alive some enormous feeble bird he had.)
No money to buy his milk, he said. I heard her breath,
felt her glance along my naked leg, and then away.
She sat hunched and silent, child across her lap. She rose
at last, and sighed: "Wait. I have to dry my clothes. I'll keep
the coat." And gave my son her child, moving into the
smoking, summer shadow of the barn. As she undressed
ah my God I could not taste again our ancient sweet
yearning in the flesh, now soft as underthighs of frogs,
and thought I was already dead. I wept. She walked close
wrapped in her wool coat of wine red. I shook my head. Yet
she lay beside me on the crushed, yellow shoots of hay
as though to rest, and loosened on one side her gold breast,
full as pears the drunken bees tremble for in the fall. She
drew down my giant skull. There, she said. There.
And I felt her fingers stir, weaving their life in my hair.

4

In my dream I know I see my father Saul a king,
the bronze gates of home shot open with a ram of oak,
my parents' private rooms naked to the look of the
enemy, cleats of their tough boots clacking in the halls,
packing the doors, where the mothers cling and seem to kiss
the wooden jambs in the hope of saints. The inner house
stirs with cries. The court shunts toward the cope of sky (and its
cold stars) the women's keening. Fifty bridal chambers,
extravagant boast for his children's children, their doors
thick with spoils of carved barbaric gold, smoke to ruin.
My father fastens round his aged, shivering breast
the dull arms of his youth, binds on his sword and sheath
and bends toward his death. See, beneath the open dark sky
a massive rock altar by a years-old laurel tree
that holds all of our loved household gods in its shadow.
My mother and sisters hover at the altar stones,
as doves driven by the hot storms, clutching husks of gods,
and when they see the king dressed in his rust streaked armor
Mother scolds him for his madness, asking where he goes
and sits him down softly by the sacred lights to pray.
Suddenly along the echoing colonnades my
screaming brother runs the gauntlet of the enemy!
Chased by a mocking giant hacking at his young limbs
with swords. He circles through the court and long rooms and
    comes
last, moaning, before my parents' altar to pour his life
in pools as wasted semen or sacramental wine
shattered on the stone. My father cries that he has lived
to see his sons bled before his eyes like slaughtered pigs.
He curses my brother's murderer and flings his spear. It
rings the shield weakly, sticks and droops from the bronze belly.

The giant drags my father to the altar, shaking
and obscenely sliding in the blood of family—
he twists the old hair in his left hand, raises his red
sword in the right and buries it in my father's heart.
My father does not die a death of fame. His white head-
less trunk rolls on the shore without a name.

5

If the half moon stamp of a sacred hoof showed Cadmus
where to found the town of Thebes, so what: Medea's love
has left me Corinth, as she careens into the sun,
her murdered kin (I think again of that hot, young niece
I had in bed) like a white and awkward albatross
about her neck—or like the dead ducks of poets, stretched
across a virgin lap. She fled mad in a flame red
chariot knit with copulating snakes, as the fake
staffs of medicine, rods of Mercury or Aaron
(whose brother came to life again out of a box a-
mid the holy human grass). It was this scene of snakes
god damned Tiresias to his female half of life!
So then my sweet son Bellerophon do not play mad
as David did, fellow in your art, who let his wife
lower him out of the house in a wicker cart. Oh,
I know how Saul himself (no artist) foamed in the mouth
and lay down nude all one day and night to prophesy
when David cut his shirt privily—he who played out
on the melancholy lute psalms of every man's heart.
The lame and ugly son of Jonathan, father dead,
and ignorant of his father's friend, sweat like a girl
to David's face, without faith the king had ever loved
in his youth, or first possessed the poet's gentle curse.
Oh my well loved son Bellerophon, you too have reined
the winged horse—your bastard brother Odysseus
lurked inside a wooden one, and waited to be born.
You would not stone as him the martyr Greek or wander
over his ancient, arrogant, labyrinthine route.
Odysseus I got on the daughter of a thief.
(The little, burnt moons I branded on the cattle's foot
printed down the road toward her house). Odysseus
was gored when he visited the crook, and you like him
are lame my son and beg for your poor bread, pushed at last
off the back of soaring Pegasus, who now is walked—
a tender-eared ass!—to pack the thunderbolts of Zeus.

You fell into a bramble bush like a horny saint
to blind your looking eyes and break the legs you dance on.
Yet no more than Orpheus or drowning Arion
could you escape the women, and one you had refused
lied like the wife of Potiphar—once you shot with lead
the disconsolate Chimera's female jaw, whose hot
breath smoked and began to melt the ore down her sucking maw.
Ah son, on the moaning beach Xanthian bitch on bitch
mad with juice they took from the smears of mares in rut, ran
at you, lifting up their skirts, to cut your manly parts!
For they hoped a poet's blood would fountain in their wombs
and make them quick. See, I weep for you my eunuch son,
beloved Bellerophon, and up the mound roll
back again the gradual rock of my grieving heart.

February 1960

TO A YOUNG POET WHO FLED

Your cries make us afraid, but we love your delicious music! —Kierkegaard

So you said you'd go home to work on your father's farm.
We've talked of how it is the poet alone can touch
with words, but I would touch you with my hand, my lost son,
to say good-bye again. You left some work, and have gone.
You don't know what you mean. Oh, not to me as a son,
for I have others. Perhaps too many. I cannot
answer all the letters. If I seem to brag, I add
I know how to shatter an image of the father
(twice have tried to end the yearning of an orphan son,
but opened up in him, and in me, another wound).
No—I say this: you don't know the reason of your gift.
It's not the suffering. Others have that. The gift of tears
is the hope of saints, Monica again and Austin.
I mean the gift of the structure of a poet's jaw,
which makes the mask that's cut out of the flesh of his face
a megaphone—as with the goat clad Greeks—to ampli-
fy the light gestures of his soul toward the high stone seats.
The magic of the mouth that can melt to tears the rock
of hearts. I mean the wand of tongues that charms the exile
of listeners into a bond of brothers, breaking
down the lines of lead that separate a man from a
man, and the husbands from their wives, in these old, burned glass
panels of our lives. The poet's jaw has its tongue ripped
as Philomel, its lips split (and kissed beside the grave),
the jawbone patched and cracked with fists and then with
          the salve
of his fellows. If they make him bellow, like a slave
cooked inside the ancient, brass bull, still that small machine
inside its throat makes music for an emperor's guest
out of his cries. Thus his curse: the poet cannot weep
but with a public and musical grief, and he laughs
with the joys of others. Yet, when the lean blessings come,

they are sweet, and great. My son, I could not make your choice.
Let me take your hand. I am too old or young to say with you,
"I'd rather be a farmer in the hut, understood
by swine, than be a poet misunderstood by men."

II

THE THIRTY-THREE RING CIRCUS

I
1

The wife of the clown,
a disconsolate performing goose,
is held by a rope
to a stake, like a hippopotamus.

2

The two and trio of hammer men,
torn dirty jeans and shirts,
poised black arms raised naked in the sun,
bow and gesture with the ancient grace
smashing iron stakes, in counter-
point of two or three strokes.

3

A carnival kid in white
cotton training pants
(perhaps the son of a gnome?)
is not spanked for fiddling with wires
at a socket on the shell of his home.

4

If we try to see in the curtains
of a performer's trailer, before
the circus, it is with the hope
of sneaking a look
at some slobbering freak.

5

An old, slop-hat, melancholy
father, no Telemachus found,
rushes weeping about the tent and ground.

6

The circus leopards start
electronic echoes.

7

The snake that can crush a pig
lies thick in a tank, its big
eye turning white, and its hide
which glowed with silver and red
on a sunshot Indian bank,
has begun to stink.

8

In the sawdust
nest of the ring
a small car spawns
a litter of clowns.

9

One grabs his hat and loses his pants
and grabs his pants and loses his hat
and grabs his hat and loses his self-
respect, his wife, and every mark
of his former art and life.

II

10

The elephant, ill with fatigue,
straws of its bed on its back,
nudges in the ring
with a kind of stupid tenderness.

11

The camel, improbable
on the face of the earth,
behind the glazing eyes
in its small skull a dream
of sand, has placed its hump
thru a hole in a flag
advertising salad oil.

12

Not even shot
from a cannon,
the clown shivers
inside, peeks o-
ver the rim and
throws out
his human hat.

13

The woman in a blue bustle,
man in a blue blouse,
are skating on some thin ice
at the top of the house.
(Zeus crashing to earth
would take his spouse.)

14

The man stands up
behind the woman who stands up
behind the boy who stands up
behind the child who stands
on the bench beside its mother.

15

The girl has lost her face.
It blurs with her brown hair
as her body spins a sheath,
by the skin of its teeth.

16

The drummer, belly sweating
thru his shirt, conducts
with ease an inane waltz
of death or life on the trapeze.

17

Two fairies teeter
on the high wire.
In despair one leaps
over the other,
breaks his fall, and swings
solo, head over tail.

18

The man with a white parasol
walks a rope (in a white
suit) sloped from the floor
to the top of the highest pole
in the tent, and vanishes
in a cloud of light at the vent.

19

The lion hides his dung
and swings under his flank
his leather genital
unable to pump the furious seed
in a steaming African glade.

20

A harem of a hundred girls,
lavender veiled, their navels
and tops of breasts exposed,
beautifully die
before the stands, and rise
on ropes to Mohammedan heaven
where they play in unison
their tiny xylophones.

21

The man who
stands on one
finger, on
one edge of
a ladder
on one leg,
on a ball,
tentative
as a soul.

III

22

Twirling her beads and plumes
she rears and jumps the horse
and tries to make him dance
(not a chance).

23

Unarmed a clown,
separated from the men
of his battalion,
is lost and shot down—
his dumb head blown clean
from his trunk. He trudges home
sorry and alone.

24

The giddy ostrich man
with his huge, orange ass
and bent bodice, his neck
hairy and slim (a gift
ribbon on its original apple),
scurries drunk and shy
avoiding our argus eye.

25

Clowns in adult, big feet,
red wigs and print dresses
with no hips
hang out their wash in the noon
August heat of the tent,
their sweating upper lips
hysterical with
hatred of their sons.

26

She swings out
into the audience
with swimming hair:
tights cuddling

graceful breasts,
her belly, and her
ravenous, universal
crotch—just
visible for an instant
above the crowd.

27

Black maned, the magnificent golden
Filipino, stripped to the waist, chest
oiled and smooth as a boy's, rides aloft
with his family. He takes the hand
of his wife, gliding past his brother,
who catches a perch and sweeps past him
to the wife, and they fly together
for a while till she exchanges them
in mid-air and he guides her again.
At last he turns toward his brother, and
throws a triple somersault, and fails, flop-
ping harmless into a nlyon net.

28

Six ponies have burned
a circle into the ground
giving rides to kids.
(Their trainers trace
the radius.)

29

After the tent is down,
the circus owner, having
slept over, sets out
in his red car, feeding
his silver slug of a house
over the waste he is lord of.

30

Kids on bicycles
gathering bottles
and a dozen bent,
thirty-five-cent fans
from the Orient.

31

By a dead bon-
fire lies the charred
button-down
shoe of a clown.

32

Between the well
and the hill
is the skull
of a doll.

33

So gored a thousand times through the heart
and mouth and thighs our earth smells of the death
of worlds, for the sulphur dung of Royal Bengal
tigers, the droppings of birds of paradise
and thin llamas from the rare plateaus
mingle on the local lot
with popcorn and the vomit of a dog.

HOMAGE TO CHRISTINA ROSSETTI

1

Christina (seven) skipped a stone
  in a small pond by her home:
  a frog came up from the dead
  or sluggish waterweed, tossed

  to his head (enormous eyed!)
  his green and ivory hand
  and moved away from there—with
A touching, still too human air.

2

If Christina found a dead bird
she would with pity bury it.
Once being tempted, bad and young
she came back to play a small God
uncovering the graceful mound,
but soon fled (crying) from a worm,
a thinner and more awful form.

3

"How she loved to catch a
  cold, little toad
or caterpillar

in the hollow of her
  beautiful hand,"
said Christina's friend.

4

A white peacock
on the Rossetti's lawn
   shook its gorgeous
watching plumes up and down,

   crying out with
sharp, inhuman pleasure.
   A fallow deer,
priestly, grace full creature,

   was overwhelmed—
and following the bird
   trampled each eye
tropical and absurd.

5

Christina received
   from her lover
who went down to sea
   in the summer

A gift for her house:
   the small sea mouse
delicately haired
   and colored green,

preserved in some wine.

6

When Christina turned sixteen
  she began to dream:
it was Regent's Park at dawn
  as the sun dropped down
its cold, almost moon-like light
  shattering on the
stone to a rose or gray pond;
  and through the clean sun,
through the blurred, green, naked limbs
  of trees, suddenly

yellow waves of light are swept!
  All the canaries
of London fly their cages
  to flock in the spring-
chilled day's halfawakened trees,
  their small ecstasies
letting undulating light
  rise like an odor
from their lean, golden bodies
  hovered together.

*For Marya Zaturenska in gratitude
for her book on Christina Rossetti*

III

ON READING CAMUS
IN EARLY MARCH

I discovered inside myself, even in the very midst of
winter, an invincible summer.

—Camus

That boy in the red coat packing snow
mixes in my mind with the obscure
taste for beauty Camus' writing stirs.
I don't say the beauty of the boy—
open only through his naked face,
only his eyes drawing the full stores
of his emerging life, that seems to
root deeply back toward the dead. (See
how the boy stands footless in the snow,
like some smashed piece of Italian stone.)
Not that, but what he does to the cold,
pure seed or sand through his muffled hand:
how he brings the Midas touch of art—
I don't care how crude he seems to mold.
Not sad or old, not adult, the boy
has no more need of art than a saint;
and as he throws against the wall, shat-
tering what his hand could form, I feel
the older, more yearning child's alarm.

SONG ON THE DREAD
OF A CHILL SPRING

I thought (and before it was too late)
my heart had begun to turn, that was
shut to love, for I was adamant
as saints, and tough as the martyr's heart,
as a wooden statue of a god,
where my father sat in the straight pew,
my mother bowed to the stone, bearing
flowers she had cut out of the earth
of my life. Ah the candles bloom cold
in the earthen air of early Mass,
like the tops of wan hepatica
that lift their light cups in the first time.
So shy we touch at these Ides of March!

Winter was too long and cold. The spring
is brief. These tulips offer up their gold
and the purple plum our grief.

LAMENT IN SPRING

Oh I have felt these same
yearnings in myself—
the tiny dark and yellow
hairs lit with wet
at the center of the May Day
violets Elizabeth held
in her seven-year-old fist
some six or seven years before
the grace she gave the afternoon

(her hand stemmed in mine)
at the topaz time of day
when children doze and she,
Elizabeth, waits breath-
less at the edge of the well.
She was my brother's girl,
and so I let her go.
For who can stand these old stirrings
in himself, and that one too?

LINES ON HIS BIRTHDAY

I was born on a street named Joy
of which I remember nothing,
but since I was a boy
I've looked for its lost turning.
Still I seem to hear my mother's cry
echo in the street of joy.
She was sick as Ruth for home
when I was born. My birth
took away my father's wife
and left me half
my life. Christ will my remorse
be less when my father's dead?
Or more. As Lincoln's minister of war
kept the body of his infant boy
in a silver coffin on his desk,
so I keep
in a small heirloom box of teak
the picture of my living father.
Or perhaps it is an image of myself
dead in this box she held?
I know her milk like ivory blood
still runs in my thick veins
and leaves in me an almost
lickerish taste for ghosts:
my mother's wan face,
full brown hair, the mammoth breast
death cuts off at the bone—
to which she draws her bow
again, brazen Amazon,
and aiming deadly as a saint
shoots her barb
of guilt into my game heart.

January 23, 1961

THE EXPERIMENT THAT FAILED

It is probable that mutual transfusions were first performed in 1492 between Pope Innocent VIII and two healthy boys, an experiment culminating in deaths of all concerned including the Pope.

—Source Book of Animal Biology

I have not written my poem
about the Pope and the two young men
the obscure, muddle-headed muse
first sent when I first read
histories of the transfusion experiment.
And I do not know why,
except for the bitter fight
in me—about the fact
the boys died. (But so did he.)
The two youths look alike
in my thought. Though one is good,
one bad. Both are dead.
I may distinguish yet
between the dark and light.
One shouldn't have to kill them both.
What do we kill them with?
A knife and tourniquet?
A porcelain dish,
its white edge flecked with dirt
causing the blood to clot
(so he demands more
from one or another)? A tube
of some fifteenth-century rubber?
God, the irony.
This was the time of discovery!
The very year the Catholic Columbus
tried for a splendid shore
in his three, piddling ships.
Together they made one—

Columbus was a man.
His Canary Island docking
was an imaginative mistaking.
But what can *I* find out?
I don't even know what killed them.
Or him. And I do not want
to think it was the loss of the blood
of manhood. There is always more of that.
Besides it is really feminine
to bleed and be afraid.
Well, what then?
The one old and the two young
men. Two fresh stones, or wells—
and the powerful, untried pen.
What cut them down?
Columbus…Washington…the mythical tree…
the recurring blade…. No.
I don't see.
Yet my mind keeps holding back
with its bloody axe of stone
another idea
nobody wants known:
that it was the hope of a fresh, transmuted life
for which the Pope
and Columbus and the two sons died.

TALE OF A LATER LEANDER

Great display guts. Fine young man come from America swim Dardanelles which had not seen daytime and especially this late in year. I say "Yashaa" to this young man.

—Turkish Captain Quoted in *Life*

1

If thieves got your bags at Istanbul
you flew across the sea of Marmara
and banged on the gates of the little shops
at dusk, hollering for aid. The minaret
of a mosque, gathering the last light,
glowed above the blue-and-gold mosaic arch
like the torch of Hero at her point of watch
high over the killing Hellespont.

2

You raised the dead to fill your need.
You rode over the rock strewn plain for hours
near Leander's mythical home, to climb
aboard a scow manned by a mad team
of Turks, veterans of the cold swim.
The ship's cabin was lighted by a single,
urine yellow lantern, and an old Greek
steered by hand her length of thirty-six feet.

3

Midnight beneath an ancient Asian moon
you strip to the heroic, gold muscle and bone,
smear your belly and chest, swollen sex
and flanks with the scow's own engine grease,
and like a naked dancer poise—to dive
into the heart cold sea, its water
dark with Shelley's or Leander's blood,
its waves lit with pearls of their spent seed.

4

Your foot feels for the bottom of their grave,
rich with the silt of poet's earth,
Edward King and Hart Crane, and of other
wanderers to the sea: sailor, coral,
dolphin, anemone. And you rise again,
flesh flashing white! and black! in the pharos'
broken light. Eyes haunting, intent,
you start to crawl across the Hellespont.

5

Soon your bones cool to the core, and your face
aches and changes in that awful chill.
You rest on your back playing the girl
to the current and the moon, and drift downstream,
until you hear the Turks scream gibberish
from the scow, and turn to fight with the sea
again, heading north to the Bosporous—
moved as Io dogged by the lust of Zeus.

6

Once I hear you groan, see you are gone
beneath the surface of a wave, one hand
caught around the big, quivering stone
of your leg, stroking it, caressing
it, as a lost boy, toward your heart,
and treading water like a broken bird,
one winged. Ah, melancholy Icarus I feel
the sea's chill at the quick of my own skull.

7

Faintly they shout. You won't turn back
toward the ship, but drag your leg
as Jacob struggling with some abstract strength,

with Proteus, or the devil of the ice. Byron
circles his grotesque foot in the Hellespont—
as you watch the mouths of the madmen work
furious in the gaudy jets of light,
hearing how the cold has made you deaf!

 8

A rope crawls on the skin of your back,
and you turn panic-struck into the phosphorous wake
of a black ship that bears its harrowing screw
just beyond, huge and spirit silent...
Weak as a tin boat you faint at last
on the rocks by the base of Hero's tower,
and the Turks haul up a frozen, shuddering, oily
beast of the sea: its twitching limbs still gesture
in the old, flesh-remembered motions of the swimmer.

IV

ON A PHOTOGRAPH
BY AARON SISKIND

Te Deum laudamus
O Thou Hand of Fire!

—Hart Crane

1

After some miserable disaffection
of the only human heart and human hand
we'll ever have, we move to this pictured glove
or hand (ghost by absence) of Aaron Siskind,
a small spirit by image, able to shape

eloquently in the air—as though
to tell, "a man stands here"—able to meet
a handsome and beloved guest, or turn
so tenderly on a wife's face and breast.
Thus this glove, flecked with white paint that glints like

the unnatural light of an angel's scale
brushed off at Jacob's crippling, desperate fall…
pale froth on the wrist and palm of a proud youth…
of the pearls that whisper through the Doge's hand.
It is the left glove, the hand of The Magus,

of all who come late or by devious ways
oblique to honor Christ, all who have stopped
to see the sure, more customary king,
having set some ridiculous gift apart—
as frankincense or myrrh, gold for the child, art.

2

The glove's backed by grained wood
it is in some light held
molded at the lid

as the arm of a Saint in amber and glass
in another cast it rests
laid by with the love of a man
to be caught up again
or it will float out toward us from that rich wood
like the hand of him who draws life
deep into the massive limbs
of Adam gesturing
to name all the gorgeous animals of earth.
I know it is this hand
or glove of God that teases us
so that we must change our life.

3

Yet in certain lights it is a melancholy hand
sloughed off with the body's green flesh. It is the stone
glove of Keats, its thumb and first finger fast angled
in that last, inexorable geometry,
unable to tell a quill or fix the rush of wine
that has made the reader mad and left him graced again,
his face caught in a gentle, momentary peace.
Ah Christ where is that grave hand this glove has left behind?
Once it held a brush heavy with the hope of beauty.

4

It is a hand that has already waved good-bye.
By it we know
we have missed our joy.
The glove is waste,
relic of a little work long since done.
The fingers bend stiff upon the palm
for it lay doubled on them as it dried,
a dead hand of Nietzsche's dying god.
Ghost of the Master's hand!
Glove of Aaron Siskind! I
feel your canvas touch

flicked with lead spots of paint
upon the cold point of my heart.

This picture is a fist.
I feel it is a thing
Siskind had cut out of my quivering chest—
out of my huge, furred stomach,
It is a fist. It is a face
in the mirror I no longer watch;
and its light flecks have now the glint of tears
I have never wept
out of the tender, bald knuckles of my eyes.

A SUITE OF SIX PIECES FOR SISKIND

1

The tip
of a leaf
is the wing of a bird
pinned (stretched) to a board.

2

A white notch as of bone
for a lost gun,
its prongs as roots
of a mammoth overturned tooth—

or like the odd feet
of some ultimate, melancholy freak—
looks into a profound honeycomb
the texture (odor?) of a morel mushroom.

3

A smashed piece of terracotta
shaped as the bottom
of a whale's mouth
(edges shorn of teeth)

stands upright
like a little, sacred shrine.
And on the shattered tongue
of this relic is

the impress of a stone chalice.

4

A glowing spi-
ral of white
paint

across a concrete post
or telephone pole
lights up this solemn, chalk tale:

I love mama.

5

A luminous, thin
long winged worm

or trout
like an animal of light

swims into the deep humours of my eye
bringing this fish pale day.

6

Why a film of mud
blisters into the shape of a sun!
its black
rays like a baroque work

of sculpture seem to shiver
when an ancient,
fair cloth
is stripped off.

EIGHT POEMS ON PORTRAITS OF THE FOOT

after Aaron Siskind

1

It is the wish
for some genuine change other than our death
that lets us feel (with the fingers of mind)
how much the foot desires to be a hand.

The foot is more secret, more obscene,
its beauty more difficultly won—
is thick with skin and
so is more ashamed than the hand.

One nestled in the arched back of the other
is like a lover
trying to learn to love.
A squid or a slug, hope still alive

inside its mute flesh
for the grace and speed of a fish.
Sperm in the womb quickens to a man.
The man yearns toward his poem.

2

With its over-long
profile lines of bone
and dark stem at the top
this African foot

is an avocado turning sweet,
or a hand-carved, upturned boat.
An idol carved of ebony wood.
I weave before it in the sand.

3

The broad, high palm ta-
pered, with its top
toes shadowed into a ridge

is like a hooded figure.
I find I don't want to picture
underneath that cloak

the hidden face of the foot.

4

One thick
foot is fixed
across another like an ancient

occult monument
of basalt
all of its meaning lost.

5

At the top of crossed foot branches
two rows or bunches
of small, fat birds are hunched.
Somehow they manage to touch

with tenderness. Short,
bundled up, squat
peasants,
they begin to dance.

6

One humped
foot, heel up,
lolls heavily on another.

Feet are members of a natural pair
and on these
(left and right)

sand has the glint of wheat.

7

The turned toes
in a rococo
scroll together form
continuing curves, one last line

after another,
with a final spiral of vapor
(or of light)
beyond that.

8

Held toward a water colored sky
full of birds and gods and souls
of the young,
the whole, lyrical foot bal-

ances, with its heel
on the great toe of its mate.
Watch! Next that earthen foot
will step into flight!

V

THE WOODEN MIRROR

For if anyone is a hearer of the word, and not a doer, he is like a man looking at his
natural face in a mirror; for he beholds himself and goes away, and presently he
forgets what kind of man he was.

—Epistle, Fifth Sunday After Easter

I wait beside the fount.
My God whispers in the box
where a fellow sinner still confesses.
Again my mind caresses
with my hand the iron fence
that protects or that ornaments,
out of art, caution or some
paradigmal wisdom,
the dish kept for our baptism.
I had forgot this fount
has eight sides of highly rubbed wood,
each with a Gothic arch in relief
leading nowhere
but to my own natural face
shadowed in its mirror.
Yet I could not forget
between these trips, as grace
wings more niggardly
(or simply goes) this
pressed, iron rose
black as the hope of the melancholy
brother to our sins, who spent
all his beautiful coins of light—
and heavy as a body
whirled through the dark
outer petals of our world....
The voice of the father
a little louder
as he absolves inside his cell
is like the gentle dropping of a waterfall.

God this grill is tall as I!
This oaken pedestal and base
as many-faced.
See the brass opening in the wood
where the priest may turn his ancient key?
The line of penitents shifts
to me. Christ I know this shut,
double-locked fount
is like the hidden basin of my heart
inside its guard of ribs and skin.
Bless me Father for I have sinned
against love,
and now near middle age,
hang guilty on the rods of my own cage.

LINES FOR HIS SON IN SATIN

The tragic hero is a man afraid of his own beauty. —Gordon Quinlan, student

So my son I would have given my right arm
to have carried the queen's train
with a gloved hand, when I was young—
the queen up ahead, me
unafraid, in a blue satin suit
my grandmother made, and tennis shoes of new white,
white knee sox, a fancy mesh in them,
and a blue silk hat with an ostrich plume!
But what would I have done
if like you I had to find my place alone
(because a page can't mix
with others present
for the Virgin's crowning pageant)?
I doubt I could have sat in the pew
with such grace as you,
full of my absolute duty
and calm with the sense of my own beauty
luminous as stone, with a blue stone's light,
my solemn, sweet page.
Let me show you a picture of me
at your age. This boy is handsome too.
His arms drop with ease. But look close.
See how his brown hair, light as a girl's,
too fine to comb down in the small wind,
pushes against the side of his head
as though it were caved in
by some forgotten chance,
and the tight cotton pants banded at the knees,
as are yours, above the calves bare to the touch of grass,
the young genital full against the leg.
But why is there such a rage in his face?
A mere boy standing in the summer grass

caught there with a boy's grace....
My son, page, I feel you bear a message
to me (though I am no king)
like a magnificent, blue stone ring upon a pillow
or a courtier's melancholy song:
that it is this very youth himself,
the summer wind and grass
gentle at his legs and face,
whom the boy's brown eye hates—
for though he wears no satin suit
or thin page's glove, he has
too much beauty, and can win easy
too much love.

REVISIT TO THE ROOM
OF A SAINT

Yesterday in Chicago for the moment
penitent, vigilant for her ancient feast,
I visited her place of death
and found the blood of a saint she left
on the flesh colored mat
beside her tiny bed. What a doll she was.
Even her rolltop desk
with its postal scale seems small.
Her letter opener, paper clips, picture of The Pope,
blotter—and the folded, remarkable
eyeglass and ruler! I wanted to touch her gold-
topped pencil like my father's
but could only slip a finger
under the edge of the celluloid cover.
And there's a celluloid box
around the little, lifeless wicker chair
where she rocked
her self into the better air.
Beside the saint's spoon and cup
and her final clothes
are her ugly little shoes.
They stand without a step inside a glass case
skin cracked from twenty-seven trips over seas
and once over the angular, ivory
Andes. Her small, folded linens
have in them an aura of the gold mountain sun,
of fresh opened earth, of firs and rain,
the odors of The Virgin Queen.
A thing she wore, a kind of sleeveless shirt,
is feathered at the edges
as with lace, or with the brush
of her tiny bones as she moved,
habited and in her black

crochet-tipped hat or coif
over the earth, like an earth-bound little bird.
White doves wound above the field at her birth.
Now wine, gold, and turquoise doves
rise surely for her death. Their tissue wings
thin and lucid as her light hands
make a light wind.
Let it breathe on my hidden face
as my beast
kneels a moment in this child's place.

The Shrine of St. Francis Xavier Cabrini in Columbus
Hospital, Chicago, December 22-25, 1961

SPRING OF THE THIEF

But if I look the ice is gone from the lake
and the altered air
no longer fills with the small
terrible bodies of the snow.
Only once these late winter weeks
the dying flakes
fell instead as manna or as wedding rice
blooming in the light
about the bronze Christ
and the Thieves. There these three
still hang, more than man-
sized and heavier than life
on a hill over the lake
where I walk
this Third Sunday of Lent.
I come from Mass
melancholy at its ancient story
of the unclean ghost
a man thought he'd lost.
It came back into his well-swept house
and at the final state that man
was worse than he began.
Yet again today
there is the faintest edge of green
to trees about St. Joseph's Lake.
Ah God if our confessions show contempt
because we let them free us of our guilt
to sin again
forgive us still…before the leaves…
before the leaves have formed
you can glimpse the Christ and Thieves
on top of the hill. One of them was saved.
That day the snow had seemed to drop like grace
upon the four of us,
or like the peace of intercourse,

suddenly I wanted to confess—
or simply talk.
I paid a visit to the mammoth Sacred Heart
Church, and found it shut.
Who locked him out or in?
The name of God is changing in our time.
What is his winter name?
Where was his winter home?
Oh I've kept my love to myself before.
Even those ducks weave down the shore
together, drunk with hope
for the April water. One spring festival
near here I stripped and strolled
through a rain filled field.
Spread eagled on the soaking earth
I let the rain
move its audible little hands
gently on my skin...let the dark rain
raise up my love.
But why? I was alone
and no one saw how ardent I grew.
And when I rolled naked in the snow one night
as St. Francis with his Brother Ass
or a hard bodied Finn
I was alone. Underneath '
the howling January moon
I knelt and dug my fist
full of the cold winter sand
and rubbed and
hid my manhood under it.
Washed up at some ancient or half-heroic shore
I was ashamed that I was naked there.
Before Nausicaä and the saints. Before myself.
But who took off my coat? Who put it on?
Who drove me home?
Blessed be sin if it teaches men shame.
Yet because of it we cannot talk
and I am separated from myself.
So what is all this reveling in snow and rain?

Or in the summer sun when the heavy gold
body weeps with joy or grief or love?
When we speak of God, is it God we speak of?
Perhaps his winter home
is in that field where I rolled or ran...
this hill where once the snow
fell serene as rain.
Oh I have walked around the lake
when I was not alone—
sometimes with my wife have seen these swans
dip down their necks
graceful as a girl, showering white and wet!
I've seen their heads delicately turn.
Have gone sailing with my quiet, older son.
And once on a morning walk
a student who had just come back
in fall found a perfect hickory shell
among the bronze and red
leaves and purple flowers of the time
and he put its white bread into my hand.
Ekelöf said there is a freshness
nothing can destroy in us—
not even we ourselves.
Perhaps that
Freshness is the changed name of God.
Where all the monsters also hide.
I bear him in the ocean of my blood
and in the pulp of my enormous head.
He lives beneath the unkempt potter's grass
of my belly and chest.
I feel his terrible, aged heart
moving under mine...can see the shadows
of the gorgeous light
that plays at the edges of his giant eye...
or tell the faint press and hum
of his eternal pool of sperm.
Like sandalwood! *Like sandalwood*
the righteous man
perfumes the axe that falls on him.

The cords of elm, of cedar oak and pine
will pile again in fall.
The ribs and pockets of the barns will swell.
Winds and fires in the field rage
and again burn out each
of the ancient roots.
Again at last the late November snow
will fill those fields, change this hill,
throw these figures in relief
and raining on them
will transform
the bronze Christ's brow and cheek,
the white face and thigh of the thief.

March-April, 1962

VI

WHISTLING WINGS OR
WHITE TURTLE IN THE WATERTREE

1

"Whistling Wings." Jesus Christ.
Can you imagine that?
We thought we were so smart.
Had the turtle in a cage
for birds, till I couldn't stand the image
longer. Then we thought
the copper mesh around his pen would always flop
him back again
when he reached a certain point of compensation.
Like a younster on a birch
he crawled up, catching each improbable turtle foot
(which the limbs of doves and wrens reflect).
But we must admit he won. He's gone.
Myth of the eternal return!
Perhaps he carries the world upon his flank again:
When we climbed up the back of Castle Rock
to take a long, leisurely look
all the maiden hair fern
shivered in the sun,
and the dry sweet pine
scales snapped like crusts of bread.
I felt the turtle's great wing shudder overhead.

Then again I saw the clams
try to put out wings
of a whitish meat (like small, phlegmatic souls)
from the Sisyphean shells
they always bear
even though abandoned in an auto tire.

The lean frog fled too.
Oh, we knew

he'd never feast upon the sun
blasted grass one kid put in,
wouldn't like the tone
of weeds against his precious slime.
Still we had a right to hope
he'd like the shallow hole
we dug, with its handmade pool.
But the frog's not anybody's fool.
Now (or thus)
as with Breughel's Icarus
I can see, in the green flowing
of my mind, his white, human legs flashing!
They leave a melancholy ring
like the abandoned whippoorwill's song.

He starts up at nine o'clock
each heartbreaking night.
The partridge has some sadness or other
knocking softly in his throat as a missing motor,
but the whippoorwill's music is the shadow, is the moon
of the last sheen of light in the meadow after rain.

The field itself leaves us blest
in an unrelieved length of pine forest—
like the baroque squiggle in the sand
of baby clams
toward water,
track of partridge with the cock's delicate trailing feather,
or turtle's print before (and after)
the shore has smoothed with weather.

2

Off the pine path
we found a pair of gray clad
wood cutters (work shirts and pants,
heavy hats
to keep off bugs and sun)
whose nagging saws had broke the peace of the afternoon.

The kids and I watched them
hack an arm
and leg from trees they'd felled.
"Pulp" I've heard the living trees called!
I held
my breath when one took off his hat
to mop the sweat
and suddenly instead a woman was there,
her hair
falling round a rather pretty face
gaunt with tiredness—
and in her blue, metallic eyes, as in a cage,
an absolute feminine rage.

There was masculine fury
at the Inn just off the highway
(like the inn of Joseph and Mary,
as the natives tell)
where a husband sent six Indians to hell.
The man and his wife, who had two daughters,
were the tavern owners.
He took the wagon into town for salt and bread,
came back to find his wife and daughters dead!
Four Indians had killed them with a tomahawk,
robbed the inn and were quickly drunk.
The husband slew the four
with an axe right there,
brought two more back
and placed six heads about the inn on pikes!
Now they have a marker at a wayside park.

3

With my own wife and kids
visiting the local Indian burial grounds
I find I wonder
at the penny-strewn boxes stretching over
graves recently dug
for Billy Walking Bird and Nora White Dog.

I would guess
a kind of halfway house?
They are buried on a low, wooded hill
where bluegrass seed and plum blossoms fall.

In another small area of cleared wood
across a net like that our turtle had
the kids hit a plastic badminton bird.

On a rope outside our concrete block cabin,
clean and damp and open
the many colored swimming suits sway,
all shapeless after joy.
At the beach, girl is clearly girl and boy, boy.
The motorboats buck across the lake
and root about the skirts of sails, who walk
by so slow
and turn so delicately now.

A blue and red and yellow and brown
and green and black paper chain
my daughter makes
to drape
across the drab stove in the corner,
each color repeating in a perfect order.
Yet this doesn't make plain to me
her genuine, womanly intensity.
See how she
bangs and shatters the dinner bell!
Which here is on a pole.
The house or cabin key now hangs upon a hook
over the kitchen sink.
These new juxtaposings make you think!
The baby's crib's back by our bed again,
and the other kids—blankets fluffed and clean,
shook from plexiglass bags—
all are rearranged.

4

At Whistling Wings our oldest son
gets up early to fish, for the first time,
or stands gold with summer sun
plumed in a gaudy summer shirt
like a splendid, tropical bird
none of us know,
to draw back his brand new bow
and shoot forever
the first slim arrow of my quiver.

That one late night,
only a hint
of moonlight,
Ruth and I
(our children all asleep)
ran down from the cabin to the beach
and dived together
naked in the summer water.
I asked her out to swim with me because
I knew how small and white she was.

His hair too long and yellow for the wood
the baby walks
quite drunk,
or else bending back
on heels like a pregnant lady
round and round a small tree,
or like a cub bear,
paws clumsy in the air,
nosing honey,
or like a grounded baby bumblebee.

Our young son Stephen looks
like a small anchor seated on the stoop,
his back to me, knees drawn up
and spread, arms hid
at some uncertain game he made.

5

I have seen them strain and wheeze
to pull down young shoots of trees
they carry before them,
tiny drying limbs
held out,
as they circle slow and chant,
like elaborate candelabra in a rite.
(Once I thought
I saw my kids carried in their own trees,
parked there like ancient, shrieking harpies.)
And once in a low fog that rolled toward the wood
like those long sighs of the dead
I saw my charmed kids
conjure up or lose a voice, an arm, a head.

The girls put a puppet together
out of cork, sticks, string, and a feather.
They painted gentle or horrendous masks
full length on paper cleaning sacks.
And I have seen them push
or wish
a full cardboard carton
like a wagon
up a hill of sand,
and down at last
into the sweet valley of grass.
Have watched the boys build
a blunt sloop of board
and make it sail!
Saw one pound a nail
in a tin squash can
and tie fish line
to make a toy filled with stone
he dragged all around the cabin
yard.
Then (though I was gone) I've heard
our eleven-year-old

pulled an eighteen-pound
carp on a clothesline
straight down the main street in town
to weigh it in at the grocery store scale.
(Small, external Jonah. Revised whale.)
Once they nailed a brown bullhead
to a board
(through the snout)
and worked out his guts
having peeled off
the skin, like a man's sox
with pliers from my toolbox.
And they say the whole business is orthodox!

6

Except for the littlest one
all my sons
and I went out to fish one night.
Couldn't wait
to try a new lure,
sweet little thing from France we thought of her:
La Vivif.
No Jitterbug, no Cisco Kid or River Thief,
or black or flesh colored rubber worm
to bring the small-mouth bass home,
a weedless hook hid
inside its dull head.
Blue, red, bronze, and cream shapely *La Vivif*
would bring more beautiful strife.
We walked from the cabin east
toward the Ghost
for whom the boys had named the trail,
which leads to the water for a mile.
In the dead of night walking near
we were startled by a startled deer!
Then, past a turn, at a sudden quirk,
that Ghost showed up in the germinating dark
hovering in the limbs of a ginkgo tree,

its great awkward silver body
like a snagged cloud
or enormous bird,
faintly glinting in the thin moon.
If it was a wounded weather balloon,
I felt it could still detect
the climate of my heart.
We joked too much (as they play
with bones on Corpus Christi Day).
Past the balloon, bird, cloud, or ghoul
we came to the walleye hole.

Putting that *Vivif* to the test
almost at the first cast
a good pike
flashed out of the lake!
I let each boy touch
the pole to feel the fish's tug,
and fought and landed it
luminous and foam wet,
the great eye without a lid
perhaps alive, perhaps dead.
Drunk with the success of our allure,
following some heady, ancient spoor
of ourselves or it
the older boys and I quick-
ly stripped and fell
into the cold, walleye hole,
like shining gold
bugs or clumsy newborn birds
hopping from a black limb (abandoned nest and shell)
into a blue black pool.
I hit a snag of weed,
was caught like an anxious white turtle hid
in the branches of the water's trees
for a long minute of time,
then dressed and went home.

Necedah, Wisconsin
Summers: 1961-1962

THE ZIGZAG WALK

POEMS 1963–1968

for my father, my brother, my six sons and for Michael

I

THE ZOO

1

Like a child the wise porpoise
at the Brookfield Zoo plays
in the continuous, universal game
of fish becoming man.

2

Llamas pray to the gods for snow. They chant
that it shall fall upon their artificial mount.
The llamas do not yearn
for tossed gumdrops or for popped corn.

Look,
even the great brown handsome official Kodiak
bear
has caramel in its hair.
Incomparable as he knows he is
the tough, tall golden lion looks at us
indifferent across
his molded hill, his helpful moat;
and, pregnant with a beast it ate,
the vicious, obvious and obscene
greedy-eyed old python
hauls itself along.

3

Gorillas lope and glare and crash
the glass in the Primate House.
The steaming place is packed
with folks who want to look
as at a wedding or a wake.
We advance. We retreat. We test. We wait.
We hope to see something masturbate.

We want to find a kind of King Kong
(magnificent but wrong)
caught and salted safe as us
behind the bars of flesh,
behind the glass of the face.

Twenty charming little tropical monkey kids
jabber in the phony trees. The gibbon is unkempt.
The yellow baboons bark, and they travel in groups.

There, ugly and alone,
awful and no longer young,
is that ornery thing
an orangutan.
Disconsolate, contrite,
red-haired widow who was once a wife
you pace and turn, and turn and pace
then sit on your repulsive ass
and with a hairy hand
and thumb delicately pinch an egg and
kiss its juice deep into your head.
Oh misery! Misery! You wretched bride.

Why only the silver monkey
glows and rests quietly,
nearly everything well,
a bit back in its tunnel
(which is lit
with its own created light).

This Primate House echoes
with our mixed cries;
it reeks with our ambiguous breath.
Each one caged as an oracle
I feel each upright animal
can tell
how much my life is a human life,
how much an animal death.

South Bend, April 1963

THREE MOVES

Three moves in six months and I remain
the same.
Two homes made two friends.
The third leaves me with myself again.
(We hardly speak.)
Here I am with tame ducks
and my neighbors' boats,
only this electric heat
against the April damp.
I have a friend named Frank—
The only one who ever dares to call
and ask me, "How's your soul?"
I hadn't thought about it for a while,
and was ashamed to say I didn't know.
I have no priest for now.
Who
will forgive me then. Will you?
Tame birds and my neighbors' boats.
The ducks honk about the floats...
They walk dead drunk onto the land and grounds,
iridescent blue and black and green and brown.
They live on swill
our aged houseboats spill.
But still they are beautiful.
Look! The duck with its unlikely beak
has stopped to pick
and pull
at the potted daffodil.
Then again they sway home
to dream
bright gardens of fish in the early night.
Oh these ducks are all right.
They will survive.
But I am sorry I do not often see them climb.
Poor sons-a-bitching ducks.

You're all fucked up.
What do you do that for?
Why don't you hover near the sun anymore?
Afraid you'll melt?
These foolish ducks lack a sense of guilt,
and so all their multi-thousand-mile range
is too short for the hope of change.

Seattle, April 1965

TWO PRELUDES FOR LA PUSH

1

Islands high as our inland hills
rise clean and sheer above the chill
April seas at La Push.
In a hush
of holy fog
the lean trees along their tops
(inaccessible to be climbed)
are offered up in flames of salt and wind.
And at La Push
the white, furious waves mass and rush
at each earthen island base.
These waves
are sudden, violent, unpredictable as grace.
They change White then
Blue then Green
swift as in Raphael's great wing!
I've seen it here where it has always hid:
Light, the shadow of our ancient God.

2

In the late afternoon light
even our human feet
start halos in the sand:
soft flashes of mind.
From the occult shore where you can see or feel
only a few shells
(shattered) among the lively stones,
we walk home.
I follow my younger brother,
for I am the visitor.
He knows the maze of fallen trees
that back up the blasted beach
for blocks: whether

this path or another.
Here the logs lie like lovers,
short by long, benign,
nudging gently in the tide.

Further up all the logs have died.
We walk through graves of wood
which are so oddly
borne out of the fecund sea,
each piece a last marker for itself,
each tomb planted with bulbs and whips of kelp.
Now as the water light fades,
I feel the monsters rage
again in this abandoned wood—gray
on darker gray.
Sometimes the flesh of the drifted face
is almost white! They seem to lift
their awful limbs,
broken from their lost hands.
Now the grotesque, giant shapes all
whirl awhile!
In the final light
the hard knots
of eyes scowl and brood
above the smaller dead
animals of wood.
I am afraid.
My brother walks ahead,
I reach for land:
the driftwood logs heavily shake
underfoot, and I awake,
balancing between my youth and my age.

THE PASS

Buttercups about the rocks and the sky
colored lupine lies

quiet in the brilliant grass
on the island by Deception Pass.

My young brother, his friends and I carefully
walk we

walk carefully along the edge
of the high flying bridge

and all look down
where gulls fall and rise over The Sound.

The awful height stirs in me
the huge, uneasy

gull
of my own soul.

I will not lean farther
over the bridge's sill with the others

(who can savor such a thrill). I will go back
and read the plaque

upon the rock.
But first I watch

a small, red speedboat hurry
beneath, pulling white, excited water flurries

like a living flag.
It passes a tug,

black and brown
(newly painted green

door) moving sure
as an old shepherd goes, before

a tremendous family of floating logs.
I wait until the tug's

completely underneath the span
(by then

even the wake of the younger boat is gone)
and turn

to walk back
alone toward the rock.

CARMEL: POINT LOBOS

"It's called God," he said.
He is young and he had
walked or flown ahead
to the violent crag.
"When I see beauty like this
I want to die for it." —
Jump
to the far rock home
where the white, roiling foam
seethes,
rolls one eddy on another, and retreats
to lie still
in a momentary peace or pool.
A little way above and to the left, the gull
folks form
quiet lines of their own.
They wait along the brilliant height,
and then, when it's time,
fling them-
selves off into the wide
arcs and dips of their angelic suicides.
Against the overcast skies
their wings and bodies
weave
a gentle, shifting spiral figure
as of light — like the faster
nebulae of froth along the blue black water.
Suddenly the sun is out! and colors
brighten all about the iridescent Point
with its prehistoric birds and plants,
Santa Lucia rocks, its hints
of whales. Everything's more intense!
I feel afraid in this
shattering new light.

Dread drifts like fog around my heart.
Why? The sheer, terrible height?
Eerie glint and glance of mica in the rock
which catches in the glittering sea below?
The rough, long time ravaged coast
here and yonder, yonder,
yonder
far as you look? Or the unlikely cormorant
never so near or rare, so gaunt.
I see the seaside daisy
die so beautifully
here. It loses its nunlike coif
as the lavender leaves fall off
and tiny yellow rockets burst
about its heart
till only the perfect-
spiraled flower skull is left.
Last I touch
(as if with hope) the odd, succulent lettuce-
of-the-bluff.
Its gray-white rubber flower
leaves a chalk stuff on my finger
like a soft kind of death.
I feel stark
as this Point Lobos rock
where I sit and wait, older,
while you climb higher
among the hundred-million-year-old boulders
in search of the precious nest. I rise
in this beautiful place,
look about me like an anxious kid
or a hopeful god
and give what I have into the sea ahead.

BIG SUR: PARTINGTON COVE

for Jim and Sara Johnson

the eyes of fire, the nostrils of air, the mouth of water, the beard of earth.
—William Blake

1

We three park by the Big Sur Road
at Partington Cove,
disregard the furious note
(ALL TRESPASSERS WILL BE SHOT)
and begin the long, dancing trek
—I mean a zigzag walk—
toward the creek,
the tunnel and the Smugglers' Cave,
hoping to return somewhat more than alive.
In the light air of early June
transistor sounds rise and weave thin
from the stream
where we guess the guard catches fish, or swims.
I'm glad one of us knows the signs
to find the old tunnel.
A large, white half shell
hangs from a branch with a hole
in its middle
(which has been filled with metal),
and a little farther on
hangs
a stranger
omen woven of many-colored yarn
and shaped like a little kite.
The Indians say it is "God's eye."
Now with our shoes off

we soft slosh
across the creek,
toes a school of fish.
A brief, final
push
through the young brush
puts us at the aged tunnel.
The guard is safely ditched, we hope.
Short trip
through the moist dark
under artful, handhewn
timbers, and suddenly we are borne
out onto the brilliant cove
the thieves (and landscape) made a secret of.

2

Hidden as the middle of night
still this cove is bright
as day. The drop is immediate,
sheer to the shimmering sea,
and now you cannot get down
to the little half-moon
beach
bleached white. Blackbearded thieves
and smugglers
swagger.
Dressed in the ancient leather
they heave and hustle boxes there
and pour
out of a giant demijohn
of green
glass flashing in the sun.
They drink and sing.
They strip and swim

and huddle round the small fire
on the shore
in their human skin.
Then they dive away and are lost
into the glis-
tening eels of water weeds,
brown and supple as a leather whip.
Oh these are men that could make you weep!
We see the great, rusting iron hooks
in stone, and the broken links
of chains they used once to shinny up the rocks.

3

The risk is great around the cliff
beneath the cave of the thief. I almost twist
to my own death
stretched in the sea's long and stony bed,
where anemones lie lovely as an egg
and open up their mouths like downy chicks;
where poisoned thorns
pierce the purple flesh of urchins.
We single file about the hill's edge
and the pointed, dangerous piles
of rock. At last we climb
to the high, secret, hollow eye
of the cave and drop inside
where the smugglers hid
and stayed
like tears we never shed.

4

Anxious here, shivering, I find I need to love.
I am the father in the cave,
and I am drunk as Lot was in the shelter

made of skin the day he loved his daughter.
My sons squat in the dark together.
I know they will not hurt each other.
My mind heavily reels in time as I hover
on my haunch like an enormous bird.
And now I rise and stir to find
what I can for lunch—
or for our life in this long dark.
The belly of the cave is large!

5

We eat and sleep
and get up to bathe
in light at the mouth of the cave,
while one goes off to think
alone on a point of rock
over the smashing sea. I watch
from my place on the slab of stone
in the sun
beside, where I lie like a lover,
father or mother,
and look over
his naked hills at the black, wandering seas,
or I shift to watch the face
of the sky with its crags
and beards of clouds.
I see the slopes of his weathered head,
and all the tawny
hair along his body
blows
and lifts like shoots
of fern or grass.
Gulls jabber about his nests.
Eyes hold the little lives of the sea
in their pools of blue or gray.

The starfishes of his hands loll and soak
the sun on the rock,
and his foot
juts out
like a foot-
shaped cactus plant.
(I want to touch or catch
the glowing thing that lives in the cleft
at the root of the throat.)
Muscles of the belly
break like fields along this golden country!
For like the lost or stolen flesh of God,
the self, more alive or more dead,
opens on to the truth
of earth
and sea and sky—
and the thieves' cave yawns empty
of our smuggled body.

San Francisco, May 1967

LINES ON LOCKS
(or Jail and the Erie Canal)

1

Against the low, New York State
mountain background, a smokestack
sticks up
and gives out
its snakelike wisp.
Thin, stripped win-
ter birches pick up the vertical lines.
Last night we five watched the white,
painted upright bars of steel
in an ancient, New York jail
called Herkimer
(named for a general who lost an arm).
Cops threw us against the car.
Their marks grow gaudy
over me.
They burgeon beneath my clothes.
I know
I give my wound
too much thought and time.
Gallows loomed outside
our sorry solitary cells.
"You are in the oldest of our New York jails,"
they said.
"And we've been in books. It's here they had
one of Dreiser's characters arraigned."
The last one of our company to be hanged
we found
had chopped her husband
up and
fed him to the hungry swine.
They nudged the wan-
ing warmth of his flesh.
Each gave him a rooting touch,

translating his dregs
into the hopes of pigs.
And now with their spirited wish
and with his round, astonished face,
her changed soul
still floats about over their small
farm
near this little New York town.

2

The door bangs shut
in the absolute dark.
Toilets flush with a great force,
and I can hear the old, gentle drunk,
my neighbor in the tank,
hawk
his phlegm and fart.
In the early day
we line up easily as a cliché
for our bread and bowls of gruel.
We listen, timeless, for the courthouse bell,
play rummy the whole day long
and "shoot the moon,"
go to bed and jack off to calm down,
and scowl harshly, unmanned,
at those who were once our friends.
The prison of our skins
now rises outside
and drops in vertical lines
before our very eyes.

3

Outdoors again, now we can walk
to the Erie Locks
("Highest Lift Locks in the World!")
The old iron bridge has a good bed—
cobbles made of wood.

Things pass through this town everywhere
for it was built in opposite tiers.
Two levels of roads
on either side
the Canal, then two terraces of tracks
and higher ranks of beds: roads where trucks
lumber awkwardly above the town—
like those heavy golden cherubim
that try to wing about
in the old, Baroque church.
The little town—with its Gothic
brick
bank, Victorian homes with gingerbread frieze
and its blasted factories
(collapsed, roofs roll-
ing back from walls
like the lids of eyes)—
has died
and given up
its substance like a hollow duct,
smokestack or a pen
through which the living stuff flows on.

4

So we walk the long, dead-end track
along the shallow, frozen lake
where the canal forms a fork
(this time of year the locks don't work).
And now and again we look back,
for the troopers haunt the five of us
out the ledges toward The Locks.
(We know they want to hose
our bellies and our backs.
Or—as they said—
"Play the Mambo" on our heads.)
We do not yet feel
quite free—
though the blue and yellow, newly

painted posts
for ships
bloom gaily
in the cold, and the bulbs
about their bases bulge
for spring.
Soon the great, iron gates
will open out
and the first woman-shaped
ship,
mammoth, silent, will float toward
us like a god
come back
to make us feel only half afraid.
Until then,
though my friends will be gone
from this dry channel of snow and stone,
I'll stay here
among the monuments of sheer,
brown and gray rock
where you can read
the names of lovers, sailors and of kids
etched in chalk,
and in this winter air
still keep one hand over my aching ear.

Buffalo, March 1967

II

HELIAN

after Georg Trakl

The lonely times of the soul
It is lovely to walk in the sun
Along yellow walls of summer.
Our steps click lightly in the grass, but in the gray
Marble the son of Pan sleeps on forever.

Evenings on the terrace
We made ourselves drunk with tawny wine.
The peach glows red among the leaves.
A tender sonata...joyful laughter.

The silence of the night is beautiful.
In a dark meadow
We sometimes meet shepherds—and white stars.

When fall has come
A quiet brightness spreads in the wood.
Calmed we walk along the walls now red.
Our eyes grow round with the flight of birds.
At evening the white water sinks in burial urns.

Heaven has a holiday in naked branches.
In his clean hands the farmer carries bread and wine,
And the fruits ripen peacefully in the sunny room.

Ah, how solemn is the face of the beloved dead!
Still the soul takes delight in righteous vision.

■ ■ ■

The silence of the wasted garden is powerful
As the young novice crowns his head with brown leaves
And his breath drinks icy gold.

His hands touch the age of bluish waters
Or touch the sisters' white cheeks in the cold night.

A walk past friendly rooms is like a lilting harmony.
Solitude—and the rustle of the maple tree,
Where perhaps the thrush still sings.

Man is beautiful. In the dark his self
Shines if he moves arms and legs, suddenly surprised,
While in their purple holes his eyes roll silently.

At the hour of vespers the stranger loses himself
In the black ruin of November—
Under decaying branches and along the leprous walls
Where formerly the holy brother went,
Sunk in the soft string music of his madness.

How lonesomely the evening wind dies,
And his head bends down
Dying in the dark of the olive tree.

      ■ ■ ■

The downfall of a generation is a staggering thing.
At such a time the eyes of the watcher
Fill with the gold of his stars.

In the evening the chimes die down
And do not ring anymore;
The black walls have collapsed in the square,
And the dead soldier calls us to prayer.

A wan angel (the son)
Walks into the empty house of his fathers.
The sisters have all gone away to the white old men.
The sleepwalker used to find them

Under the posts of the entrance hall at night,
Home from a sorrowful pilgrimage.

Their hair! How studded with filth and vermin!
He stands inside on his silver feet
As the dead sisters step out of the barren rooms.

Oh you psalms in the fiery midnight rain!
When servants strike the tender eyes with nettles
The childlike fruits of the elder tree
Bend down astonished over an empty grave.

The yellowed moons softly roll
Over the sick sheets of the young man
Before the winter's silence follows him.

      ■ ■ ■

A lofty destiny looks down on the Kidron River
Where the cedar, delicate creature,
Unfolds itself under the blue brows of the father,
And at night a shepherd drives his flock over the meadow.
Or there are cries in sleep
When a bronze angel comes up to the man in the grove
And the flesh of the saint melts on a glowing grate.

The purple vine creeps along the clay hut,
And bundles of yellow grain rustle.
The humming of bees. The flight of the crane.

In the evening those who have risen from the dead
Meet on the rocky paths.
Lepers look at themselves in the black waters
Or they open their garments flecked with filth,

Weeping, to the fragrant wind
Which blows from a rose-colored hill.

Slender girls grope through the lanes of the night
To find the loving shepherds.
On Saturdays gentle singing rings in the huts.

Let that song also tell of the boy,
Of his madness, of his white brow and of his going away—
Him whose flesh rots, as the eyes open bluish.
Oh how sad it is to meet again like this!

　　　．　．　．

The grades of madness in black rooms.
Shadows of the old ones under the open door,
As Helian's soul gazes on itself in a rose-colored mirror,
And the snow of leprosy drops from his brow.

On all the walls the stars and the white
Shapes of light are put out.

Bones of the graves rise from
The silence of fallen crosses on the hill.
Sweetness of the incense in the purple night wind.

Oh you smashed eyes in black mouths,
When the grandson, gently deranged,
Meditates alone on the darker end,
And the silent God lowers his blue eyelids over him!

SEBASTIAN IN THE DREAM

after Georg Trakl

The mother carried her child in the white moonlight
In the shadow of the walnut tree and the ancient elder,
Drunk with the juice of poppy, with the lament of the thrush,
And silently,
With pity, a bearded face bent over them.

Gentle in the darkness of the window. All the old household goods
Of the fathers
Lay in ruin. Love and autumn's dreaming.

It was a dark day of the year in melancholy childhood
When the boy went down secretly to the cool waters,
To the silver fish, to peace—and a face!
His star came over him in the gray night
As he threw himself like a stone before black wild horses.

Or when he walked in the evening
Across the autumn graveyard of Saint Peter's
Holding his mother's icy hand—
In the dark of the burial house a fragile corpse lay silent
And the child opened his cold eyes over it.

But he was a small bird in barren branches.
The bell rang in nocturnal November.
Ah, the peace of the father when
He went down the winding, darkening stairs in his sleep.

2

The soul's tranquility. A lonesome winter evening.
Dark figures of the shepherds by the old fish pond.

A little child in the hut of straw; how gently
The face falls with the black fever.
Holy night.

Or when the boy climbed silently up the gloomy Calvary Hill
Holding the hard hand of his father,
And in the dark crevices of rock
The blue shape of The Man passed through his own legend,
Blood flowed purple from the wound under the heart.
Very quietly the Cross grew up in his shadowy soul.

Love. In the black corners the snow melts.
A blue breath of air, caught brightly in the old elder,
In the shaded arch of the walnut tree: and a rose
Colored angel softly appeared to the boy.

Joy. When a sonata rang through the cool rooms at evening,
On the brown wooden beam
A blue butterfly crawled out of her silver cocoon.

Oh the nearness of death! Inside the stone wall
A yellow head bowed. The child was quiet
When the moon fell apart in March.

3

Glowing Easter bells in the grave of night
And the silver sounds of stars,
So in a shuddering fit
A dark madness dropped from the sleeper's face.

How quiet the walk down the blue river.
Thinking of what has been forgotten, while in the green branches
A thrush cries the ruin of an unknown thing.
Or when the boy walked in the evening by the fallen walls of the city
At the bony hand of the old man

Who carried a tiny, pink child in his black coat,
And the ghost of Evil appeared in the shadow of the walnut tree!

Groping across the green stairs of summer. How softly
The garden falls down in the brown silence of autumn;
The fragrance and the sadness of the old elder tree
When the silver voice of the angel died in Sebastian's shadow.

TWILIGHT LAND

after Georg Trakl

1

The moon stepped like a dead thing
Out of a blue cave,
And many flowers
Flutter all along the rocky path.
A sick thing weeps silver
By the pond of evening.
Over there the lovers
Died in a black boat.

Or the footsteps of Elis
Sound through the wood
Hyacinth-colored
And die away again
Under the oak.
Ah, the form of the young boy
Fashioned from crystal tears,
From shadows of the night.
Jagged flashes light up the forehead,
Which is forever cool,
And now on the hill just turning green
The echoing
Of the year's first thunderstorm.

2

So gentle are the green
Woods of our home,
The crystal wave
Dying along the broken wall—
And we wept in our sleep.

Now we stroll and linger
By the thorn hedge,
Singers in the summer night,
In the holy quiet
Of the distant, radiant vineyard.
The shadows of the cool castle
Of night are mourning eagles.
A moonbeam closes gently
The crimson wounds of grief.

3

You great cities of stone
Built on the plain!
Mute, his face dark,
The man who has no home
Follows the wind
And the barren trees on the hill.
Distant twilight floods!
The mighty, terrifying sunset glow
Is shuddering
In a mass of thunderheads.
Ah, you dying peoples!
A pale wave
Shattering on the night shore,
Falling stars.

THEY'VE BLOCKED EVERY WINDOW

after Tibor Tollas

Only this much light was left from our life:
The stars in the sky and a fistful of sunshine.
We watched for this day after day from the depths
Of the dim walls, every evening and every afternoon.
But they stole that too, our handful of sun:
They've blocked every window tight with tin.

I feel my eyes grow wide as I see the blue water
Of Naples. Above its shimmering shore
Vesuvius still waits, smoking—nearby
Are deeply suntanned, happy men. Do you see them?
But we live in darkness like the blind.
They've blocked every window tight with tin.

Ten of us lie smothering in a narrow hole.
Our ten mouths starve for air,
Gaping like the gills of fish
Driven to shore. We lack heart to breathe in,
Along with the stink, what would sustain.
They've blocked every window tight with tin.

The Alps send with their cool
West Wind sprays of the odor of pine
And your soul is rinsed by the purity of space overhead.
You can track the smell of snow to the smiling hills,
But yesterday my cell mate coughed up blood in pain.
They've blocked every window tight with tin.

The sound of whistles from pleasure boats shat-
tering the silence, girls' laughter glancing off the walls,
No longer echo musically in our ears.

We do not hear the thousand reeds of summer's organ.
Our cells are deaf. Every sound is gone.
They've blocked every window tight with tin.

The warm voice of a dark, Barcelona woman,
Humming at twilight, filters through the
Distant gardens as she strums
Her guitar where dancers still color and dot the road.
But to our ears only the leaden days flow in.
They've blocked every window tight with tin.

We would probe for the velvet sky
But our fingertips drop with blood.
We are nailed up as in a coffin,
Only touched by burlap clothes or bugs.
We would stroke the beaming shoots of sun!
But they've blocked every window tight with tin.

At London dances in their silken dresses
Girls are gliding over the beautiful floors.
The bright down on their gentle hair
Glows in the graceful arcs of antique furniture.
The West is dancing! Maybe they have sold us then.
And they've blocked every window tight with tin.

Our tongues are awash for the fresh spice of spring
And we swallow drafts of swill, groaning.
Each stale, stinking sip would make your
Belly turn and spill.
Yet we suck every mouthful in.
They block every window tight with tin.

We gorge our starving guts on full
Dreams. The delicate taste of pastries
In Paris shops. Above their neon lights

I seem to see the silent terror creep.
And you will never again have dawn.
They will block every window tight with tin.

Let the radios howl hoarse about freedom
And the rights of men. It is here
That my self walled in—with millions more—
Feels the knot of Moscow's whip.
From Vach to Peking hear the prisoners moan.
If you are not careful throughout the world of men
They will block all the windows tight with tin.

PRISON POEM

after Tibor Tollas

A spider is sewing the silence;
He stitches up my shabby loneliness.
In the world I would not have seen you,
but here I greet you, fellow of my solitude.

First living thing I've seen for months!
I can talk to you!
Please look on me as a gigantic fly. Believe
I am caught in your web.

Suck my blood! What do I care?
I know. I know it is agony
to be hungry. But this is dinner for me—
to be able to give myself to you.

See, they appear through the air slowly:
Poison spiders with two legs.
When they bite me with the hate
in their eyes, or choke me in their iron snares,

I let them. Ejaculate all your poison!
A weight of fluid now protects me,
and the beauty in my heart moves toward the sun
though I am trapped by webs of stone.

THE OWL

after János Hegedüs
and for Jill Bullitt

The moon is in sight
On a poplar rotting in the night
Two lamps of eyes catch fire
Two clawed feet clutch at their desire
The profound owl
Ferocious and gray
Grotesquely feeds
For he is hungry as can be
He is hungry as can be.

HOMAGE TO
RAINER MARIA RILKE

for George and Finvola Drury

I love the poor, weak words
which starve in daily use—
the ordinary ones.
With the brush of my breath
I color them. They brighten then
and grow almost gay.
They have never known
melody before who trem-
bling step into my song.

      ■ ■ ■

I remember my early poems.
In the silence of vine-covered ruins
I used to chant them to the night.
I linked them happily together
and dedicated them
as a gift for a blonde girl,
a fine golden chain of my poems.
But as a matter of fact
I was alone,
and so I let them fall
and they rolled like beads of coral
spreading away in the night.

      ■ ■ ■

My mere desire shall reach
of itself into rhyme.
My ripe glance will softly burst
the stone coats of seeds

and my silence bring you ecstasy!
Wait! Someday the public
will drop to their knees
struck with my lances of light.
Like priests each will lift
the baroque chalice of his heart
out of his breast
and gladly give me blessing.

■   ■   ■

I am so young
I give myself to every sound.
My desire winds
its way
like the turnings of the garden
walk in the wind's beloved force.
I'll take up arms
at the call of any war.
From the coolness of this morning
at the shore
I will let the day lead
me next
toward the land-locked field.

■   ■   ■

At dusk, in the dark stone pines
I will let my shirt
fall like the lie it is
from my shoulders and back,
and pale and naked
plunge suddenly into the sun.
The surf is a feast
the waves have prepared for me.

Each one shakes like the last
about my young thighs.
How can I stand by myself?
I am afraid.
Still, the brightly joined billows weave
a wind for me
and I lift my hands into it.

■   ■   ■

O thou wakened wood amid the raw winter
you dare to show a brave sense of spring,
and drop your silver dross delicately
to show us how your yearning turns to green.
I don't know where I'm going,
but I will follow your needle paths
because the doors
I felt against your depths
before
are no longer there.

■   ■   ■

Put out my eyes! I will see you—
Close up my ears! I hear you still,
without feet will go to you
and without a mouth will cry you.
Break off my arm!
I will take hold of you with my heart's hand:
Stop my heart! My brain
will beat—or ring my brain round with fire!
Still I carry you along my blood.

■   ■   ■

If it were quiet once—
if the casual and the probable
for once would cease their noise—
and the neighbors' laughter!
If the clamor of my senses
did not so much
disturb my long watch:
then in a thousandfold thought
I could think through to the very brink of you,
possess you for at least
the season of a smile,
and as one gives thanks
give you back again.

∎ ∎ ∎

This is the day when I reign
and mourn. This is my night.
I pray to God that sometime
I may lift my crown from my head.
For my reward may I not once
see its blue turquoise,
its diamonds and rubies
shivering into the eyes?
But perhaps the flash
is long since gone from the gem,
or maybe Grief, my companion,
robbed me. Or perhaps, in the crown
that I received there was no stone.

∎ ∎ ∎

Lord, it is time now,
for the summer has gone on

and gone on.
Lay your shadow along the sun-
dial, and in the field
let the great wind blow free.
Command the last fruit
be ripe:
let it bow down the vine—
with perhaps two sun-warm days
more to force the last
sweetness in the heavy wine.

He who has no home
will not build one now.
He who is alone
will stay long
alone, will wake up,
read, write long letters,

and walk in the streets,
walk by in the
streets when the leaves blow.

April 23, 1967

THREE POEMS ON
MORRIS GRAVES'S PAINTINGS

1 *Bird on a Rock*

Poor, thick, white,
three-sided bird
on a rock
(with the big red beak)
you watch me sitting on the floor
like a worshiper
at your melancholy shrine.
All you can do is look. I mean
you lack any kind of wing or arm
with which to go home.
The three-toed foot of each odd limb
forms a kind of trapezium
about its edge
(though there is no web).
Oh bird, you are a beautiful kite
that does not go up.
You cannot even get down.
Because you've lost your mouth (it's gone)
only your great eyes still moan.
You are filled with the ancient grief,
fixed there lonely as a god or a thief.
Instead of limbs to bring you nearer
Morris Graves has given you
the sudden awful wings of a mirror!

2 *Spirit Bird*

Looking at Morris Graves's Spirit Bird
(1956), suddenly I
understood the structure of angels!
They're made of many colored streams

of the most intense, most pulsing light,
which is itself simply the track
of the seed of God across the void.
Each length of light seems to be a thread
that forms this angelic or spirit
stuff. But it's not. It's finer than that.
What gives the light its substance and shapes
the streams into the spirit thing
(apparent limbs and parts of body)
is the heavy, almost solid and
somehow magnetic *eyes* of angels.
These create the dark into which they glow,
and pull and bend about these sweeps of light.

3 *Moor Swan*

I'm the ugly, early
Moor Swan of Morris Graves.
I'm ungainly. I've got
black splotches on my back.
My neck's too long.
When I am dead and gone
think only of the beauty of my name.
Moor Swan   Moor Swan   Moor Swan.

III

THIRTEEN PRELUDES FOR PIONEER SQUARE

1. At the aged
Pittsburgh café under the street
(it's open only during the day)
the ragged pioneers get more meat
for their money.
A coat and tie gets hardly any.

2. Cigarettes die in
salmon tin
trays of gold and silver
and you pour your sugar
from a mason jar glint-
ing in the morning sun.

3. Moe's loan
keeps the pioneers in wine.
There's a trail of blood in the alley behind.

4. In the Florence Family Theatre
through the triple feature
the oldsters sit and cough.
Or they sleep it off
stretched across three seats:
they laugh and speak
loudly
out of their dreamed-up movie.
Some wake and go to the john,
where they solicit the young.

5. In the Six Fourteen the queers
think *they* are the pioneers.
When they dance they bleed and swallow
trying to decide who should lead
and who follow.

6. Next door the highly dressed men
with their highly dressed women
go
into the Blue Banjo.

7. Indifferent or reckless
(male and female)
two pioneers hail
and meet.
Near the street
in a stairway
they make it, their way.

8. One aged fellow, smashed
at a corner of the square
sits against the wall
(he doesn't stand)
and feeling the need
hauls it out and pees,
no longer a man.

9. The tall American totem
in this triangular square
scowls with its mask upon mask
at the Victorian shelter near.

10. The Square's mixed light
part-aged-gas, part-mercury unites
the drunk and beaten, swollen
Lady Indian
and beau a block from Brittania Bar,
the Negro weaving home from the B And R,
and the white man who can't
quite make it out
of the lounge at Rudy's Restaurant.

11. The great, garish,
painted concrete parking garage
fills in
across the street from the ancient building
where Bartleby worked and grew wary.
Its ruined lower halls have formed a marble quarry.
The upper floors are rich with pigeon shit,
and on a kitchen shelf still squats
the hunched up skeleton of a cat.

12. The oldest pioneer
still reigns not far from the Square
among tops, totem poles
on sale, little ash-tray toilet bowls,
lemon soap,
cups and knickknacks in the shop.
A real wooden Indian still stands
petrified at dying in the desert sand.
Six odd feet of bone
and tanned skin,
a purple cloth across his drained
loins (a little dry blood
is brown about the arrowhole above).
"Look Dad a real live dead
man," said a kid
and, tiptoe, tweaked
the king's mustache, which is red.

13. In the basements under the bars
about the Square
you can see bits of ancient stores
before the street was raised up in the air.
Pioneer Square
alone survived both water and fire.
Now the freeway named Aurora soars higher
and Seattle's ghosts settle in another layer.

WHITE PASS SKI PATROL

His high-boned, young face is so brown
from the winter's sun,
the few brief lines in each green eye's
edge as of a leaf
that is not yet gone from the limb—
as of a nut which is gold or brown.

For he has become very strong
living on the slopes.
His belly and thighs are newly
lean from the thin skis.
Tough torso of the man, blue wooled.
Thin waist. White, tasseled cap of the child.

Beneath the fury of those great,
dark panes of glass, that
seem to take a man out of grace,
his gentle eyes wait.
(We feel their melancholy gaze
which is neither innocent nor wise.)

Like those knights of the winter snows—
with a healing pack
(sign of the cross on breast and back)—
serene, snow-lonely,
he patrols the beautiful peaks
and the pale wastes that slide like a beast.

Sometimes still blind from his patrol,
you'll see him pull down
from the dangerous Cascades his
heavy sledge of pain,

its odd, black-booted, canvas-laced
shape alive or dead, without a face.

Colors blooming in the sun, he
caroms down his own
path, speeds (bending knees), dances side
to side, balancing.
Under-skis glow golden in the
snow spume around his Christiana.

And as he lifts away from us,
skis dangle like the
outstretched limbs of a frog in spring.
He swings gently in
the air, vulnerable, so much
the "poor, bare, forked" human animal.

And now he slowly rises up
over trees and snow.
He begins to grow more thin, and then
vanishes in air!
as, high in the lithe boughs of pines,
the silver leaves flake silently down.

There are the shadow tracks he left
down the long, white hill
beside the lift. Wait! Look up! Cloud
trails in the bright sky!
Breathing a wake of snow ribbons,
something has just flown over the mountain!

Washington, February 19, 1966

HOMAGE TO HERMAN MELVILLE

for Guenevere Minor Logan

I

1

Yearning for the time, trembling with the hope of Isabel
(and then with the fear of her)
David came out of the woods above his sister's house
to begin a last, brief watch. It was early evening—
the end of the dark day's rain, and of his wandering.
He'd thought and wept and walked it seemed for weeks, ever since
Isabel told him who she was. And now he was resolved.
He'd leave his mother and his childhood home, his father's wealth.
And he would not marry Beth.
There was only one way left he could live with Isabel.
For he could not murder the memory of his father,
name Isabel his bastard sister. (Nor for that matter
hurt his mother so much.) Nor could he, with his long desire
to have a sister, ever give her up now he'd found her.
There was only one path. Thus he could not marry Beth.
Now David stood a moment at the skirt of the woods
in a faint road used only by dredges in the snow.
The trees formed an arch for fields sweeping down to the lake.
Scattered pasture elms seemed to shiver in the wet world.
The lake beyond was a sheet without a breath over it,
without the life to reflect even the littlest thing.
Only in the sun David knew the lake caught the quick,
green images that changed the blank
mirroring of a faceless heaven. On either side
the long mountain masses rose over the lake's farther shore,
their shoulders shaggy with hemlock and pine, the mien of the
mountains strange with a kind of aura or exhalation
in the dimming air. At their base black forests lay, and from
the owl-haunted depths of caves

and unused inland overgrowths of decaying wood,
odd intermittent moanings
came: rain shakings of trembling trees, underminings of rocks,
final crashes of great rotting limbs, and the devilish
gibberish of the forest ghost.
On the near shore (semicircular and scooped with fields)
the small farm home lay in the moist air, its ancient roof
a bed of bright moss, its north point, where the moss wind blows,
also soft with the furred growth—like the huge trunks in the groves.
A single shaft of vine waved up like a lightning rod
from a tangled web of plants
at one gabled end—against the other the dairy shed,
sides netted with Madeira vines. If you come close, perhaps
peeping through the lattice and the tracery of plants
that bar the tiny window,
you might see the mild captives, jugs of milk and the birch
white cheeses in a row, molds of gold butter, and the pans
of lily cream. In front of the house stood three immense
policing linden trees!
For a long way up they showed little foilage—almost to
the ridgepole of the house. But then, like three vast balloons,
suddenly their great, green, rounded cones float into the air.

2

On the rise over the house David waited the time
of Isabel. He felt more disembodied as the hour
grew near and shadows began to shoot slowly, deepening.
He tried to conjure the coming scene with his sister
as he told what must be done.
But fantasy failed, and only her face began to
appear to him (beautiful with the flesh of his father
whom David remembered from a beloved picture),
her face mixing with the shapes of air and crowding the air
away so that it was difficult for him to breathe.
The sweet form, buried in him since he had last seen her,

seemed to glide from a grave, fine hair sweeping far down her shroud.
Once just after they met he turned from her out of care,
began to leave, but she had caught his arms with her hands
and held him so convulsively her long hair swept side-
ways over him and half hid him.
"I'm so afraid," she said, "that the shadow of me will fall
over your whole life like these dark vines, dry tears of my hair."
But David had gently kissed her.
Now night shadows grew more thick, began to move to one black
and the place was nearly lost
under his feet as he circled down closer to the house,
only the three dim and hovering lindens leading him,
his mind serpentining like his path as he left the life
of his youth forever—and the rights of his birth. His walk
grew less quick when he saw the weak, single lamp in the house
struggle with the ancient day.
And then suddenly it was night. David was at the step.
Silence exuded from the small house till he stopped it
with his human knock. The light flickered and he heard the
creak of some inner thing in the room. David's heart shook
as he saw the outer latch
lifting near his touch, and—light in hand—Isabel was there
standing at the open half-door!
Nothing was said. There was no one near. David stepped, he
almost fell into the house,
and sat down pulling at Isabel's hand as if for life.
Quite faint he raised his eyes to her melancholy gaze.
Then, the fresh, rich sound of her voice played into the room,
slightly alien. She almost asked, almost stated,
"My brother…David." And she added, "But you seem so weak.
Am I a Gorgon blasting those who look? Wait. Rest here.
And I will bring you some wine."
"No," David said, "Don't leave. I'm weak for what I must say,
what we must do. But I have never been so strong. Please don't
take away your hand." He rose and caught her. Isabel's head

dropped against him and his whole form changed in the glossy light
of her long, ebony hair.
He felt a faint tremor in his arms, and with both hands
David parted the shadowed seas of the hair and looked
into her eyes, which were afraid.
She stopped shuddering, and the lovely eyes closed. It seemed
to David then that she was dead.
The deathlike beauty of her face! The death that leaves untouched
the latent calm and sweetness of the human countenance.
But not he felt her tremble again, and her eyes opened,
and she spoke. "David, I don't know what you mean, but your hope
is also mine. I will do what you want. For though I feel
an outer evil lowering
over us now, I know you will be careful with me."
David said, "My love touches yours.
Trust me, Isabel, in whatever strange thing I may ask.
Together, we will find the truth of our own life." Side
to side his eyes turned in his skull, but his voice stayed strong.
"And we will find our own glory."
Watching his face, she asked, "But is love cold and glory white?"
"It may be, for I believe to God that I am pure.
Let the world think what it will when we have made ourselves sure.
Listen!" David stood back from her. "This is what we want.
Do I not speak your own hidden heart, Isabel? Listen!
You know I cannot be an open brother to you,
for that would injure the memory both of us honor.
Yet if either of us left the other both would die.
Listen! There is only one way.
Let me hold you, and say." He gathered her into his arms
and she bent over toward him. His mouth wet her ear
as she felt his breath blow on her face, felt his whisper,
heard but could not believe the ancient words, "Be my wife."
Isabel did not move, except to fall closer, the thin
vines of her hair forming a kind of darkened arbor
over him, giving shape to the inarticulate,

248

suddenly intense love she felt.
All at once a terrible self-revelation shot
through David's mind. He kissed Isabel's mouth and he kissed her
hair and eyes again and again, his hands moving under
the black, delicate robe that dropped from her head.
One last change, and the two of them stood mute, coiled together
in the awful burst of light.

II

Toward sundown one night David stood in the Black Swan Inn,
the writing desk and blue-chintz-covered chest before him,
great brass lock glinting in the fire
he lit when he came in, to freshen the long closed room.
Fruitlessly his hands stirred through his pockets for the key.
How unlock the vision of his father—the picture
buried under bits of cloth
and other relics of his father's past. Combs. Portrait coins
of gold. David smashed the lock with an andiron. The lid sprang
open over his father's face
with its nameless, it ambiguous, unmoving smile.
It was David's first look at the loved face since he learned
his father's lust had got for him a bastard sister.
Now he swallowed with nausea, for he found certain lines
of Isabel's flesh glowing soft under the father's.
Painted before she was born, still the figure seemed to
level a finger at the air from which she had emerged.
David could not remember the lines of Isabel
from his memories of his dead father's face. Thus it was
the *picture* which now seemed to him to be her father.
Suddenly to David's eye
it quickened with an obscene life, and he hated it
with passion he felt full as his love of Isabel.
David lifted the portrait over his head a if to
smash it. His hands hovered there. But for now he turned the face

toward the wall and began to walk
about. He thought, "The picture shall not live. I've always kept
fragments and monuments of the past—a worshiper
of heirlooms, filer away of letters, locks of hair,
the thousand and more things love and memory make holy.
That's all over now. If any memory becomes
dear to me I'll not make a mummy of it again
for every passing beggar's spit and dust to gather on.
Oh, love's museum is foolish as the catacombs
where the laughing ape and abject lizard are embalmed
as if significant of some imagined charm—instead
of the decay and death of endless generations.
It makes of earth one awful mold.
And so much even for mementos of the sweetest!
As for the rest, I know now the twilight fact of death
first discloses (secretly) all ambiguities
of the departed thing. It casts
oblique hints and insinuates gross guesses never cleared.
By God, death should be the last scene of the last act of man.
The curtain inevitably falls upon a corpse.
Therefore I will never again play the vile pigmy
and by my small memorials
attempt to reverse the decrees of death. Let it all die
and mix again! There's no reason to keep this picture.
It must go—to keep my father's public memory
unviolated, because it tells the terrible truth
that is trying to drive me mad.
In the old Greek times before men's brains became enslaved
and their arms and legs, bleached and beaten in Baconian
factories, lost their barbaric tan and beauty—when the
round world was fresh and spicy as an apple (wilted now)—
in these old times our dead were not dished up like a turkey
in a trencher and set down with garnish in the ground
for the god-damned Cyclops to glutton on like cannibals!
Instead the friends who stay alive would cheat the anxious worm

and gloriously burn the corpse,
letting the spirit spread visibly up to heaven."
David stopped his pacing about.
He turned toward the small heap of embers still alive.
With his knife he slit the picture
clean, out of its faded gilt frame, dismembered the body
of the wood and laid the four lean pieces on the coals.
Soon the dry stuff caught the spark, and he rolled the canvas
into a scroll, tied it with a scrap of gold ribbon
from the trunk and committed it to the gathering flames.
Carefully he watched the first crispings and blackenings
of the painted tube. Suddenly unwinding from the burst
string, for one swift instant his father's freed face writhed up-
wards and stared at him, beseeching,
horrified. Then, shrouded in one broad sheet of oily fire,
the figure disappeared forever.
David darted his hands among the flames to rescue
the burning face, but had to draw them back, smoking and
turning black. Heedless, he crossed the room to the gaping chest,
scooped up old letters and other relics of paper
and threw them one after another onto the fire.
Shaking, David watched his private holocaust flame to ash,
putting an end to his paternity and to his past.
The future is an untraveled gulf.
There David stands, twice disinherited, his present self.

IV

POEM, SLOW TO COME,
ON THE DEATH OF CUMMINGS
(1894–1962)

"I care more about strawberries than about death."

"Herr: es ist Zeit."

1

Lord, it is time now. The winter
has gone on and gone on.
Spring was brief.
Summer blasts the roots of trees and weeds
again, and you are dead
almost a year. I am sorry for my fear,
but you were father's age, and you were fond;
I saw it in your eyes when I put you on the plane.
Today it is too late to write
or visit as you asked.
I feel I let you die.
I chose the guilt over all the joy.
Now I know you cannot hear me say,
and so my elegy is for me.

2

I knew your serenity. Compassion.
Integrity. But I could not feel your death
until I visited your wife.
She is haggard with the burden of your loss.
I wish I had not come
before, when you were there,
and she served currant jam
on toast and you poured brandy in the tea
and laughed, slapping your thigh

and hopped, like a small, happy boy,
about your newly painted Village place.
Now the color on your walls and hers
is not fresh. It has peeled with the falling
of your flesh. Your paintings in the house already date,
especially the soft, romantic nude you did
(although I love it best):
Her dark hair full to hips,
girlish, unsucked breasts,
rather pensive belly, skin
a lucid gold or red like a faded blush.
Her beautiful, jet feminine bush.
And the limbs you made, thin with their own light,
with the glow of that other world:
Women. Estlin, your poems are full of love—
you wanted to know that other world
while you were still alive.
All poets do. All men. All gods.
Inside a woman we search for the lost wealth
of our self. Marcel says,
"Death is not a problem to be solved.
It is a mystery to be entered into."
Then you have what you wanted, Estlin,
for Death is a woman,
and there is no more need for a poem.
Your death fulfills and it is strong.
I wish I had not died when I was so young.

3

Your last summer at your farm
like a young man again you cut down
an aging, great New England oak.
Oh you are big and you would not start to stoop
even on that absolute day.
I feel you are a giant, tender gnome.

Like a child you came home
tired, and you called your wife
asking to be clean. Still tall you tossed
the odd body of your sweaty clothes
to her down, down the ancient stairs,
and it was there as the ghost
tumbled, suddenly you were struck
brilliant to your knees! Your back
bent. You wrapped your lean,
linen arms close around your life
naked as before our birth,
and began to weave away from earth
uttering with a huge, awkward, torn cry
the terrible, final poetry.

July 1963–August 1964

ON THE DEATH OF KEATS
Lines for Those Who Drown Twice

I am recommended not even to read poetry, much less to write it. I wish I had even a little hope.

Send me just the words "good night," to put under my pillow.
—Keats to Fanny Brawne

I do not care a straw for foreign flowers. The simple flowers of our spring are what I want to see again.
—Keats to James Rice

1

The last month in your little Roman house
your eyes grew huge and bright as those
a gentle animal opens to the night.
Although you could not write or read
you were calmed by the thought of books
beside your bed.
(Jeremy Taylor your favorite one.
Plato and the comic Don.)
"How long is this posthumous life of mine
to last," you said.
What is a poet without breath enough?
The doctor made you swallow cupfuls of your blood
when it came up
out of your rotten lungs again.
Your study of medicine
made you suffer more the movements
of your death. One tiny fish
and a piece of black bread
to control the blood
every day you died. You starved for food
and air. For poetry. For love.

(Yet you could not read her
letters for the pain.)
One night you saw a candle flame
beautifully pass across a thread from one
taper to start another.
All month you heard the sound of water
weeping in the Bernini fount.
You asked your friend to lift you up,
and died so quietly he thought you slept.
They buried you with Shelley
at a cold February dawning
beside his drowned heart
which had survived a life
and death of burning.

2

Ruth and I visited your grave
in Rome's furious August rain.
The little old Protestant plot
beyond the pyramid the Romans, home from Egypt, made
in the middle of the city.
All the names are English,
which nobody knows or nods to
in the awful noise and light. Nobody speaks.
This rain springs for ancient seas
that burst
behind the bones of my face
and wash in salt tides
over the small shells of my eyes.
Since my birth
I've waited for the terror of this place.
The gravekeeper in his hooded black
rubber cloak
wades ahead of us toward your tomb.
The streams that shape and change

along the tender's rubber back
light in the thunder flash
into grotesque slits of eyes.
They see my fright. Ruth's hand
is cold in my cold hand.
You, Keats, and Shelley and Ruth
and I all drown again
away from home
in this absurd rain of Rome,
as you once drowned in your own phlegm,
and I in my poem. I am afraid.
The gravekeeper waits.
He raises his black arm.
He gestures in the black rain. The sky
moans long.
His hooded eyes fire again!
Suddenly I can read the stone
which publishes your final line:
Its date is the birthday of my brother!
"Here lies one whose name was writ on water."
Oh Keats, the violet. The violet. The violet
was your favorite flower.

ELEGY FOR THE REV.
MR. JAMES B. HODGSON
(1892 – 1963)

I haven't talked to you since your death
but your picture still breathes
and flames in my dreams and at my eye.
I can tell you as a boy
folding back and back the loam
of your family's farm
as the beginning morning light grows like grain
in Yorkshire or as wind-blown fur
changes texture—
while your mother
turns again the parti-colored
fields of quilts along the beds
and furiously sweeps your little room.
Or see you following the great, slow team
while you memorize the paradigms
of Greek
you pasted on the wooden wagon seat.

As a man you shepherded a white
Presbyterian church, pointed and at rest,
a unicorn among the Iowa farms,
penned beside a field of marble colored blooms.
But I will surely not forget
that you also taught.
Small, lean body, annular face and eyes, metal rims
and a fixed (false teeth) grin
make up the picture
of my first beautiful teacher.
You taught us to listen to a book
like a lost, ancient father's talk,
and from the light in your eyes we knew

you
would become aroused
if a handsome library passed.
You gave me Goethe's *Faust* in German
and together we struggled over "time" in Bergson.
(Still for some instruction you were not so strong—
walked away from a film on sex for the young.)
And you paid
the favorite praise to my poems when you said,
small eyes gray with peace,
"You have experienced deeply both of nature and of grace."

I left the school, tried my young luck.
But I kept coming back
as if to beg someone's pardon.
Your wife made lunch in the garden
while you caressed the flower beds,
patting the dirt and pulling weeds—
or talked of your son studying abroad,
of your wife's portrait paintings on the wall,
and of your own apocalyptic book—undone until you would "retire
and have the time."
Twice I stayed the night.
But you would never break
reserve, and said at last,
"I shall follow your career with interest."

Sixty-five came, and you bought a tiny farm
where you turned
your father's earth over in your hand
and cherished close your aging wife.
But she gave up her life
the very first, quiet year,
and you would not stay there
by yourself, nor finish up your work.

Soon you too took sick
and died—with your mouth and cheek
all caved in like a hill of earth
under the heavy disc of a stroke,
unable to talk.

Still it isn't this I remembered on the afternoon
I learned your final lesson.
I was filled with an ancient image
seated on the stage
as you waited to speak at school.
You seemed to curl
forward into a ball;
your heavy head fell,
hands were born farther down between the knees
as an infant is
before he leaves his early night.
You seemed to become more taut,
more formal
or compact, more integral.
And as the mass of your body bent,
and folded some, I saw it give off bright
streams as of language or light!

THE WEEPING

for Thomas Morgan 1873–1948

Why do I still run
from the grandfather in my dream

I thought my love for him
died when I was young

Oh Grandfather you are alive
in the huge houses of my inner eye

Like the sudden yellow gleam
in the windows of your farm

When we come around the turn
and in the summer sun your high ancient home

Looms on the hill
I remember you cried like a young girl

Standing by the well
after Grandmother's funeral

Your mountainous beautiful
Welsh face all filled

And the roots of your hands still
Grandfather you blessed me once when I was ill

In my dream it was you who died
as I thought you did

And it was I who cried
as I never would.

November 12, 1963

GRANDMOTHER DEAD
IN THE AEROPLANE

for Abigail E. Logan 1875–1968

Grandmother after that late eclipse
when I lay drunk in the weak, April grass
and watched the moon on the last, best Friday night
grow awful and cruel and then lean
slowly out of the light
(become an odd, dark rock
under which some of us
still have our moving lives)—
after that you can hold the very first
of your favorite Easters.
At least a good and gaudy card
came each year before you died.
There is no message yet this time.
Instead I feel you addressed
and mailed *me* on this Saturday plane.
Grandmother you have verified the myth
inside my head.... Inside my head
I carry your gentle, senile hunch-
back and your swollen ankles
still shuffle here in the airplane's halls.
Your rheumy, red old eyes leak out all our tears.
Look out, Grandmother!
Or else I will look in. The plane
window angles near us (well, between)
and your face
reflects. You are spread
thin and shiny over all this Holy Saturday.
Grandmother is there ever any Easter
without a hope? And will the moon
be light
for the Saturday dance again tonight?
I am angry since you died.

The 727 motor at my ear
is joining me fast to Detroit
on my Easter trip,
and it has quite
disoriented my small, waning life.
Everything has died.
I'll learn how to mourn quite mad
if never to rave in love.
I want to stay up here forever,
Grandmother. For I am tired of the fogged earth
down there
with its esoteric itch of flesh.
"Time Flies." I swear my soul has just turned
ninety too. On the night I visited
and stayed
in your sad, old ladies' home
I really shook. Sick, I shivered
from the barbed, tiny animals of dread.
I kissed you and I cried
and tried to sleep
in the ancient woman's bed
(your absent friend)—
her family plastered to the wall.
Something flickered back
and forth in me, black and white,
and I touched myself heavily
again and again
to see if the young
man (I was twenty then) was anywhere around.
Oh you and I too have had our scenes,
since I was the chosen one.
When I was ten
and you visited the farm
you unwrapped your long,
red, lacy velvet doll
and then undid the bones
of china for its tiny house.

You took the picture albums
out of the attic trunk. And took that
milky, moon-shaped paperweight.
We squatted cross-legged on the attic planks
and swayed and wept for what
you made me think
the two of us had lost.
Was it really only you
who were not young
and who no longer had a home?
Oh, I did love you my ardent old Mom.
It was the second time for me,
my first mother gone.
You pushed me proudly in my pram,
and I remember this:
right in front of your friends
I wet my pants
until I knew you noticed me.
You fixed the rockers on my broken horse.
And just before the picnic once
put a poultice on my swelling thumb
to draw the sliver out.
Now I watch the nail's moon
blacken by my pen.
Look. My plane has never gone
far: it hovers in your air.
Christ what am I doing here?
Communing with you I guess.
Well then, come on,
my beloved crone. Open up.
Now I lay me down
in your aged lap and sleep
clean through this Easter.

Easter, 1968

V

LINES FOR A YOUNG MAN
WHO TALKED

But I wish you would not hang your head.
It is that image lags inside my mind.
If you had known how much we need
to help our friend (Oh I think in some old
innocence perhaps you did),
you would not hang your head.
It was out of your own gentleness you cried
for aid. And it's not because I'm fond
of you (although I am) as if you were my son instead
of my young student and my young friend
that I do not want you to hang your head.
It is this: the bit you told—
no, not *what* but simply *that* you said—
was like a gift! An ancient gift of horses or of gold.
It was a grace. Oh I suppose you thought you had confessed.
But I am not a priest. To say you had been bad
and young and let you hang your head.
Use me to find in what way you are good.
Christ, listen to your own charitable word!
We spoke so that you might understand
and be merciful to yourself. Here, give me your hand
for it is I who must feel ashamed
again, until you do not hang your head.

South Bend, April 1963

THE RESCUE

for Roger Aplon and James Brunot

I doubt you knew,
my two friends,
that day the tips
of the boats' white wings
trembled over the capped,
brilliant lake
and fireboats at the regatta
rocketed their giant streams
blue and white and green
in the sun just off the shore,
that I was dying there.

Young jets were play-
ing over the lake,
climbing and falling back
with a quick, metallic sheen
(weightless as I am
if I dream),
sound coming after the shine.
They rose and ran and
paused and almost touched
except for one
which seemed to hang back in the air
as if from fear.

I doubt if you know,
my two beloved friends—
you with the furious black beard
your classical head
bobbing bodiless above the waves
like some just appearing god

or you, brown, lean, your bright
face also of another kind
disembodied
when you walked upon your hands—

That as you reached for me
(both) and helped my graying bulk
up out of the lake
after I wandered out too far
and battered weak along the pier,
it was my self you hauled
back from my despair.

SUZANNE

You make us want to stay alive, Suzanne,
the way you turn

your blonde head.
The way you curve your slim hand

toward your breast.
When you drew your legs

up, sitting by the fire,
and let your bronze hair

stream about your knees
I could see the grief

of the girl in your eyes.
It touched the high,

formal bones of your face.
Once I heard it in your lovely voice

when you sang—
the terrible time of being young.

Yet you bring us joy with your
self, Suzanne, wherever you are.

And once, although I wasn't here,
you left three roses on my stair.

One party night when you were high
you fled barefoot down the hall,

the fountain of your laughter
showering through the air.

"Chartreuse," you chanted
(the liqueur you always wanted),

"I have yellow chartreuse hair!"
Oh it was a great affair.

You were the most exciting person there.
Yesterday when I wasn't here

again,
you brought a blue, porcelain

egg to me—
colored beautifully

for the Russian Easter.
Since then, I have wanted to be your lover,

but I have only touched your shoulder
and let my fingers brush your hair,

because you left three roses on my stair.

LOVE POEM

Last night you would not come,
and you have been gone so long.
I yearn to find you in my aging, earthen arms
again (your alchemy can change my clay to skin).
I long to turn and watch again
from my half-hidden place
the lost, beautiful slopes and fallings of your face,
and black, rich leaf of each eyelash,
fresh, beach-brightened stones of your teeth.
I want to listen as you breathe yourself to sleep
(for by our human art we mime
the sleeper till we dream).
I want to smell the dark
herb gardens of your hair—touch the thin shock
that drifts over your brow when
you rinse it clean,
for it is so fine.
I want to hear the light,
long wind of your sigh.
But again tonight I know you will not come.
I will never feel again
your gentle, sleeping calm
from which I took
so much strength, so much of my human heart.
Because the last time
I reached to you
as you sat upon the bed
and talked, you caught both my hands
in yours and crossed them gently on my breast.
I died mimicking the dead.

ON THE HOUSE OF A FRIEND

for Robert Sund

Under the lightly leaved
April trees,
your small red house seems to speak—
mildly. It lets you come down
into it from the easy sloping lawn.
Your house is very clean,
for each room
has been well swept by your young friends.
You gave up your bed to them
because they are in love: the lean,
glad girl with long hands
who shares easily all she has
with her blond, gentle boy.
It is this the house seems to say
at the Dutch, open half-door:
their love and yours.
Look, a hapless slug
suns and glows on the madroña stump
beside the porch. So slow, so
slowly it goes
toward the great, full mushroom
resting there. That home
shall keep him from harm.
Beside the rhododendrons in the yard,
your red, Iceland
daisies make a light sound.
Their music seems to change and go
between the flowers and the glass in the window.
Robert, now this small
red house (as in a child's
book) smiles
with the smile of your own face.

LINES FOR MICHAEL
IN THE PICTURE

*There is a sense in which darkness has more of God than light has. He dwells in the
thick dark.*

—F.W. Robertson

1

You are my shadow in the picture.
Once I thought you were my brother,
but to be honest, he and I were never friends.
(Even our boyhood secrets never brought us closer.)
Odd the way you stand behind and to the side,
like a shade. Still it is your own
darknesses you stay in.
You generate shadow like a light
or like an odor
falling from your arrogant shoulder,
eddying into your eyes.
The great eyes almost seem to glaze.
Look! They seem to tip!
Your eyes are alive with the gestures of death.
You've got something of mine shut in there, Michael.
I must enlarge the picture
and let it out
of your ancient, melancholy face.
My shadow yearns for peace.

2

You came to my house
just separated from your life,
your clothes still burning in the chimney
(fires tended by furious women),
books piled or bent ("She has made

me stupid," you said)
or lost. Dishes in boxes, smashed.
Pieces of your life gaped from paper sacks.
Shelves were stripped like flesh,
letters from your friends destroyed—
family scowling, all utterly annoyed.
Who was to blame?
Your marriage already gone
at twenty-one,
you said, "I have abandoned myself," and wept.

   3

Something binds every kind of orphan.
I could find my own loneliness in your face,
hear it in your voice.
But there is something else,
some lost part of myself I seem to track
(did you know I used to be called Jack?),
so I follow like a blind animal
with hope (and with fear)
your brilliant, shadow spoor.

   4

I followed in the sun
until we reached the silent pine
the day we climbed the mountain.
We were with your friends, Marie, Jim.
I was jealous of them
for they had known you longer.
It was then I began to wish
you were my brother. We cut
some sticks and walked behind.
Suddenly the pied fields, farms
and iridescent waters of The Sound

blue or black
simply fell away from where we watched
like the holdings of a haughty god,
and from the mountain top
I found an island in a lake
on the other island where we stood.
That is the way you seem,
there is your home.
Your eyes are like the inwardmost island
of that inwardmost lake,
and your tears are the springs of that.
Ah well, we all weep, Michael.
One of our eyes cannot even know the other
(except, perhaps, with a picture).

5

Down the mountain again
we stopped to swim
in a cove of The Sound—the water
actual ebony beside the brilliant sky.
You walked away from the rest
for you had seen
another hill you hoped to scale
rising down into the sea.
Marie sat on the steps behind
as we undressed.
(She wouldn't swim with us.)
Tall, classical, you poised at your own place
on the stones black from the wet
of waves, and dove suddenly
into the heartcold sea.
And for a silent while
you were gone with no sign,
the time of a cold change.
Coming back you brought up

a part of the dark
of the seas in your eyes
and some of the blue, obscure snow of the hill
drifted on your thighs and arms
in the shattering sun.
Jim and I dunked briefly,
chattering and quickly pimpled.
We carefully kept our backs
to Marie as we dressed. You
simply stood, naked and plumed,
half hard
on the bridge of the rock
and (almost as an afterthought) turned
toward the steps.
Marie looked easily at your body
and smiled. You grinned
and climbed toward your clothes.
Suddenly I felt that she
had watched the dark
rich-haired shadow of me.

6

You and I, Marie and Jim
that night on the island shore
piled up log
on log on log (we couldn't stop)
and built a driftwood fire so big
I think it scared the four of us
into dancing barefoot on the sand.
The greatest fire we'd ever seen!
We didn't join our hands,
but the eyes of flames
grew huge
and struck us blue,
then red. Blue. Then yellow.

Blue. And as we danced and danced higher
the freshly made fire
threw our shadows each on each
and blurred us into a family
sometimes three, sometimes four
close as lovers on the beach!

7

It was the last ember
of that transforming island fire
that seems to fade in your eyes in the picture.
It makes you brother, friend, son, father.
If it isn't death, it is change,
and in that fine shadow flame
what was locked is yours, Michael, as much as mine.

Seattle, May 1965

SAN FRANCISCO POEM

"A pier," Stephen said. *"Yes, a disappointed bridge."* —James Joyce

1

We moved like fingers
over the curved arms of the rock
pier at Aquatic Park,
saw the black-
haired, half-stripped boy haul back
from the sea the huge, live hand
of a crab. It charmed
and scared a playing kid.
"O-o-o-oh," she said
and jumped
right straight up
in the air,
where she changed
into a low, light limbed star.

2

And where we walked
in that watery park
the formally
happy families
fished on the pier.
From his one good eye a floored flounder
gazed with long despair,
and the dogfish shark
writhed on the concrete walk—
shucked aside

by the female touch of time.
Half-dissected by a gull
he bleeds his tears of oil.

3

Purple flowers shadowed the island prison
(windows closer than I had ever seen).
The small harbor freight train screamed
along the sand
across
from the curved pier, across
from us.
Its racket shook the ancient circus
sprawling in the sun:
the bursting muscle man,
a lovely, light-haired gamin
of a girl in blue (and little else)
whose breasts were never false
to man;
it nudged a midget growing like a stalk of corn;
an old salt who blends
with the sand, living out of sacks,
purple bats
and mothers inked along his back,
once-bright snakes
dying in the heat blackened
flesh of his aged arms.
(And other oldsters roll
their bocce ball
about the nearby green.)
When they hear the train
stark-naked kids all pause in their paradigms.
The little girls tell the little boys.
Gulls wheel about the dinging buoys.

4

At last we walk
to the far end of the break-
water pier, which turns
so gen-
tly in the sun
of the long, April afternoon.
There is some grotesque, giant thing
still there
left behind by a war
(or a very melancholy sculptor).
At the circular edge
of this stone stage
I can hear the little herds of fish
be still, or stir and shift to graze
on the sea's beautiful grass.
The pied, ambitious ducks dive
and are gone away
(long or shorter as the case may be)
under the mild surface of the bay.
One sleek,
brown-and-black duck
suddenly comes back
with a meal quivering in its beak.
Another dives and appears,
dives and reappears,
still poised but quite pissed
off at the absence of a fish.
The few colorful birds
(absorbed)
dive and dot
the black,
shimmering canvas, alive, abstract.

5

You and I sit on the concrete bench
at pier's end and watch—
each
other and the far folks upon the beach.
They watch you as you take a leak
with no attempt to hide.
We read Roethke's "Words for the Wind,"
smile at the faggot with the fat behind,
admire together
a white, three-masted schooner,
and read the signs that tell us where
we are.
"Ghiradelli Square." "Drink Hamm's Beer."
"Cable Crossing. Do not anchor here."
Because the concrete spot
where I sit
suddenly grows too hard
(and because I am really tired)
I tuck the body of your coat under my head,
curl up on my arm
and fall easily into a dream:
Two people surface and begin to swim.

San Francisco, April 1966

LINES FOR A FRIEND
WHO LEFT

*"Ich starre, wie des Steins
Inneres starrt."*   —R.M. Rilke

Something vague waxes or wanes.
I have been grieving since you've gone,
and I am stark as the heart of the stone.
I have this grief because you are a ghost
and a thief. Since you left I have missed
my own self. For your absence
steals my presence.
Next I lose my dignity. At night
I put on the dirty shirt
and coat you left
and go out
to hunt for you in the bar or street
feeling your private warmth. Last night
I thought I saw your very face
(voice of another)
in the place of a folk singer.
(The heavy mouth almost seemed to sneer
at the end. I could not be sure.)
I have not heard
since you've gone, so I still yearn
for any sign
of your life. For if you died
I did too. I
Can no longer quite
make out your body's breadth and height,
and there is something vague that grows in me
like a dead child.
Write
or come back, before I forget
what we both look like.

LETTER TO A YOUNG FATHER
IN EXILE

When I last wrote
I was so hung up with old guilt
or fright
      I could not think
what *you* might need—you who are
caught by this fucking war
in another land,
gone from parent, from calming scene, friend,
who had to leave school just as that
began to help
        shape
the keen blessing of your insight,
which is bright and quick
with presence as a fresh, dawn-white
drop of milk.
        And now you have a son
whom you are also exiled from
double-walled away
          by
both an outer and the terrible inner fight
(more bloody than any human battle, yet,
Rimbaud said).
Sweat, tears and sperm
press together from the muscles of a man
such as you are in our time—
an age which is only made
(it seems) for the old
who dare to send
        their gifted young
off to the predicted geld-
ing of a war, or jail, or to some other land
from which as you they never can
come back.
So you've become a lumberjack—

and undertake
the most dangerous of lumber jobs
choking, hooking, lassoing logs,
risking your young arms and legs
because you are not afraid.
Better to take the lives of bears and trees
than any of those
you feel inside yourself or in the eyes
of brothers, or in your own
yet unseen son's
                    burgeoning flesh.
He learns to nurse—
a sharp and tender boy
we have the hope to say—
and grows out guts, limbs:
desires to return what his mother gives.

Next, as do all kids, I guess,
he will try to learn to piss
with all the strength of giants, Gulliver
and Pantagruel, heroes who could stop a war
alone, or Leopold Bloom, higher
than two hundred fellow scholars
against the white wall
of his elementary school.
(Or the young man in Freud's dream
whose powerful river could rinse clean,
as in a famous, ancient marvel,
the filthy Augean stable.)
And one day your son will learn to swim and ski
with your own passing grace and beauty.
And perhaps in a heavy, red
woolen sweater and a massive, black beard
he will hunt swift and kill (as you) the lithe
heavy bear, and pose squatting alongside
its great, steaming, brownfelled thigh.
Michael, your son's rifle will resound
and resound

though you may only see his young kind
and not himself,
since you are banned, and since you do not have
his mother for your wife.
And you have lost one daughter or son
already, under
the murdering stress
of our own human hopelessness.
After the tender pulsing in
of your full tide of semen,
with the clouded image of a son
(which always brightens when we come)
once there
was the fusing of the sea and shore—
meeting of another half
                                    life
to carry yours.
But then war
on the womb, solid hits—
and death for the quick new part
of you and her.
And now again the grotesque hidden scars
that form and grow in all our hidden wars.
With this slow grief and your present loss of roots,
with all your unwritten books
and your rock hard, exiled life
(its vicious, black, summer logging flies):
Jesus, how in hell do you survive!

And finally this, my own thoughtless role:
you write me a note
                              about your first son,
a bastard like the rare and brilliant one
of St. Augustine,
and in my brief reply I do not even
mention
              him. Well, I see (sadly) I am cruel.
And I too know how to kill!

For when I last wrote
and said I wanted to forget

      (abort

your image out of my mind)
simply because you are not around
for my solace and my life, now
I see I raised what came

       into my hand

against you. Thus
I am loving and as treacherous
as parent or as child—in the black
ancient figure you and he may fight to break.
Oh my lost, abandoned brother,
 you know you had a father.
Now let your son
say so with the jets of milk
he has drawn from yours
and from the breasts of a mother,
whose fecund spurts
of white
as in the Tintoretto work
where young Hercules is nursed
by a god—have formed the brilliant wash
and brush

    of stars across the dark, inner wall

of our still radiant, woman world.

Buffalo, December 1968

THE SEARCH

But for whom do I look?
The whole long night you will see me walk
or maybe during the day
watch me pass by.
But I do not wander—
it is a search. For I stop here,
or here, wherever people gather.
Depot, restaurant, bar.
But whom do I seek?
You will see me coming back
perhaps at dawn. Sometimes
the faces seem like tombs.
I have tried to read the names
so long my eyes darken in their graves
of bone. (The bodies of our eyes
lie side by side
and do not touch.)
But for whom do I look? My search
is not for wife, daughter or for son
for time to time
it has taken me from them.
Or has wrenched me from my friend:
I will abruptly leave him,
and I do not go home.
For whom do I seek? Out of what fear?
It is not for queers,
for my search leads me from their bars.
It is not for whores,
since I reject their wares,
or another time may not.
Then for whom do I look?
When I was young I thought

I wanted (yearned for) older age.
Now I think I hunt with so much rage
that I will risk or lose
family or friends for the ghost of my youth.
Thus I do not know for what I look.
Father? Mother?
The father who will be the mother?
Sister who will be the brother?
Often I hunt in the families of others—
until hope scatters.
I will call up friend or student at night
or I will fly
to see them—will bask and heal in the warm
places of their homes.
And I must not be alone
no matter what needs be done,
for then my search is ended.
So now the panicked thumbs of my poem pick
through the grill. They poke
the lock
and put out a hand and then an arm.
The limbs of my poems
come within your reach.
Perhaps it is you whom I seek.

NOTES TO *THE ZIGZAG WALK*

1. I grouped these poems on the basis of person and address. Sections 1 and 3 are made up of pieces addressed primarily to a general audience where the speaker uses the first person (1) or not (3). The poems of Sections 4 and 5 are addressed secondarily to a general audience but primarily to given persons whether living (5) or not (4). (The speaker uses first person throughout these last two sections.) The pieces in Section 2 are all translations mixed in person and address—except for the Morris Graves poems which however are derivative in another way. Poems are roughly chronological in the order of each section.

2. "The Pass," "Thirteen Preludes…" "White Pass Ski Patrol," "On The House of a Friend," and "Lines for Michael…" were written in Washington State except for the last, which however was begun there and which cites places there: Mount Erie on Whidbey Island and beaches on that island and at La Conner. Deception Pass is a waterway between Whidbey and Fidalgo islands. La Push is an Indian community on the Olympic Peninsula. Pioneer Square is the oldest section of downtown Seattle, and White Pass is a ski resort in the Cascades.

"San Francisco Poem" names the aquatic pier in the marina there. Point Lobos extends into the sea near Carmel, California, and Partington Cove is in the Big Sur area near the Hot Springs, California.

"Lines on Locks" speaks of Herkimer near the Erie Canal in eastern New York State and thus blurs that town with Little Falls (not named) just to the east. "The Zoo" is Brookfield Zoo in Chicago and "The Rescue" was staged on the shore of Lake Michigan in that city.

3. "Homage to Herman Melville" is based closely on scenes from Melville's *Pierre*, while "Homage to Rainer Maria Rilke" is based on fragments and in some cases on complete poems from several of Rilke's books. One such complete poem is "*Herbsttag*" which

concludes my "Homage" and which also figures briefly in "...on the Death of Cummings" in the epigraph to that poem. The translation of "*Herbsttag*" was published in an earlier version dedicated to Paul Carroll in the old "Chicago Magazine." The Rilke epigraph to "Lines for a Young Friend Who Left" is from his *Das Marien-Leben*.

4. I am grateful to several people involved in the translations: James Wright suggested I choose the three Trakl poems included here, "*Helian*," "*Sebastian im Traum*" and "*Abendland*." Their translations in earlier versions were commissioned by The Bollingen Foundation with the help of Elizabeth Kray at the YMHA Poetry Center. Mrs. Stephen Rogers (in particular), Robert Bly, and Max A. Wickert at one time or another swelled my small German.

The translations from the Hungarian poets were undertaken at the urging of David Ray and were included in *From the Hungarian Revolution*, which he edited for Cornell University Press. Since I know no Hungarian my work was done from German translations and from literal Englishings by Watson Kirkconnell.

5. The three Morris Graves's paintings which I used I saw in a Graves's show at the Seattle Art Museum in 1966, and they are owned by collectors in the Seattle area. The Seattle Art Museum owns "Moor Swan."

6. If Morris Graves is my favorite older American painter, Jim Johnson is my favorite younger one, and I dedicated the Big Sur poem to him and his wife because early paintings of his first conveyed to me concretely the concept of the rapport between landscape and the human body which that poem uses.

Like Blake in his *Prophetic Books* (Epigraph to "Big Sur..."), Freud also speaks of such a rapport in his *Interpretation of Dreams*.

7. It was in Freud's *Interpretation* that I read the account of his own dream (which he analyzes) referred to in "Letter to a Young

Father..." This poem also quotes Shakespeare's Sonnet Number 13 and cites a painting by Tintoretto entitled "The Origin of The Milky Way," which I am grateful to Dr. Zelda Teplitz for calling to my attention.

8. The quotation from Gabriel Marcel in "...on the Death of Cummings" is from his *Homo Viator*.

9. The quotation from the theologian F.W. Robertson as epigraph to "Lines for Michael..." was given me by Michael Rust from the latter's journal. The photograph on which this poem is based was taken by Robert Sund, and was first published in England in "Agenda."

10. The reference to Bartleby in "Thirteen Preludes..." alludes to the fact that George Bluestone made a film based on Melville's story in an ancient building on Pioneer Square. This poem was first published in a college periodical at Eastern Washington University and then in "Literature in the Arts and Society."

THE ANONYMOUS LOVER

NEW POEMS (1973)

for my three daughters

CAPE ELIZABETH:
A PHOTOGRAPH

In pools
along the wide terraces of shards of shale
shot
    with white
amid the rock colors of a lasting fall
there
    are
        these very gentle moves
of life—
        a wonderful solemnity:
see the secret algae,
mussels and the mottled dark
barnacles
that open up their mouths like baby birds
among the darting, delicate fleas of God.
At the edges of the sea's expanse
loom giant clouds of silent ships,
and just on
        beyond
           the horizon
waits the little light-
ship I cannot quite
        see.
But watch with me—
for soon it will show up
in this filtered picture that I snap.

ABSTRACT LOVE POEM

All the heavy
               wet-
                     ness
of the long rain
is held in deep green
spring grass
               gathering it
to capture all the light
which through ground
glass clouds
               has fail-
ed unmarked
                   and now the sky is dull
more dark
          than
               the damp
                     green
but lighter than
the great trees that stand
immensely black
               cast-
ing in
      the green
             glow
of grass
        no
           shadow.
I hesitate
           to hurry up the path
disturbing the in-
               timacies there

between
      green,
          black,
the last
    light
        and the moist air.

ONLY THE DREAMER CAN
CHANGE THE DREAM

Riding on his bike
in the fall
or spring Fel-
lini-like twilight
or dawn, the boy
                    is moved in some way
he does not understand.
A huge gray or green, long porched house
(he's partly color-blind)
crowns a low hill: rise-
s silent as a ship does
before him.
The vision makes him yearn
inside himself. It makes him mourn.
So he cries
              as he rides
                          about the town.
He knows there are other great homes
and other beautiful streets
nearby. But they are not his.
He turns back.
                  He gets off his bike
and picks
          up three fragments of unfinished pine
adrift on the green
                      (or gray) lawn
thinking—hoping—that perhaps
there is something some place he can fix.

POEM FOR MY SON

1

Well, Paul, when you were nine
I wanted to write
and now you're nearly twelve.
For too long I have shelved
this fact
      in an
           in-
accessible part
         of myself.
And the presence of it there
is like a blush
        of shame or
guilt inside the flesh
of my face. A fall
bloom of bril-
        liant gold about
to wilt
    beneath
obscure,
     heavy breath.
Your breath is sure
as the hearty new born
filling up your bronze horn
in the junior high band,
and your cheeks puff with it.
Your pockets bulge with hands
as you grin in the picture
about to speak
balancing on the side edges of your
                 feet.

I have seen your new
beau-
   tiful
     body dive

and dance one and a half times
into the pool.
My mind moves back
to where at nine I sat
in the bus on the big girl's lap.
And more than once
                              forgot my lunch
so the one ahead
                        in the fourth grade
(believe
        it
            or not
named Glee!)
would give me sections of her
or-
    ange
not knowing it was all prearranged
inside
        my mysterious head.

            2

When I was young
I lived on a farm grandfather owned:
I remember in the cold
my small damp tongue
stuck on the hand-
                              le of the pump.
My cousin Clark
and I got the calf to lick
us in the barn,
                    but then
his father caught
                        us and caught
us too smok-
ing big
        cigars behind the crib!

I carried cobs
                in buckets for the cook-
stove and cranked the separator hard.
Oh, I did
all my chores with a genial hatred.
Sometimes at night I lay
in waves
                of summer grass
feeling inside my chest
the *arching*
                of the search
                                light *shin-*
ing from the distant town.

3

When I was ten
                nobody said
what it was the dogs did
to each other, or the bull
(whom we never could
                go near) and
the cow with the gentle bell.
                                The good
                                nuns told
me (I didn't ask)
that my dick
could only carry waste.
But they were wrong.
My son, you shouldn't have
to wait
        as long
as some to learn to love
and find for yourself
a bright, a sweet, calming wife.
There are some things not all fathers know
but if I could I would tell you how.

4

Oh I remember times I wish
I could forget.
Once when the family took a trip
and stopped
            at a motel
you cried and cried.
We thought that you were ill.
Then at last you said
"Why did
        we have
                to move
to this small house?"
And the vacation time
when you got left behind
in the car while the other kids and I climbed
the mountain side.
When we came back you did not feel
well.
        You fiddled with the wheel.
My mind's eye
                goes blank as yours that day.
And once after the divorce,
confused, you asked in a small voice
(a mild one)
Daddy, do you have any children?
I do, Paul. *You* are one.

CHICAGO SCENE

for Roger Aplon

At the bar called
                    Plugged
Nickel in Chicago
red, blue and yellow hammers
on its honky tonk piano
easily make their hits.
A boyish drummer ticks
his brush
              and pushes
back
      a shock
              of brown hair.
He draws lightly from his glass of beer.
A heavy scholar of the sax
mounts his giant bass
and together they begin
to snort,
            smoke,
                      and carry on
like a Saint George with dragon.
This certain beat
pulses to the puff of Bobby Connally's cheek.
And now the sweet and sour sauce
of the old New Orleans Jazz
potent as our father's jizz
permeates the air,
seems to knock us in the ear
and starts
              melancholy thoughts
(it is too loud to talk).
Behind the bar,

          oracular,
a bushy bearded (black)
and muscled man
            works
and broods. No one has ever seen
his face!
      For he's gone,
               proud,
to the dark side
          of the plugged moon.

SATURDAY AFTERNOON
AT THE MOVIES

Movies are badder
                than ever
in San Francisco.
Man, if you wish to go,
then perhaps you should listen
to what a midwestern
buff has to say:
They
      showed nude girls before
(crotch shots looming up near)
and, usually on alternate days,
they showed nude guys.
Next they let the naked fel-
low pretend to ball
(rather softly)
          the wildly
frenzied, faking girl.
But some of these
          amateurs could
not help taking their scenes
harder than they were told.
So now there's no pretense—
and, hence, this melancholy singing.
Frisco's dirty flicks are really into something!
Fucking, blowing, sixty-nine.
          And, *che sera*
             sera
let whatever comes, come.
Trouble is
      I'm not at all at ease
with the technicolored sur-
          facing of sperm,

sentimental music piped
     behind.
Trouble is
the patterning of pubic hairs
is not
  abstract.
Trouble is inside the cunt
I see more than a hint
of a human face
hooded, primitive, unfinished.
And there's a face in the head
of the erect
cock. A changing face rolls
in the balls
   as they make a further thrust.
Also a face at the breast
that will
   gather
round the eye or
the little
tough nose of the nipple.
There's another, more hairy face
in the man's chest.
Or in the back of the cares-
sing hand,
    the hollows of the thighs.
And
  always there is this
face
  in the *face.*
For our conscience views itself
in the mirror of the flesh.
Satur-
  day after-
    noon at the
movies. A far cry from the
Grande Theatre in Red Oak, Iowa.

Shit. With the porn
there's not even any popcorn.
So what should a boy from the Iowa farm
do when
        he finds himself in San
Francisco at a pornographic film?
Well, I guess
        he should just face the facts
and get his ass home.

MARCH. THE MUSEUM. BUFFALO. de CHIRICO

after "The Anguish of Departure"

The two short,
                straight
bushes
        from de Chirico's brushes
neither reach nor touch,
                    do not stretch.
Perhaps
        they are people?
Surely they are dwarfed,
are stalked by a forced,
rust red
        and
                naked
grotesque giant
                steeple.
(Chimney.)
            Masculine sex
(that is)
        quite empty of mystery.
The gently roll-
                ing bell-
y and thighs
                I
see
    briefly
            land-
scaped in the background
                        behind.
The white
        clust-

er or cloud
which could
be a sign
of hope
will not go up
over deChirico's building with its
three arches.
The arc of dreams is black
and streak-
ed with gray as dead as hair is
or as the dawn empty streets
of early March.
And even the arch
of despair's in shadow.
Ah, I know
that near arch of woman.
It's in the front by the foreshorten-
ed mathematic modern railroad car,
horse drawn,
not brazen,
not far—
but iron wheeled to the ground in
the foreplay of the painting.
This arch of woman
more than
half-lit
he left
(more than one might have wished)
quite unfinished:
a poem cannot,
no, it *does* not
want
to utter
how eerily closed
de Chirico
kept the louvered shutters
over each of those

          three arches.
We all grieve behind them
in the anguish of departure—
each of us
       in his own
              anxious room.

HEART TO HEART TALK
WITH MY LIVER

1

Listen here,
            liver,
let's stop hurting me.
Okay?
I'm fed up with you
and your unsatisfied
demands
            for special foods
and highpowered drugs.
Don't you feel well?
I'm told you can't take pork or eggs,
and Carter's little pills
(our fathers' famous reds)
just aren't enough—
you want the hard stuff.
For my part
            I thought
we were once close
                        friends,
but you've become a dope
fiend,
      liver,
and made me your pusher.
Thus, I protest your changed
and your more ingrained
                        attitudes.
Like somebody writing ads
you've been giving me the hard sell.
I suppose I'll have to explain
if you've been listening at all
to my harangue:
"Hard cell" is a pun. Well,
do you know that can lead to cirrhosis?

and don't you agree
                    that would be
too much for the both of us?
I wish you'd consider
all the good times we've had together,
liver.
        Remember?
Please bear with me for awhile and
forgive me if I get mad.
I think you'll find I am dead right.
Which is preferable to being dead. Right?

        2

First I'd like to try
                  to pacify
you, liver,
          not just with a lecture
but with a poem—
and get you to heal up your xylem
and phloem.
             Oh, I'm
aware those are parts
                 of plants
(I was a biology major)—
but I speak in a circulatory metaphor.
Or, similarly,
             I might have used a simile,
which is a word like "smile."
But again I'll
have to expand what I mean
for, obviously,
               considering pain,
you know little about poetry.
Get this for one thing:
"Poets like
        to drink."
But then you invoke

your damned Victorian ethic
and I hear the reply:
"You do something I don't like
and just wait—
I'll make you smart!"
It seems the philosophy
of your physiology
       is in an infantile
stage still.
May I point out this then:
an infant never wrote a poem.
Really, liver,
    why not
just admit
    you're an ig-
norant and selfish boor.
You have to have what you desire
or things get rough.
Before long you just want to go off
into the wild blue yonder
and take me with you.
Well, no
    wonder,
my poor, pining liver.
For you and I have been lovers:
I mean we really cared.
Now, truth is, you've got me scared.

   3

Liver,
   I know that
you and I are stuck
in this thing together
and we're alive—
but if you are such a fart
that you insist
     on hurt-

ing me,
       then I say
I want out
      of this
          relationship.
I want a divorce
(get back into circulation).
Don't you read the newspaper,
              liver?
Find out what's happening in the nation?
Have you ever really faced
the fact that you can be replaced?
I tell you this domestic hassle
is not for me. I'm bored.
I say it's for the birds.
Gaggles of geese or vultures,
So, get off my back,
             liver!
Or at least stop peck-
ing at me.
Who do you think
          you are. Zeus?
Well, I'm not Prometheus.
Fact is
     I have a reverse
           Prometheus complex.
For instead of stealing fire
          I lose it.
"Give me some light!"
(Claudius to Hamlet).
Or "Mehr Licht," as Goethe said
when he died
      shut in
          behind a curtain.
Or contemplate
       the sense of that
phrase
     the Ancients use:

"liver and lights."
But…I'm afraid I'm not getting through:
You
    just can't see
poetry.
        Well let's simply look at
some biological, even financial, facts:
Did you know that if you stay longer
you accumulate more gold, liver!
The richest source of Vitamin A ever discovered
was the liver of a snake (python)
estimated to be a hundred years old
when it died
        in a zoo in London.
And the halibut liver
        is richer
than cod, as scientists hint,
because cod is a mere adolescent
at the time of the sale of it
as contrasted with the older halibut.
Oh, to hell with it—
the lecture
        won't work either.
I'll tell you where you're at,
liver, you're illiterate.
But, after all, you're as old as I am—
Why, as it seems,
must I "come back to tell
        you all?"
Thank God you know me at least
as well
    as any body.
So why give me such a bad time?
Did you forget your very name
signifies
    that which lives, not dies?
For Christ's sake, liver,
what are you, an Indian giver?

Why don't you just cut it out? Stop
complaining and do your job?
Are you so choked with bile
that despite
    my obvious fondness
you took on all my proposals with jaundice?
Or do you just like to hear me rave?
Still, I feel our relationship
       can be saved.
I don't want to say "this is it."
You can understand that.
Now, I hope you feel ashamed.
I hope you change your ways.

   4

You'd better!
Because when I took
you down to the doctor
he clucked
    (as you pecked)
and said you were growing larger.
Now, when a doctor says that to a kid
he usually pats him on the head.
The Doc
   did not
      pat
       you—in fact
he pounded you a bit.
Liver, what the hell do you think you are?
Just a growing boy? Jesus—
perhaps you're going into your oedipal phase
and that's why you're so mean.
You're getting just too big for your britches.
That's
   why you hurt
      and have these itches.
You know if you were

                the liver of a polar bear
bounding
        down
some glacial hill,
they say you could
contain enough vitamin to kill!
At any rate
        you've got
too large for what the docs call
your "capsule."
But, with me,
it's not just that
old cop
(out)
    attitude—
              that you have to be stopped
and slapped
          back into your cage
(rib).
     That would be just too glib:
The *sad* thing is you've begun to change
                 my image.
For when I heard you were getting bigger
I looked at myself naked in the mirror,
and it's to you alone I have now confided
the fact that I appear lopsided.
I mean to say
you have ruined my symmetry!
Destroyed my manly beauty.
Because of your increased heft
my right side is twice as big as my left!
And you've made me a freak!
So, in conclusion, I say fuck
you, liver.
Do you think my heart is going to grow larger?
Or that this will affect
brain, glands, neck?
Stomach, balls and cock?

God, I'd be like that ten foot
                    fake
Fourth Century Etruscan warrior at The Met.
You've Oedipus-wrecked me
both horizontally and vertically!

          5

Wait, I'm raving again.
(Dionysius without gin):
And now it's me who feels ashamed.
What I really want to remind
you is this: the side
you're supposed to be on
                    is *mine*.
For side is not a physical
concept. It's spiritual.
I think
          this confusion becomes habitual
whether or not we drink.
And like a dark mirror
                    this reflection, liver,
brings me to self-recognition:
For I have to be on your side
too: I have also hurt
                    you
and injured *your* image
with a passion very much like rage
(of which you are the seat).
I can see it makes sense
it was the angry liver angry Zeus
attacked.
          Prometheus
                    is shackled
like a goose that's gorged
with corn to enlarge
its gland for the special feast.
That goose's feet

are nailed to a wooden floor
spiked through the poor
fragile webs
like the bird of the Christ Fable
prepared on the giant table
of the cross, whose crumbs, whose dregs
of wine the priests and poets drain:
they munch the body of the young bearded
man
    (thirty-three) who hangs suspended
over the twelve men banqueting
in Dali's painting:
           robes stripped from him
he has hair beneath his arms
              that are
spread-eagle in the clear air
of truth.
      For thirty days the goose's
liver grows, force fed.
And perhaps three days later that bird
with his pried open mouth and throat
is like us, twice dead.
I say let's decide
        instead
to be twice alive.
I want to open (willingly) the mouth
of my youth
      and breathe musical breath into it.

6

Therefore
let's stop this war
within the body politic,
a conflict
neither of us can win.
I want to atone
and speaking less

as angry father to a son
(or the reverse) —
and more like a priest
                    or brother
say, "Let's cease.
Let's forgive each other."
                              Finally
in my lecture, sermon, letter, poem
(which, like you has grown over-long)
I speak for the poets and the mothers,
                  as one of them
and simply plead, "Let it be born,
for the time has come:
Let my belly return
flat as a man's belly again
so that at least for here
and now (perhaps for ever
if God is no deceiver)
you and I
            may be
our own
          deliverer."

THREE POEMS ON AARON SISKIND'S PHOTOGRAPHS

1

The louvered lids
of the still lived-in, hard
Roman House behind
(its old household heroes whole
a bit longer
        in the shelter
of their niche along the inner wall)
are heavily shut
          against
the sad, weathered stone
of the father and his shadow son,
whose curled head and torso have already gone.
The father's eyes still stare at God,
and his face is furious with hope.
His shattered arm once gestured
to protect
        his beloved son, now dead.
The father's still alive although the pocks
of time deepen and grow black
along his rock thighs, and time
too has broken down
his jaunty Roman prick.
But the stony hair remains
upon his belly and his son's—
like moss or winter wheat
as from the north of Rome
weaving from the graves of the brain.

2

Into the wet, brief,
                    green and white
flash of weeds
your ancient stone shade now leans
at dusk
sick as a melancholy youth,
the blind too-smooth face
stained
with moss and memory both,
the strong, graceful feet first
taking on the color of the earth.
This ghost seems never to have had a nose.
Yet it has the bearing of a once
beautifully formed man:
Roman student, soldier, citizen,
toga carried back proudly
from the perfect, nude body
and hung loose from the young shoulder.
Now the flesh has gone slack from weather,
the face and loins made flat
by the terrible wedge
of a very slow sculptor,
and muscles of the back and legs
copied in an athletic prime
are made old and impotent by time.
A thousand and a thousand years since you are gone,
and then the long decay and death *of the stone*.
Must your face again go blank in a poem?

3

I could not decide
                 in this either hot or iced
weather
          or both (of the heart) whether
you stare wide-
eyed with fear,
                 surprise,
                           or shock.
Sure it's a surprise
this leading so many lives
when you thought
                 you'd chosen
one of them,
               not
                    two or more
or
    none of the above—i.e., tried
suicide.
          So I eyed
your nose
            again but could not recognize
whether it was aquiline
(as
    my brother, that tease,
used to say of mine)
or smooth, since,
                   as if by some contin-
uing token, your
                  stone
                          nose
is broken.
          The unfinished poem
moves to your mouth, sensual as a ripe,
thick-veined scarlet
                      fruit,

pert,
or finally
    just surly.
                And is your
long, marble hair
        a boy's or a girl's?
It is the two curled
                lines—
one bright,
        greater,
and one smaller—
pouring out of your
            mouth rather
                    than in
which seem
        to sum
            or sym-
bolize
    what stone,
            camera,
and poem try:
for these streams of water
gather
        back again
                in
your teeming, unbroken basin.

NEW POEM

1

The beautiful, bodiced
                              yellow dress you had
and your long
                    brown hair in the late
spring
        your eyes glint-
ing with wet
                    that was not tears
(it
    was the moisture
of ferns,
            their
young, light haired fronds
unwind-
            ing, bending in the wind
together). So it began
We walked, we two, married (just)
in the Iowa City street
                              quite aware
of our
        rings
                whose new gold, glancing
in the sun, seemed to make the fing-
er
    lighter:
            we hoped
they'd be seen by others.
We climbed on the bus and sat side
by side
        weaving
our hands together, reaching
for the feel of each
other
        through the small but fierce

intervening flesh.
Off the bus
         we walked on, and we wished.
Long, almost silent walk,
the always whoring or always virgin
sun
    blazing blue, gold, orange as it dropped:
and the long, inarticulated wish
like a many-toned print or watercolor wash
yearning, anxious, strange—
the eternally ancient
                (yet
in some sense young) hope for change.

    2

Just as the light
           began to be lost
we walked beside
             a freshly growing field,
and then at once turned
together as we heard
a very gentle, shuffling sound
with
    an unmistakable feeling of breath.
A breathing.
          Huge, dark figures were quiet-
ly moving
      through a gate
and spreading themselves still and
great through the field.
Some of them bent
          ghostly, beaut-
iful, to brush along the ground
with their long, lean heads.
Some few stood alone quite
                self-possessed
in the failing light

and others stretched
themselves to touch.
                    The gate closed
as the last colt
                    lurched
slightly drunk or mad or wild
through the soft, half-light.
Then the groups simply stopped
moving
          and were caught
it seemed
          in a steaming
or fogged, fleshed and powerful tableau
in the twilight's
                    thickly purpled glow.
The meadow
          now
                    dark and filled
(I should
          say the fulfilled
field)
     blend-
          ed itself with each of them
as we walked away
               along the shadowy
disappearing fence

          3

to our first house,
               Home.
The honeymoon room.
                    Structure now gone—
with my records, an
               un-
gainly four-legged phonograph
                    with doors, height
and all that

                    (a kind
                            of absurd shrine)
    and my books:
                    a second floor
                                bay window
    with a chair
                    from which the libido
                                    floats, looks;
    heavy tapestried, linen
                        curtain
                                on
    the wall behind
                    a candled
                            altar,
    for we were
                religious then.
    And a bed.
                I took off my shoes
                                and wiggled my toes
    lying on the floor in that first room
    excited by them
                    (toes I mean)
                            and fascinated,
    flabbergasted
                by you—warmed
    together by the presents of our friends
                            around us
                                    in our new house.
    Shy, we
            undressed separately
    you in our room
                    I in the bath down
    the hall. "My god,"
                    I said
    to myself (not quite pajama clad),
    "This is exciting as hell."
    The knowledge that my hard-on
                            would soon

have another use
               than in the past
(terribly tired of loving a fist)
made
      me paradoxically calm. And glad.

        4

I must tell something more
                    of her.
For she gave up much to be with me:
School (she was a junior
when I met her),
brief affair with another lover. Family.
Her
     brown hair
                is long as I have said,
and that yellow dress she made
herself; besides she was very good
at seeing what is real and necessary—
a kind of
          anguished god-
                       dess at managing money.
She
    had the nearly haughty
look and bearing of aristocracy.
To tell the truth her
                    hauteur
half turned
           me on.
Invited to the Caribbean
by her father
             in the summer
she chose my own
                less colorful, slowly drain-
ing ocean.
          The profile line
of her neck and face

had a Pollaiuolo portrait's grace.
And the aura of her presence and her talk
brought meaning, memory and hope
                                                        back.

                    5

I was a virgin
                        when
we went to bed.
                        (Not that this
is
    so unique or sacred.
All of us were virgin once.
And many spend years along the fence.)
Oh, I know words cannot catch
much
            of the experience of sex.
On the other hand
painting, sculpture and music can—
the first two because we see or even
feel the textured flesh through them;
music because music's sound
like time
                moves behind, together with, or runs ahead
of spirit and mind.
It was the tenderness of meeting
that surprised me. Going
from my known man's land
into the flowering country of woman.
Part of myself moving inside you gent-
ly or thrusting, kicking like an unborn child
in its development.
Or like a live fish of silver or gold
now darting, now suspended quietly,
in your rich, profound, uncharted sea.
And you—you danced with me,
sometimes led

sometimes followed.
I knew what loving meant
and for the first
time pointed myself toward your woman's heart—
tried to touch it with my groping, masculine hand,
as I felt you grip
      me
          and ungrip me
with your closing and opening body.
You and I felt
     that we were lost
          (or for a time spurned)
parts of each other now perfectly returned.
Predictably,
    I suppose,
        we
came too soon
    that honeymoon time
and shrank
   back
     into our own tight skins.

   6

The great, bright, moon shaped crab creature
rests, having just crawled up on the shore.
Land leans away from the sea.
A giant cloud, changing shape, leaves the sky
black or blue or gray.
The crimson crowned, great eyed king is dead,
but long lives his shriveled child!
Every troubled, dreaming young man
lets go the girl in his hand.
And the tired parents of each of us
turn over to sleep at last.

THE DEAD MAN'S ROOM

My hand clicked on
                the dead man's
                      lamp.
Its hanged crystals weak-
                ly rang
(did not weep)
            out of shape
under its shroud of dust which
covers too the plastic
fern and fake, foolish rose.
If those
        live
spirited lilies
            one sometimes sees
are real presents for the dead,
then what weird grave
                  could these flowers deck?
I'd guess
        the tomb
              (his or mine?)
of him who took sick
              and died
never having been alive.
Here I still stay
and look
        at (soak up)
his relic stuff.
            His books—
one's a not
so NEW DICTIONARY (1928).
And one of them's in
            Ovid's Latin.
And there's an ENCYCLOPEDIA OF THE WORLD
beside

a cardboard
mounted photo of mother and child.
A milk glass wedding jar
                              for
the nuts and candy he once ate,
mouth and eyes turning more
and more
                out of the light.
I sleep
          in his bed trembling with chill
while the little rolls
                        of lint shed
or blow together again
along the ashen, old
brocade-papered wall.
On one dresser laid out
                          neat
the dead man's
ball-point pen.
In the same line,
a tiny, brass
                ceramic box (to keep his stamps in,
although the letters all
                            are mailed),
scissors, screw driver, and file
for his finger nails. (They'll still
grow for a little while.)
There's a darkening
                        rather heavy chain
with a silver dollar (1896)
for the keys, now laid separate
and flat,
          that fit
the dead locks.
And in another line's
                          his magnifying glass,
aluminum flashlight case
(batteries yanked out safe

and lined up or ranked); retractable measuring tape
snapped back from the length of his life;
pocket knife, machine file and an awl,
some used and unused screws and nails,
paper clips for his uncompleted works.
At the side a still
elegant sil-
              ver comb and brush.
A cache of drugs
drying, such as cough drops,
and some wash
              for the dead man's mouth.
Tie pins wait, one plain, one pearl
and the garish ties of which he was fond
(I mean the ones that do not bind)
line up limp along the wall
beneath a rack of family plates
recording souvenir sights.
A bit far-out
              the pictures on the opposite wall:
A luscious Renaissance girl
nude, leered at by her
              elders—
and a photo of a classic sculpture,
a naked youth
              lean muscled arm upright
pulls his sword out of the throat
of the enemy (or friend) he quarreled with.
The sampler with its embroidered carriage—
its colorful Victorian couple who hope or hoped
once for marriage
              and its message:
"All to myself I think of you
"Think of the things we used to do.
"Sometimes I sigh, sometimes I smile
"But I keep each olden, golden while
"All to myself."
And on a shelf

           this lonely dead man's
framed
    himself
from far back as his own youth:
in undershorts, muscles soaking sun
being just as alive as the young body can.
Here are the clothes
              he throws
off: shoes
          someone shined and gave trees
to: a pair of pants
lying formless as a ghost
with the pockets all turned out
(offwhite like the balls of eyes)
and a still dirt-
           y, red woolen shirt
which has already lost
               its human smell.
His tables, candles, clock and bowl.
His mirror
      losing silver,
where now, this day I stand
               and
suddenly am afraid!
For my god I see in the glass—
only the contoured back
            of my own head!
And here, here is the bed
where I have lain these three nights past
and felt the mirroring pillow fit
closer and closer to his
the hollows of my own face.

TWO POEMS FOR WOMEN

1   for my daughter

This red
      Italian hand-
blown glass
          vase
narrow as the very young
stem
   of your age,
Theresa, has a flame-
shaped
      flaw
white
    as the stark
movement in
           my scarlet brain
when
    I think forever
(like a curse deliver-
          ed *to* me)
of the fire screaming in the Christmas tree
New Year's Day night
you fled tall
      with your beautiful
fire
   colored hair
(your face white
even in the heat)
into the flaw-
         ed snow
with its wrong
      red tongues.

2   *for Phyllis*

At my best I'll
                drive
around
        that island
just with you again and
wade
        in the glinting warm
Hawaiian
            waves,
put my hand
around your nicely naked waist
as it shimmers with wet
about the islands of your breasts
and drink champagne
letting it spill
                and surf a little
on my chin
when I'm
startled by your living face
beside me suddenly at the beach cafe.

POEM FOR MY FRIEND PETER AT PIHANA

1

We all live
        on islands.
And you and I've
                wand-
ered far this day
on one: on Maui
en route
        to Hawaii
which they call
                the Big Isle.
I've gone farther than you have
because I find myself
catapulting away
from you as if afraid
                        to meet,
then back.
                Though it is
a horizontal zig
                zag,
I thought
        of the vertical drop
of young men,
                a rope of hemp
around their feet
in the initiation ceremony
down a sheer hill
that (without skill)
could easily crack the skull.
We've seen the beautiful
                        pink
anthurium plant,
                part of it
erect out of its broad

adamic leaf, the scarlet I'iwi
bird
   and the strange-boned
gorgeously formed
          and mixed
native girls with hibiscus
in their dark hair.
        That far
sheer, ancient wind-blown
             mountain,
lush
   at its base,
       its long
feminine
     erotic lines
partly shrouded
       hushed
in mist,
     the sun sometimes just
catch-
    ing for a moment
the rocketing red
        ohi'a-lehua flowers
which spring up
      in the wake
of volcanic fires,
the yellow mamani
clustered like a family
       of friends
on their stalks in bril-
       liant patches
along hills
    and roads above
the native
   houses
or the falling terraces
       of taro fields that
run

                stretching down
                              like quilts
or tawny animal pelts
toward the sea again.

        2

You are patient with the pain
I keep
        which I can
neither explain
                    (even to myself)
nor escape. And therefore I half
begin
        to love you, as your
quick black hair
lifts as gentle
                    as your brown eyes still
seem
        in the wind
that shifts from higher up the sacred ground.
At Pihana you stand
                    where Kamehemeha shed
the blood of young Hawaiian men
in thankful sac-
                    rifice
some few of his bat-
                        tles won. (He was
turned on to blood
                    by Captain Cook—
who was torn apart—
and he showed
                    a tenacity like
that of the later ministers
                            of Christ.)
The stones of the *heiau*
                        now
are the horrid black

          of that
old
   dried blood.
Once before, you said,
          you took
three
   of these
holy stones away
        and they've
caused you more cursed grief
than
   you deserve, Peter, my friend,
well-meaning thief.
But there's just
       too much
           dangerous life
in these ghosts they've left behind.
Perhaps
    the sensual red Af-
rican torch ginger
should first have made you wonder.
For my part
I
 wonder if the urge to rape
an orphan child
      and steal
his semen,
    leaving his bones all
broken up
    and black
inside the private temple of his flesh
is like that sacrifice
by which Kamehemeha thieved
young life
    for himself
and for the wife-
       ly earth into which
it still soaks

```
                    slowly back.
                              It
drips
in the enormous mother vein
or extended island cunt
left by lava tubes
                    we found
and went
          through
                    underground.
Kamehemeha had less *mana* than
                              his son,
you said,
          my guide,
                    and less even
than his queen
whom he therefore needed
                    to approach naked
on his belly
          like a baby.
A thousand youths he threw
(or like a mad Circean swineherd drove)
over
     the Pali,
                Oahu cliff
of sheer
          fall and of
sure,
     overwhelming beauty—
where the wind's so strong
it sometimes
                hangs
you or wafts you back again
like a sorcerer's wand,
or like the spores of ferns
or the cork-
                like
seeds of screw-pine
```

the waves will float
                 for months.
My own seas, my winds,
are weak today
          and I
depend
        utterly on you,
who do not know,
           so now
you walk
         suddenly out of my sight
if only for a minute
and I begin
         to trem-
ble with the panic of it.
My eyes drop at once
from this beautiful island place
to my own two feet
which I see
         monstrous
in their blackened socks
             split
by plastic thongs
into two club shaped parts
like the frozen lava flows
from Haleakala
The naked feet of Hawaiian
men
    and women
are graceful as their hands.
But my feet
are black and swollen
because I've died in this exotic heat
that gives
        life
to all other manner of men,
                 women and plants,
the hanging red

                    heliconia, the hundred orchid kinds,
and tamarind.

        3

Peter, my absent
                friend,
the blood of boys, flowering,
may keep
            an aging king
alive, but not me.
I should have healed
                    my grotesque feet
in the silver pool
in the valley of Iao
at the green root
of its great
            rising, aged pinnacle.
But I did not.
And now again, it's too late.
For Christ's sake
                Peter why don't you come back!
If you're really gone for good
would
        you at least
                    respect my wish?
On my Maui grave
I want someone to leave
a half-
        empty bottle of wine
(perhaps some food
                for our continuing need).
And don't let
            some kid
steal it from my tomb!
Just give me that
                blood-red funeral urn
at my foot. Perhaps an uwekahuna, wailing priest,

may wander by then
                    toward home
and in the trained, spirited light
from his lean body
you will all see
the gorgeous white plumeria trees
that fill
        my cemetery up like girls.

    4

Thank
      God
           or Madame Pele
whose fiery
              goddess home has been on Maui
and is now in the still smoking
sometimes flowing
young Volcano where we head—
the desolation blasted stretch
on Hawaii.
           Or thank someone I say—
even Apua'a
          the lusty pig
god whose prick
            is like
a cork
    screw.
Thank one of them that you
are walking back in sight again.
I know you've been
            looking for green leaves
to place on
       the stones
           of the *heiau*
in hope of a safe passage
             for all of us.
But please don't

                 go
again, Peter.
           (That's my oracular
                         message.)
Don't leave,
        and don't let me drive,
but get me out
of this astonishingly bloody place
and after this
please keep such terrible beauty to yourself.

Note: "Haleakala" is a dormant volcano on Maui. "Heiau" and "mana" are Hawaiian for "sacred place" and "sacred power" respectively.

DAWN AND A WOMAN

The morning
                island light begins
to grow
        and now
the cocks cry
                at giving birth
to the colors
            of our day.
Their feathers make the dawn
blue and red and green
and they will strongly brighten up their combs,
as in the cold lodges
our women drop
naked to their haunches
                        pok-
ing at the tepid fires.
Why, they will go out bare
to bring in another log
before coming back to bed!
The flames they build
as they squat
                and hug their chilling breasts
form halos in their pubic hair
                            for
they are hunched in the ancient shape
of hope.
            The fireplace
with
    its fine wisps
                of smoke
suddenly fills with peace
opening like
            the great, God-wide
                            canyons of Kauai

that drop clean from the clouds into the sea,
their distant threads of waterfall
like darts of light playing on the wall
and on the
              body.
The woman will give us what she can.
We men will take what we are able.
(Painted blue
              the Sibyl
inside ourselves is also writhing there—
some kind of dance about the same, uncertain fire—
I do not know what for.)
These early women, wives, lovers,
leave their dawning chores
and coming back needing to be held
                    will hold
us too.
      They already see
we do not know our fathers
and cannot learn to love our brothers.
But they will do what they can
                once again
to warm our gut
           and heart
and also that secret, incomparable cold
that grows upward from the groin
when we learn
           we can lose a son.

MIDDLE–AGED MIDWESTERNER
AT WAIKIKI AGAIN

The surfers beautiful as men
                can be
ride the warm
          blue green
              swells
and the white sand is alive with girls.
Outriggers (double boats) ride the waves back in
as the native warriors did.
I tried to swim and tried to look,
but ended up just going back:
a huge, perfect black
man at the beach
somehow drove me away a block
to St. Augustine's Church.
The bodies were giv-
             ing me a fit
and I have come to seek the momentary calm
we find sometimes in the musk of Christ
(when he was awake
             and sweat-
ing blood
        as others slept,
or like a furious bouncer
hustling out the money changers).
The bodies of Mary and Christ
both still live, we're told. They're alive
and thus
must have dealt with the stress
of that long time
           of turning on
to being young.
I speak of teens.
           Fifteen and ten

years ago when I first confessed,
it was in this same church built then
as a gigantic shed
where the strange Hawaiian birds
(I forgot their names—no matter)
flew in and out of the high wood-
en rafters
like the whimsical winds of grace,
and grace gives back to sight
what beauty is—
                  as
that loveliness at the beach.
Now the church
                  has been rebuilt
in pointed stone across the street
from a much
                  higher new hotel
where at lunch
                  I almost spilled
and found I could not eat
the purple orchid in my drink.

RETURN TO THE ISLAND

Along the back farm road the
Jacaranda
      and (still on Maui) the
Bougainvillea
burst like purple bushes struck with fire,
polyps burning under water.
               And far below
the unutterably blue
"Sea
   of Peace"
bare-
   ly shows itself, a more
ancient symbol
even than the Paia Montokiji Buddhist
temple
     we just passed,
where a few
        chanting women sew.
Above us the
         fecund rain forest
and the weird loveliness
of the bright orange illness
on the gray Eucalyptus tree's
flak-
   ing bark,
whose fragrance fills
the twilight
with its bittersweet
        oils.
We walk together
       out of our
human love:
I don't mean walk *out* of
it, but

within. Still we are more separate
than either of us might
wish at the depths of our lives,
and we leave our friends
                              behind
in the car,
              their
lives and limbs entwined
like the roots of trees
apparently
                beautiful as the name of
that one: Macadamia.
Or Avocado.
And the slow,
gray sheep whose coats begin to glow
in the going light,
their faces start-
                      ling black
as they make
their yearning, childlike
                              music;
and the yet
                blacker cows with faces white
as mimes
              amble up
                          to us
pleased with the grass
                              we pull
from beside the road
and toss
into their field; in their shud-
                              dering ancient peace
these cows and sheep
quietly take their fill.
I feel
it is our love that must
                              just
nibble at the exotic hill.

There is a white
upper
      half-flower
where we walk
(whose bloom is now growing dark),
the Naupaka of the Hill.
The Naupaka of the Sea turns its other half-circle
of lower petals
from the dis-
             tant Pacific
this
    way.
Is it because of me
we both seem Naupakas of the Hill?
Or is it because of imperfect
                  human love it-
self
    we
seem two Naupakas of the Sea?

THE GIRL IN THE FOG

The fog
          stammers everywhere
along the rock
                    break-
water pier
                and in the twilight air
the Peace
Bridge has its Buffalo steel feet
nearly all cut off.
                          Therefore it walks
like a lame centipede quite
impotent at first
then on to
          Canada.
Fishermen
            are chattering in
the fog.
          It's not
just the sign of them on the shore
I hear
but also the live laughter
of those boys with their poles
moving toward us,
breaking through the holes in the mist
which then again will fill.
I turn to you.
                The two
of us hunt
          for shells
(which somehow in or through their in-
tricacy have
                managed to stay alive),
and for the April plants—
Here alone the predictable, unruly grass

sprouts again and mounts
these unlike-
        ly rocks
where the ice has only just
              broken up
again. I fix my
        hand
about your rich, young body,
your light ass.
           As we are about to kiss,
your small daughter who has run ahead
grows afraid
in the suddenly lost
           light.
She screams and tosses
           up
toward the gathering thin
             moon
the dead,
        admired fish she held
in each of her hands.

POEM: TEARS, SPRAY, AND STEAM

In Memoriam: Eric Barker

1

Peering, stung,
            bleared, hung-
over and lame,
through the waves of spray,
I feel somewhat
            panicky,
weird, about my sweat-
            ing body.
For where do we and our vapors end?
Where does the bath begin?

Strange to be able to see through the steam
(but satisfying, to the point of calm,
like the vision of the perfect, newborn)
for the first time
the whole,
            beautiful body of a friend.

Like a god
            damned eternal thief
of heat,
      clouds
wreathing round
your black, bearded head,
belly, limbs and your sex
(but no piercing eagle about,
yet)
you lie flat on your back
on the rock
            ledge bench in the bath,
Promethean in your black
                        wrath.

2

In our nun's or monk's
                    black
rubber hoods
(lace-paper coifs
                just visible at the tops
of our heads),
as if about to pray,
and black rubber coats
                        to our feet
because of the spray,
we walk the Niagara Tunnel.
You can tell
            almost for sure
which ones the kids are,
but you can't tell men from women here.
Unsexed in these catacombs we watch
for the asperges of the bath.
The damp walls bleed rice.
All dark, all si-
                lent, we all pass.
We bow, each to each,
and some,
            not only young,
give the ancient kiss of peace,
standing in the alcoves again.
We reach for rain.
The Falls' spray touches each of us.
The glass
        over our eyes
                        weeps.
Cheeks
    are wet. Lips.
Even our teeth if our mouths gape.
We are caress-
                ed with wetness
all about our cloaks,
and we sway

and float
broken out in a dark sweat,
complex, prodigious:
female, white, male, black, lay, religious.
At last we all
                    peer out the stone holes
at the back of the Falls
and see nothing but The Existential Wall:
water roaring out of the hidden hills.
Power passes us, detached,
                                abstract
except for this cold steam
that licks and teases
                    until at last
we turn our drenched, glistening backs.

        3

Aging, still
            agile
poet Eric Barker,
who has been coming
(I almost said springing)
back here
            for many years,
and I and two friends
strip at the still springs
with their
            full smell of sulphur—
here where bodies and warm water
are moon- and candle-lit, wind woven,
in a shallow cavern
                    open
to the heaving, iridescent sea
near
    Big Sur,
and we invade the great,
                        Roman bath
intimidat-

ing the Esalen teacher with his small class:
three naked girls in three corners of the big tub—
he, their leader,
             in the other.
The candles waver
as the class takes cover
                and the mad teacher
leaves with one student to find
a night watchman, leaving behind
the others:
          one of them
already slithers
in a smaller tub with one of our friends.
The third girl now fully dressed—
and for the moment repress-
ed—stares
         at the rest of us
lolling and floating our masculine flowers
as we give a naked reading of William Butler
Yeats to each other
           (taking care not
to get the book wet)
and then we read to her
as she begins to listen.
             So she too strips and
slips into the fourth corner,
becomes for a moment our teacher.
Her breasts come alive in the water.
Yeats
    will wait
and Keats—for Barker, with whom
we have been drinking wine
all afternoon
knows
      all the Odes
            by heart
as well as many
          bawdy songs:
"My long

delayed erection,"
he'd recited, laughing,
"rises in the wrong direction."
But he too is silent
for the while, and
                    sits stately,
buoyed by the
                    water: its movement
makes his white
body hair seem to sprout.
Soon,
       we begin
                to say the poems again
and to touch each other—
                              the older
man, me,
the boys and the girl read-
ing over the sea's
sounds
         by the candles'
light and the moon bright, burgeoning,
shin-
       ing time to time
                          as
the clouds pass.
                  In this gently flash-
ing light then
we all leave the tubs and run
dripping down the shore
together before
                  any others come—
as hostile teacher, watchman.
But in that warm spring
water which we briefly left, everything
                                         eventually heals:
for, by
       the sea
it flows out of these ancient, California hills,
which are the trans-

formed,
giant body of a once
powerful, feather, bone and turquoise-adorned
Indian Prince,
            and the sulphur is changed
sharp incense
            he burned daily as he chanted
year and year over for the sick young princess—
who took her loveliness
from the many-colored, fragrant trees
and the flickering sea.
Finally, unable to help,
            he thought,
the tawny-skinned prince
died of his grief,
and his body became this mount-
ain. And everybody here who comes together
            in belief
is somehow bound, bathed,
            and made
whole, e-
      ven as was she
by this gradual, glinting water,
the prince's continual tears for his sister.

So, when we return a little later
from our dance along the open shore
we find the Esalen
            teacher there again,
and the watchman,
each with a woman.
They wait
            in that gentle, lunatic light for us.
They smile as they undress.
Eric Barker takes a leak,
begins reciting Keats,
and we all bathe and sing together
in the new waters of brother, sister.

THE BRIDGE OF CHANGE

POEMS 1974–1980

---

for Jerome Mazzaro
—whose compassion, intelligence and creative
gift combine to help keep one alive in our time

The trouble with most poetry is that it is either objective or subjective. —*Bashō*

I

RETURNING HOME

POEM FOR MY BROTHER

Blue's my older brother's color. Mine is brown, you see.
So today I bought this ring
of gold and lapis lazuli flecked with a bright bronze.
His blue is the light hue of his eyes. Brown's the color
of our dead mother's long hair,
which fell so beautifully about her young shoulders
in the picture, and of my own eyes (I can't tell hers).
I loved my brother, but never quite knew what to think.
For example, he would beat
me up as soon as the folks
left the house, and I would cry big, loud feminine tears.
He was good at sports and played football, and so instead
I was in the marching band.
My brother stole rubbers from the store and smoked cigars
and pipes, which made me sick. But
once we swam together in
the Nishnabotna River
near home, naked, our blue overalls piled together
by the water, their copper
buttons like the bronze glints in my ring. I remember
once when I was very young
I looked deep into a pool
of blue water—we had no mirror—and I was so
amazed I looked over my shoulder, for I did not
imagine it was me, caught
in that cerulean sky.
Thinking it was someone other, I tell you I con-
fused myself with my brother!
Nothing goes with gold, but I can see in this rich blue
stone the meeting of our clothes like the touching of hands
when he taught me to hold my fishing pole well and wound
up the reel for me. You know,
blue is the last of the primary colors to be named.
Why, some primitive societies still have no word

for it except "dark." It's associated with black:
in the night my brother and I
would play at games that neither of us could understand.
But this is not a confession; it is a question.
We've moved apart and don't write,
and our children don't even know their own cousin!
So, I would have you know I
want this ring to *engage* us
in reconciliation.
Blue is the color of the heart.
I won't live forever. Is it too late now to be
a brother to my brother?
Let the golden snake bend round
again to touch itself and
all at once burst into azure!

—*1974*

GRACE

We suffer from the repression of the sublime. —Roberto Assagioli

This artist's sculptured, open box of mahogany
(ivory white inside) is strung
with vertical and horizontal layers of mus-
ical wires that sing when struck, and bits of bright garnet
rock tremble where they intersect.
These gems flash in the candle light,
and before me all my beloved childhood looms up
in the humming levels, each one deeper than the other.
I tip this sculpted box and my child laughs and moves there
in his own time. You'll hear me moan:
Oh, you will hear me moan with all the old, sure pleasure
of what I'd thought I'd lost come back again.
Why, we have never left our home!
On the leather lace fixed about my neck, blue, yellow,
red and black African trading beads begin to glow:
their colors all weave and newly flow
together like translucent and angelic worms.
And beneath these my neck is as alive with gentle,
white bees as is a woman's breast.
Beside and in the light river
figures come on stage exactly
as they are needed. I tell you, I conduct my own
act! A boy poses so youthfully,
so beautifully, his slim arms a graceful arrow
over his small, brown head, and he dives!
Limbs and body push supple as a whole school of fish.
And then his vacant place is taken by another—
a man dressed in denim and in boots of red rubber.
He is wrenched from the shore and pulled
through the fresh, bright stream by a kid
who tugs on one of his hands and holds a fishing rod.
And, too, this man is dragged in the opposite direction

by a red dog on a leash shaking his wet
great coat into the stippled light.
That man just sashayed: he zigzagged
this way and that. The man is me!

A bluejay does a dance for us!
He hops beside a tree that rises inside of me.
He half-glides, his iridescent,
blue back striking like a brush
of Gauguin on the bare canvas of the air and then:
he flies! leaving behind him a small, perfect feather,
which I find shades from blue to brown—
my brother's color into mine.
Now in the space the diver and the booted fellow
left, my brother and I are there
fishing together, our poles glinting in the water.
My mouth moves. My eyes are alive!
I cry to my brother with joy.
For that bluejay was a messenger of what I want!

Gregory my friend and guide on this voyage seems benign.
He brushes my chest and my stretched,
naked arms open to the sun
with a branch of the fragrant pine.
"Be healed," he chants with each glancing
stroke. "Be healed." The needles prick my skin back into life,
and I go down to bathe my feet in the stream. The veins
form a light, mottled web along my white ankle.
I feel my kinship with the pine,
the jay, the luminescent stream
and with him—or is it with *her*,
the Mother? Gregory, my oracle, my teacher.
He leans there in the door of our tent by the river,
his face glowing, hair long and shining as a woman's,
his belly fat with life—pregnant with the two of us:
my brother and I, unborn twins who lie entangled
in each other's developing
limbs. Soon we will be born! He and I will taste of milk

for the very first time! And taste of strawberry pop
and of bright bananas. And we will eat, my brother
and I, a great, shining, autumn-red apple fallen
from our father's tree as if from the long sky, and *you*
too will taste this apple with us,
for we all have the same mother, and her name is Grace.

RETURNING HOME

The Argus-eyed old greenhouse is all gone where once the black banana fronds were, come from someplace out of town (it seemed like Mars) and the sick, several-colored birds of paradise were there too stunning us Red Oak kids visiting from tough, old Miss Benware's class. And gone Cozad's oil station. I peddled there the five cent *Saturday Evening Post* before dawn, passing like a pale hero through the strong snow storms with my cap pulled down around my bitten ears, and the skin of my leg too grotesquely breathed on where the black wool sock separated from the knickers. The local cemetery has sprouted much more pine and spruce: it has put on population in the fifty years since I was born. Today I stand beside my mother's grave in the heavy rain. Did you know it took me decades to find where she was dead? I had imagined there was a place for me beside her changing body. But I was wrong. I figured out from the stone placed upon her head (like a great foot upon my heart) that she was only twenty-eight. And now, you see, already it's too late, for the plot is thick, is full. Oh well. Oh well. My grandfather took that last spot away from me when I was three. According to these graves it was very hard for him—for Otto. His daughter dead (my mother) and his son, my little uncle, had died before, when he was only two in eighteen eighty-four. Wait! Look! my grandfather's wife Ann died when his small son did! Well, no, on second look—the same year anyway. I was thinking more of me, for it was I who died and was laid in earth the same day as his daughter. She thought rather that she had given birth in a house on a street named Joy to a living son named Jack. I want that house, I want that street back! Yet in some sort of truth or other it is my mother Agnes who has died, and it is I who have stayed alive. Agnes, whose name means lamb. Of sacrifice? Oh, I did not cry. I was quiet as three mice. I was dumb before I was wise. And I was drunk before ever I was dead. Last night I read the "handwriting on the wall" in the Westerlund Cafe (that at least has stayed!). It said "Clean the wool out of your zipper you sheepfucker!" I remember here my father downed some beers on Saturday afternoons and listened to the games on the radio. My friend and I had the opera on. Christ, he would say when he came home at six o'clock fuming. Is that damn thing still going? And in Iowa, it was. Stam pipe, stam pipe, I see the stam pipe. Whoever truly sang it first won the child's play as we came back to town from rides all over Montgomery County. Now that high monument is gone as is the circular pavilion with the magical name near where it was: cha-ta-qua. Red Oak's great cock is now lost to an orange tank on stilts. And the brick house where once I went to school is gone. Where quick Lloyd Hicks always won the barefoot race at recess, and that snot-nosed Thelma ate the library paste. My homeroom is gone! Now it's a storage bin for grain. Gone the swimming pool where first I saw Junior O'Dell's new red hair and Marilyn Hughes's breasts suddenly bulged beneath her suit. I watched my young semen float thin cloud palaces of white in an isolated part of the water. And so, you see, when I came back to town I found all my boyhood things and boyhood places gone. Even my grave was robbed! And that is why I sobbed in the loose, driving rain underneath the spruce and pine.

—1975

NOTE: *"Stam pipe" is colloquial for stand pipe, a vertical water tower.*

FIVE PRELUDES FOR
BUFFALO'S OWN FOREST LAWN

1

"I say, instead of the white man
converting us let us watch *him*,
and if there is any difference to be seen, *then*
we will listen for his white God."
Seneca orator, Chief Red
Jacket's body was converted from its native grave
to the sod of Forest Lawn, where the flag of his brave
tomahawk still waves above the statue of his form
rather far from the folks at home.

2

Ominous, marble-hooded figures lean over bowls
and continually vomit out of their bowels.

3

Pyramided within glass slopes and arcs of marble,
you cannot be dead in the Blocher Memorial,
for you with your rock beard and book
opened across your chest lie life-sized upon your back—
fully clothed even to your coat—
by two mourning and scolding folks, mother and father,
both of them quite full-sized as well,
and, above: a life-sized angel!,
who, the story goes, is the girl
your parents would not let you wed.
She hovers now (forever) above your cold, stone bed.

4

About the spring pond in this elementary town,
flowering trees drop their white and purple petals down
as mallards nest and the baby ducks waddle around.

5

The angel has begun to chip
over the child's grave. To see this,
go in the Delavan-Delaware entrance and turn
left about a block. Someone who cared placed a glass box
about the angel, for it *should* be more durable
at least than the body of the child, whose flesh falls off
so quick inside his own box. His friends are unable
now—or just do not want, perhaps—
to guard his grave: some of the glass about that box is
broken. The angel guardian
dissolves in tears of falling stone,
and those who were so attached to him have all gone home
except for one who makes now this protective poem.

ASSATEAGUE

Tamar and Royce are in love.
They run up the beach and give
each other a hand. I walk
behind and brood. I'll try my luck:

Gray the beach at Assateague.
Gray the sky and gray the sea.
A white heron whirls off now
and a spider crab comes out

of its hole, scuds swiftly back
having sensed a big mistake.
I find a white plastic bit
I had thought was a devil fish.

The washed-up wood of old ships
breaks the sand, with shells like coins
lost from Spanish galleons
that used to try these awful seas.

One ship torn up on the reef
left a heritage of dwarf
wild ponies from centuries
before, and still two herds of these

roam the shores and live on marsh
grasses. The round-up is harsh
yearly, decimates the herds
driven before the waves and winds:

They swim across the channel
goaded by the boys and men
and up the beach into pens
pattering up over moist sands

and dashing the placid salt
pools into myriad drops.
Roped and with spirits broken,
the ponies are driven inland

and for the rest of their bound
lives they yearn for salt and sedge
they fed on under the ridge
of snow along the island edge

as we yearn for our childhood
or the love we never had
or else had but could not keep
until we came to Assateague.

for Michael and Robin Waters—1978

LINES FOR AN UNKNOWN LOVER

I desire to hold in my heart
(which is shaped like a child's fist) the thin stems of feelings
no one has ever felt. They'll burst
in great bouquets your touch gathers
up from the unlikely roots of my fingers and toes:
sudden, resonant, color full—
the blues, reds and golds will damage the bulb of my eye
beautifully. And I will give you back a caress
you can tell in the delicate tip of your eyelash,
feel echoing quiet at the
first and then more stridently in the hidden fronds weav-
ing upwards toward the bright trellis of your belly.
Listen to the sound! It is dis-
sonant above the musical
ground bass, the passacaglia of your humming sex.
And when we join, all these colors will match all these sounds
and the broad strings I bear in the arched rainbow of my
body will bury themselves, well, nearly noisily
in the scudding clouds of your breast.
Your breast's light lights up your unknown face.

MEDICINE BOW

Something isn't right with me.
We climb in the hot July
car three-thousand feet from Laramie
to the snow
covered sum-
        mit of Medicine Bow—
my son,
    his wife, grandsons, and me.
Despite the beauty
of the dove-gray mountains and the bright lake,
the azure columbine,
        I find
           I am shak-
ing. Like the edge of the snow,
my energy
    slowly recedes,
        although
I am in the midst of my family.
Anxious, I bend to the ground
and scoop up a shimmering hand-
ful of snow. Suddenly my mouth is
washed with ice
    and I know
I have shocked myself back to life.

A DAY IN THE SUN

The magnolias merge each to each
with unearthly ease in dance
of riotous flower among
other gnarled, leafless trunks. My son
takes a picture as I posture
in the bar open to the air.
We have had a drink or two there
where trees loom up over the walls
and ferns tumble from their tops
like waterfalls. He talks to me.

My son talks to me. He explains
the awfully intricate way
the camera works, tells its quirks,
how you focus the lens and how
for light you align the needle
in the multi-shaded circle.
Master now, I take a picture
of him, of my beautiful son.
We get in the car and make shots
all the way to Sausalito!

We park and go down to the shore.
We sit on a log together
and set it to take a picture
by delay on this sunbright day.
There is a background focused too:
eucalyptus trees just for us
and (lower) the blue flowering
iceplant. And then we smile and hug
each other for the last picture.
We hear the snap of the shutter.

We grin and he winds up the roll.
Then Stephen frowns and mutters, "Shit.
Something wrong with it!" And we find
the damn thing didn't work quite right.
None of the photos will come out.
We pause for half a minute and
then we laugh: all that instruction,
posing at elaborate ease,
and "Cheese." We turn toward the car,
our thoughts a bit reflective, far.

for Stephen Logan

COMING OF AGE

Driving the new road to Buck's Lake,
I shout toward the pickup's back
but find they cannot hear me from the cab where I sit
forward with my fond son David
in his blue turquoise brand new truck.
Young sons Paul, Stephen—and Stephen's girl—ride behind.
It's David's birthday and we plan
to celebrate it in the sun.
At the lake we leave the truck and seek a private place.
After long experience I am afraid to burn,
so I don't undress as my three kids strip to their trunks,
and fresh, nubile Clara hikes up sharp her bathing strap.
Suddenly David dives, streaks from a high, jutting rock:
a wild swan just turned twenty-one.
I flush and feel alive as he.
Paul, my youngest one, after fast-swimming a full lap,
lies asleep, and the hairs on his legs and belly sweep
as he dries and dreams in the late
summer wind. "Whew," the others shriek,
climbing up out of the cold lake.
They shiver underneath the white
fir and sugar pine while they sip
frothing cans of bright-colored pop
and beer: there's only one kind of brew they'll drink, since here,
in all the little towns about,
big David is distributor.
We chat a bit and then they swim clean across the lake!
Their voices flutter like my shadow in the water.
Clara, who could be my daughter,
has the highest voice. I answer,

"Please stay over there a while! I've not finished my thought!"
But they head home, and I leave my
reveries in the breeze-blown foam,
which wafts to the manzanita and the golden oak.
Their new lives shape in this, my wake.

for David Logan—1980

II

POEM IN PROGRESS

POEM IN PROGRESS

1
First Prelude. Dream in Ohio: The Father

My ship passes overslowly through the foreign lands
her lovers all are from. There is not much time. The boat
brushes, feels the banks of these beautiful canals. But
there is no one you will see in the unusual
houses with their strange-shaped, attractive red-and-white suites
of dining—or brownish, burnished bedroom—furniture.
Their decorators are inventive and avant-garde
though slightly color-blind. Even if they *are* empty,
nothing's ripped up from the floors and we can see that there's
no thievery. Toward the back
of the ship with its frothing, fountaining wake, I walk
underneath elaborate glass pendant chandeliers,
their candle-lit tears turned golden
with the muting dust of the last years above this old
and red San Francisco brocade.
I stand at the ship's stern chain. Sure,
it's dangerous to be here! Drift-
ing all this weird weekend through landlocked midwestern towns.
I think of that possible slip
out of the ship's fastenings
into the long sleep of the wake.
But I wave through. I try to greet,
as the boat moves on quietly through the avenues,
some aging men on corners in this alien place.
But they only talk among themselves. How can they miss
this ship in the streets, these old men—
miss *me* trying to salute them? Father, I suppose
it's you again. Why did you stop
hunting for the vivid pheasants in the fields
or having a beer with your friends
in the old Westerlund Cafe

when I was young in Red Oak, Iowa? Oh, I once
thought we might have talked, might try to have something to say.
Instead, I ran my buddy's car ninety miles an hour
down Highway 48 outside of town and jacked off
when I got home. Father, I love you still—
still yearn for your advice. Shall I turn back toward the tip
of the ship? There are people alive close by upstairs
in this many-tiered boat. I can hear them as the ageless, orange moon, ri-
ses over the small hill or houses. Well, I will go
up there to the sailors perhaps
or the families or the whores—
whoever *lives* on this ghosted ship that floats through the streets
where absolutely anything goes, and there *are* no shores.

2
Second Prelude. Reality in Albuquerque: The Son

Passing through Albuquerque where I'd read poetry,
I find myself beside a quite young drinking buddy.
Black-haired and bright-eyed Chicano kid, he wants a coke
with three cherries in it. He gets that and then asks me,
as folks next to each other in bars are likely to,
why there are no cherries in *my* glass.
"Because," I say, knowing I sound absolutely
absurd, "Screwdrivers just never *have* cherries in them."
Surreal, I think. What's this kid doing in here at ten
o'clock A.M. anyway. "No school today," he says.
"Teacher's convention." He is
only seven and his father is tending the bar.
He asks me where all my kids are.
"In New York where I live," I lie,
then tell the truth. That I am flying back there tonight.
"And your wife?" Third degree, I think. Well, part of bar talk.
"Why, New York too," I lie again.
How the hell can I tell this kid
I hardly ever see my sons
because they are three-thousand miles
away from me (and then some). Perhaps *you* understand

what I mean—but him? Both of us
in the bar at ten A.M. He walks to the juke box
with a quarter given by his father, then looks back,
admits he cannot read well. So
we select together and agree on two pieces,
playing first that morning song, "Bridge Over Troubled Water."

3

Plato in Florida: The Friend

Our car strays only for today through the Florida
highways. Sun-bronzed student named Mike,
you are my guide in this incredible place where Cape
Kennedy veers to Disney World,
and I feel sure you are a friend.
Intense, bushy-haired, your hands scal-
ing from hard work, you've taken on the archaic look
of an animal born out of the Orlando swamp,
and so you are both old and young:
millions of years and twenty-one, balancing between
the ancient, ugly, splendid figure of the almost
extinct sphenodon with its one
median eye (quite clear but dull
like the opalescent jewel
pendant on a woman's forehead)
and the more than human, quite beautiful young man, who
glows with intelligence from a point somewhere behind
the middle of his brow. You've guessed
because I grow older and you have learned from my work
that I may possess some wisdom.
Well, right or wrong, still you ask me to say what I know
of Plato. Just wait awhile though
before I say, "Love." Love, Socrates said, is a lack:
a sign, in "The Symposium," of our poverty.
You with your own love (should I say
your own need?) of music—whether
it's the hard or folk rock of your own time (some of it
androgynous as David Bowie or Lou Reed: "Trans-

former" album, that electric, angelical name),
or the classical pieces of mine—
would take to heart Bernstein's early "Serenade" he based
on Plato and his myth of that interior split:
A scholar says, "male and female created He *it*
not 'them'." In "Genesis." Then this fable that Plato
put to us—and Bernstein set—of Aristophanes
(whose name I think means "the shining vision of the best,"
but my Greek is no longer sure).
Bernstein's program notes, like poets' attempts to explain,
do not articulate well the sweep of his own sound
where, in that human or god-given miracle, he
plays out for us again also the lyrical love
song of Agathon for woman, then sings cacopho-
nously Alcibiades' tipsy, horny entry,
anxious as he was to put the make on Socrates,
his old general from the wars.
But the man went home from him at the first bell of dawn,
having drunk them all under the table—and afraid
still that he would be unable
to teach him (and us) if he touched Alcibiades.
Thus he left him unfulfilled, as
the sky moved from black into light.
The love that is a lack. Not that Socrates did not
love Alcibiades, but that he did. The other
love in Plato's "Phaedrus" is not thus: the need of man
for woman, or of man for man, woman for woman;
instead, it is the love that will be felt as fulfill-
ment, the erotic burgeoning of wings whose dry buds
become as damp again as the newborn. The wholeness
of the Trio underneath the Charioteer's mind-
ing whip, the courageous White Horse and the desiring Black.

4
Rescue in Florida: The Friend

It was poverty I felt at my reading when we
met: I wrapped my legs together, my arms surrounding

myself, fetal, vulnerable
and afraid before I had to begin to perform.
I felt beside me in the next
chair *you*, with your brown eyes and that lovely brush of hair,
felt just the glimmer of your interest and was warmed
though I'd never seen you before—except someplace else
inside myself. And so I read
to *you*. Your eyes helped the life inside me to unfurl
again, like the slow, moist tendrils of a primeval fern.
Later, driving with you, I was able to watch with ease
(before, more dead, I could not) the unbelievable
shapely peacocks shimmering in the park and road,
their graceful, crested heads moving in a kind of dance—
the albino one isolated as an exile
is—his white tail dropped but still gorgeously, formally
curled round like a unicorn's beard.
Slow as a ship does, our car moved through the hens and cocks:
blue, brown, red, purple, and with a flashing metallic
sculpture sheen among the unguent eucalyptus trees,
and their too many feathered eyes, it seemed, reflecting
in the Florida water, their elegant baroque
fans bursting occasionally in an orgasm
which fixes there, weaving in air—a frieze of rockets.
Perhaps we can guess peacocks solve
the problem of balancing their sex against their heads
or, say, their burden against their gift.

5
Interlude. The Colombian Statue: Archetype

At the picnic you drove me to in the overfull
car, I wanted to speak to you.
But you ran off with Bob, your buddy, along the stream.
Then there was the lovely interlude with two of your
friends, Jay and Kathy, who walked through the green, white and blue
Florida pastures more as a brother and sister
than as the lovers they now are. A great fig tree fixed
the wandering clouds, the colors and us there in time.

They showed me their childhood river, live water spilling
into the many-colored bed of bright rock from three
huge tunnels where, when they were kids, they had stripped and slid
through one, as a furious water moccasin slithered past and the two
played that they were already dead.
It danced, or dare we say, the water moccasin half-
stepped on their young flesh, light sparkling along it, and slipped
through Kathy's very white legs, she said. I thought of Art-
emis deflecting the sperm of Zeus along her thigh
still virgin. Kathy had no tan
then, for it was still the spring. By that light stream they knew,
Jay and Kathy gave me the wood statue of a man
from Colombia, a piece both of them loved and had
hoarded together with the few treasures of the young,
because of what they said my poems gave first to them.
(I remembered at once the story Neruda tells
of the source in his early life for his sense of what poetry
is: an exchange between strangers—
the boy he had never seen beyond the garden wall
who had left a toy white lamb in a niche, and the child
Neruda took it leaving his prize pine cone instead,
and the anonymous boy clutched it quick for himself.)
The Colombian fellow is bearded, benevolent, hatted, a sack—
like some kind of load—at his back, and the jutting folds
of his cloak like two, low wings. He carries a big bag
of gold or of fish in his, say, fifty-year-old hands
(or he's pregnant with it, with the gift which balances
perfectly the weight on his back).
This bag's tied up in some cloth that looks knotted in front.
His beard parts above the pursed mouth of the sack: the breath
he has breathed into it—or it has blown inside him—
is given back again. In him, old Colombian,
the love of fulfillment he offers us matches ex-
actly at his back the love of lack.

6
Union: Father, Son, Friend, Archetype

After the picnic, we all bought books at the flea mart;
Dostoevski, Sartre, Camus—
"The Myth of Sisyphus," that patient man whose burden
boulder, rolled up again and a-
gain, he learned to let become a piece of the given:
his shoulder or his gaunt, rock cheek.
Then, away from the others, we headed for the beach.
We were scared away from Daytona, mere sea of cars,
by the seasonal race—the one that's all too human.
Next, New Smyrna Beach, whose name suggests wars of heroes
brought down to us by Herodotus and the lucid
histories of Thucydides. In "Smyrna" there burns
a small, warm aura of figs—and of Tiresias.
That dark, absolutely rich, open place is Plato's
full love of landscape, unlike the
lack at Daytona. Here the waves moved on shore between
hills, gray on black on gray on white,
like layers of feeling, of touch, of thought, of insight
that we carry around us—
sometimes gentle, sometimes violent as the violet,
pink and red levels in that vast vagina which holds
the ancient sea between its earth-
en walls, strata of many-shaded sand brought to life
inside some goddess' hourglass.
It was beautiful but cold at New Smyrna Beach. This
somehow brought us together, huddled, holding on to
each other against the black hill. My hair (gray) and yours
(brown) blew together, mixed with wind,
almost invisible in the dark. I felt all the
elements with us and all times.
The waves rushed in again—still. You'd made love with your girl,
you said, here, this very place, in the warmer New Year.
One of the deeper bright planes of the waves was that one—
that generative giving. Friends,
father and son, brothers, we clung

together, digging our feet deep into the black soil
of the sea's hill, burrowing back
in the cave of our bodies molded
as if to feel in touch with the earth that binds us all
together and keeps us from blowing away in those
powerful winds that will fill and shake at us always,
at the old man hill with its veins of time like frozen
waves upon waves. It was as if we were his own poised
burden and gift, the young man born out of the older
or the old from the young, the two of us planted there
together beside the loud sea
at a hunched hill filmed with the fog
like that dark Colombian man's brown, aged, sculpted legs.

7

First Reunion in New Orleans: The Father as King of Revels

In New Orleans we part with cars.
We walk the blocks to Mardi Gras
and put on another mask to
catch the bright, luminescent beads
and gold doubloons flung from floats cruis-
ing the full streets in endless, fabulous parades
toward the Gulf. The tractors lugging floats for the Krewe
of great Zeus wish their way toward the engines of ships,
because these floats move quite like "ships
passing in the night." Clown shapes piss behind parades,
for thousands are drinking beer in the streets from great, white
paper cups, or they arc red and light wine out of goat-
skins into their mouths. Parades are plays before our own
audience. We watch the progress of King Proteus
who changes configurations in the dark like us.
There are floats for Zeus, Aphrodite and for Diane.
I think, well, Michael, here we go again—costumed with
painted faces like our thousand anonymous friends,
levels of beads about our necks,
wrists and the belt loops of our pants.
Why, we have so many beads we heave them back again

in an amiable exchange.
We shove and shout. We touch and dance
in the live New Orleans streets,
and the men and women both old and young *notice* us,
as we them. We are each other's dream within a dream.
After the parades and the great Cathedral of Saint
Louis, King of France, oldest in the land, on the same
site where its small predecessor
was blown apart two-hundred-and-fifty years ago
by the greater King Tornado—
after the Cabildo where our ancient father signed
in lieu of us for the Louisiana Purchase,
we go for New Orleans jazz and hear Sweet Emma
singing and still playing a mean piano at age
eighty-nine, a garter of bells on one leg, red cap,
just as she had when jazz was born
in Preservation Hall (well named!)
just off Bourbon Street with its black
lace of delicate worked-iron balconies and the
old Absinthe House where King Faulkner
met and sipped double shots of Jack Daniels with his friend,
elder King Sherwood Anderson.
On Fat Tuesday night, as the revels move to their height,
we leave and drive in the truck of a guy we had met
through the strange, moon-lighted Louisiana landscape
I had never seen by day, toward his sculptor's kiln
twelve miles out. Trees drop their gentle
debris of moss on us: we stop
only once to pick and give each other the newly
blooming, reaching azalea flowers which seem to glow
under the moon all in the same
color, although we know each fresh
pale cluster, like a feather plucked from a peacock's tail,
is radiantly different.
This seems an oracle of what we find just ahead:
a huge, monolithic concrete kiln glowing quiet
as the moon itself, all filled up
with white-hot lustrous ghosts of earth

our friend had made. We are not amazed to find they've reached
their peak of heat alone in the middle of a blue
field as Mardi Gras hits frenzy,
and consumed, burned up, everything falls away from us
under the white moon like revelers' masks and costumes,
leaving us stark naked there as for making love or art.

8

Second Reunion in San Francisco: The Lost Son

When you visit San Francisco,
it's my turn to drive: white, old Corvair—not your new car—
(mine, like a galley, even has gills, outlets for oars,
manned by machine slaves through these chiaroscuro streets).
My pistons poke and halt and fart,
show us both their need for a rest.
I remember the last time I saw you in your car:
a red, contemporary sculpture in Florida—
you living, laughing in the front as if to balance
its trunk lid, open, extending a makeshift coffin:
your own, hollow coffee table,
which you planned to climb in and out of again in an
experimental movie your friend would make at school.
We drive now for your welcoming drink at the Cliff House,
which is so absurdly painted a false water-blue,
sailboat-white, with comic-book clouds
to make us guess, sliding down streets, we'll soon hit the sea—
as we would, since it's right there where it has always been.
When I was just married a generation ago—
well, a whole life hence,—my wife and I had salmon steak
in this place. Now the saws whine to make it new again.
This House has burnt and been built and burnt and built three times!
We gaze out the corner window just over the sea,
there where the sun simply all of a sudden descends
in its golden red Apollonian last moments,
as in its first, illuminating the foam from which
Aphrodite sprang. This ocean turns, sweeps, not as on
the beach at New Smyrna, where it was dark—or as un-

seeing Homer knew of the Old
World Smyrna, quite black: he sat by the mythic river
which runs through the Melos Valley near Diana's Baths—
Diana, the virgin helper at difficult births,
patroness of crossways. Over us in Sutro Park
her statue waits, its bow-arm broke, like a flawed crescent
of her ancient moon. And below us at the Cliff House
the spread, mud landscape of ruins
of the elaborate glass-pavilioned Sutro Baths
given to San Francisco by a man wealthy but
guilty for the deaths of coolies who built his railroad
shafts through California rock.
"Super May Day Festival at Sutro Baths, April
30th, 1898. Commencing At Ten
In The Morning, Lasting All Day.
Lots Of Fun For The Little Folks!
A Beautiful Queen And Triple
Maypoles! Gorgeous Butterfly Ballet! One Thousand Kids
In Grand March And Fancy Dances.
Catch True Color and Detail in Giant Camera!"
We've seen in souvenir shops the flat, old sepia
photographs of those now-burnt baths:
all men it seems (though they were not),
bathing suits clean up to their shoulders and no mothers
around, brothers of Athene, who was born from the bones
and labyrinths of her father's brain. With their arms crossed,
they pose arrogant as hunters
or lynchers whose pictures I remember as a kid.
Diana turned huntsmen into stags and let them
be torn apart by their own hounds if they smiled at her.
Smyrna colonists, the encyclopedia says,
were from Lesbos we remember,
but let's both just fuck all this and have our drink, look out
at the kids poling on that rock
(famous for years, though the young fishers surely don't care),
joined by a pier of sorts to shore.
With the waves so white, furious, this dangerous day
we know it's cold for them. We shiv-

er sipping our champagne, which froths like the foam outside.
As we watch the play, our talk wanders easy, happy,
even if we are a bit chilly. Christ, a kid slips
quickly off the rough rock in front of our very eyes!
We gulp another drink. We blink,
listening to seals about the rock increase their bark
over shocked silence inside us
and catching out of the corners of our eyes the gulls
rising up (wings flash white on gray!).
Suddenly I realize you and I, as we sip
cocktails, do not watch the topless
and predictable entertainment of the big town,
but we are seeing a boy drown!
I put my civilized drink down
and run through the tourist-crammed bar to the telephone.
A friend of the boy is running up along the shore.
Soon, wails of police cars. Firemen
stand around in their weird black pants
not well suited for finding the drowned, but hustling still
for death or for the human, hope-
ful giving of breath, waiting to be shown to the site.
Some watchers swing coin binoculars out to the point.
Old signs in the sand say, "Fun For Everybody Here."
Pay dimes to see somebody drown?
Some people still able to manage their martinis!
We stare at the stark, old rock from the wood rail outside.
There are no Florida peacocks here, odd as they are,
no iridescent Iowa
pheasants. Giddy seagulls jabber around, and the sand-
pipers pick their way. Well, we are all voyeurs, vultures
round the boy who cannot be found,
death rising cold in his groin from the thrust of the sea
that once gave all of us our birth.
This kid gives up his life in breath
which surfaces white someplace by
that rock a little while—long enough for me to feel
your turmoil churning in myself.
The Coast Guard's sharp chopper struggles

overhead (hovering above this sunset-lit stage
before our strange audience)—fake
boat out of the dream rivers of Ohio, a ship
from the beaches near Orlando
and with a lurid-hued hint of your own red car. It
whirrs impotently, spider-like parody of God,
which has split the shot-with-color
webs of air and of human breath: jealous Minerva,
useless *deus ex machina*.
But the drama we are all of us caught up in has
let you stay alive here beside me in a blue coat,
Michael, for you have not slipped with
this six- or seven-year-old kid
off the treacherous Frisco cliff,
as we did our best to have a happy reunion
drink, not funereal sips out of that mixed chalice
all of us know. Perhaps it is
your life—or *yours*, or *yours*, or *yours*, or *yours*—I felt up-
stairs in those luminous and dark, hidden levels of
my own, still quite navigable ship!

In Memoriam William H. Chaplin (1942-1974)

III

TRAVELING

THE BRIDGE OF CHANGE

The bridge barely curved that connects the terrible with the tender. —Rilke

1

The children play at the Luxembourg fountain.
Their small ships catch wind and sail out and come round again.

2

Sometime between 250 and 200 B.C.
fishermen and boatmen of the tribe Parisii
discovered and built their huts on the largest island
in the River Seine. Celtic *Lutetia*, "Town surround-
ed by water,"
                thus was born there.
The island is shaped like a boat—
and this figure became a part
of the capital's coat-of-arms. So this was the start
of the City first named for its engulfing water
(on whose economy it depended), then after
the people themselves: members of the tribe of Paris.
We listen to these water folk and know they hear us,
for we are born out of boats and out of water.
The first sound we hear is the heart
knocking quiet as a boat docks:
and we all dissolve to island, earth and tears later.

3

And into air and fire! Once in the Latin Quarter
in a space formed for him by waves of bright loiterers
near the shortest street named for the Cat Who Catches Fish—
or who (with slight inflection) "sins" —
I watched a dark young man, naked to his thin waist, push

long plumes of flame into the air
above our awed faces raised there.
From the sharp heat inside and out,
his head and chest glowed in the night
with an aura of oil or sweat.
Thirsting, he drank again from a sponge of kerosene
and breathed out long strings of fire and smoke into the Street
of the Harp.
              Dark ash dropped back upon his face and cap,
which lay open on the cobbled road waiting for coins
from all who guessed at the mystery in what he'd done.
He built a vast pillar of fire as if to guide us,
then suddenly stopped, walked across
the space, and kissed a reaching child
(to bless and heal that amazed head),
waved gratefully to us who now filled his cap with alms,
and, smiling and burned (I saw scars beneath his raised arm),
he sailed up that narrowing street in a wildly bal-
looning white shirt we had watched him casually don
to cover his vestment of skin.

      4

For centuries that old City
ended its west boundary
in a small archipelago
separated from the main island by the Seine's two
arms. It was on one of these small islets that Philip
the Fair about the year 1314 had raised up
a stake for the grand master, Order of Templars, whom
he condemned, then from the palace window watched him burn.
These little islands, quickened with their ghost victim's screams,
were joined in the sixteenth century by the decree
of Henry Third (and by a great engineering feat
Faust could envy) to the main island of the City.
This new western tip was given the name of a park,
"Vert Galant," nickname of Henry Fourth: "The Gay old Spark."
Near there I watched in a loud street

a white-haired man stand with one foot
on the curb, the other in the cobbled street, and play
an old mandolin. He was dressed in a black and frayed
tuxedo and played with intense passion, sadly, but
this desperate, dignified man, transformed by his art
and by poverty (his case kept open for money),
could not play the mandolin. —He
just strummed the same chord again
                              and again and again…

5

It was also Philip the Fair
who created an aristocratic prison air
by building the blocks-long Gothic Conciergerie.
The best view is from the Right Bank: The Slaughter House Quay
(which now is a market for pets).
You can see the four recently cleaned towers reflect-
ed in the Seine. (At the Seine in fall, beneath the red
and gold leaves, you see the rust, mahogany and beige
boats gently jostle together at the shore and wait.)
On the right: the crenelated Bonbec Tower stays.
Bonbec means "babbler," for this place
was used through the centuries as a torture chamber.
The right one of the twin towers, Argent, held treasure.
Still the gorgeous Horloge Tower on the left corner
of the ancient building across from the Bridge of Change
houses the giant clock which gave its name to that quay:
in its field of blue the many great gold fleurs-de-lys
and the two life-sized mythical
women, one with a fascicle
of wheat, one with a balanced scale raised high in the clock,
whose silver chime used to toll the hours for the monarch.
(This was melted down in those days when Terror struck.)
In this turreted place we have shaved the graceful neck
and head of Marie Antoinette, ripped her white, ruffled
collar wide and wrapped the cuff of
rope about her hands behind her back. We made her face

the casual knitting women and men making fists
sitting on steps in the "May Court"
(where a fresh tree was placed each spring by the lawyers' clerks!)
on her way to the guillotine. Its blade was heavy
as primeval stone: she, the chemist Lavoisier,
Charlotte Corday, poet and brother André Chenier,
Madame du Barry—all 2600 who died,
having said their last farewells in the Women's Courtyard,
twelve per day underneath the blade!
and some were disemboweled beside.
Was there sometimes an image of beauty in their minds
at the last? Perhaps on white sands
beside the blue-black sea a matched pair of roan horses
galloping together in the bright spume, riderless.
Or a nude young man and woman lying together
touching in a field of flowers?

6

Nearby on this Island the gargoyles of Notre Dame
gawk in ancient horror and some
forever gnaw on stone rabbits in the parapets
or wail in winged, formal misery outside the set
limits of the orthodox Church—
all glory happening within the walls where they squat:
so hunched, so beaked, so horrorstruck.

7

A wing of the May Courtyard where the condemned waited
"Monsieur de Paris" as executioners were named
now adjoins the building of glass and light, with no walls,
it seems, jewel of Sainte Chapelle,
its windows of rose and blue, gold, green, yellow, purple,
rising fifty feet:
                    its spire piercing the foliate,
layered, many-colored egg of the vault of heaven,
showering all the primal hues and shadows given—

bright as the truth reflected in a drop of fresh blood
or the colors of the body's inner organs hid-
den before the sure explosion of light that hits them
at the moment of violent death. —This is a time
like that of the sun that once a year, just at the dawn
of winter solstice, lights up an ancient Celtic stone
grave, striking the bones spread on shelves
with all the colors of the flesh.

8

Who can stand these juxtapositions of person and place and
time? I walk across the Bridge of Change where I have so often
watched by the towers of the Conciergerie. Now, water laves a
little higher up the stair from the River to the Quay, hiding some
of the steps from me. Boats nudge at the edge. I walk along the
Boulevard past the great gold and blue corner clock, the ornate
wrought-iron gate and fence of the Place of Justice (its name
changed from the time of kings), past the shadow and spire of
Sainte Chapelle. I cross the Bridge of Saint Michel into the Latin
Quarter. But I do not look for the Street of the Cat Who Fishes or
the Street of the Harp. I turn right, wandering a bit, and
suddenly, as if by chance, find myself at *this* street, and here I will
wait, for it is our street, *Rue Gît le Coeur: Here Lies the Heart.*

for Roger Aplon—1975

AT DRUMCLIFFE CHURCHYARD, COUNTY SLIGO

1

That great feather the mind's wind drives
over the graves
and which lights
and stays on the tomb of Yeats
is made of skin and of thin stone
akin to cliff, akin to drum.

2

On this ancient monastic spot
I feel the shocks of rhythm underfoot—
gigantic hooves of heaving
Irish horses, their riders weaving
with ecstasy as their long, god-like legs
stretch
      and cleave the tight
breaking up the patterning of light
the brown,
      the black, the roan,
the mottled hides give off
like the sun shining (and then not)
through mist
      in bursts
along Ben Bulben's back. The wild long-
haired men and the wild
long-haired women ride
and merge and are gone.

3

Yeats's grave lifts to heaven
the body of a man, body of a woman—
himself, his wife, his wife, himself,

and his ambiguous epitaph
celebrates his birth forever back into life.
The great "cold eye" now opens
in the soaring brow of Man-Woman.

4

This gravesite is a bridge of sex.
It is a bridge of space
between
       the valley and the mountain—
between the long, free
flanks of the land and the fossil sea.
It is a bridge of time, for the round
stone tower still stands
where the medieval monks hovered
over the church cloths and silver
when the swift, marauding Vikings came.
And the Celtic rock High Cross
(figuring how Christian love
joins Adam and Eve
while
     Cain's hate kills Abel)
is raised along the selfsame
wall where a prehistoric standing stone
covered with its weathered skin
tapers hard toward the moon and sun,
its erect substance teeming full
of the tiny bright seed of shells.

5

Oh, I can feel the mind's wind blow still
over the graves, the church and Ben Bulben hill.
Wait! Touch your cheek!
For this feather breath breathes too
upon you.

for John Unterecker

DUBLIN SUITE:
HOMAGE TO JAMES JOYCE

1
The Bridge

It is raining. The child is waiting
for alms on the O'Connell Bridge in
Dublin. An infant cries in her arms.
She stays on the walk morning til night.
The child's eyes are hard. They're almost wild.

Her face is dirty as her dress is.
It is raining. The child is waiting.
The lid of a cardboard box for coins
begins to come apart in the wet.
Many of us pass her by. We fail

to tell how bone thin is her red shawl.
The infant she enwraps weighs heavy
in her small lap, and I tell you they
both lie *here* in the laps of us all.
It is raining. The child is waiting.

Joyce would have watched an epiphany.
His family was constantly poor.
It is Stephen's young sister who sits here.

2
The Library

This massive, carved medieval harp of Irish oak
no longer sounds in the winds from the ancient times gone out
of Celtic towns. It rests in the long, high vaulted room
filled up with one million books whose pages chronicle
the works and ages both in *our* land and in Ireland.

For a hundred years no student has bent here above
those huge, leather volumes that burgeon on the balconies
like matched and stacked rows of great pipes
for the unplayed organ of this magnificent place.
But both pipes and harp seem still to come alive and turn
Trinity College Library
into a fantastic temple when we stand over
the twelfth-century Books of Kells,
which James Joyce so loved he carried a facsimile
to Zurich, Rome, Trieste. "It is,"
he said to friends, "the most purely Irish thing we have.
You can compare much of my work
to the intricate illuminations of this book."
Its goatskin pages open up for us under glass
in a wooden case. At this place:
a dog nips its tail in its mouth,
but this dog is of ultramarine, most expensive
pigment after gold, for it was ground out of lapis,
and the tail is of lemon yellow orpiment.
Other figures are verdigris, folium or woad—
the verdigris, made with copper,
was mixed with vinegar, which ate into the vellum
and showed through on the reverse page.
Through the text's pages run constant, colored arabesques
of animated initial
letters—made of the bent bodies
of fabulous, elongated beasts
linked and feeding beautifully upon each other,
or upon themselves. Why, even the indigo-haired
young man gnaws at his own entrails.
The archetypal figure of the uroboros
recurs, as does that the Japanese call *tomoi*:
a circle divided by three arcs from its center.
These illuminations around
the Irish script of the Gospels
are some of them benign and terrible like that
Satan from the four temptations:
the devil is black, a skeleton with flaming hair

414

and short, crumpled emaciated wings, which appear
to be charred as are the bony feet—
and the reptile with such gentle
eyes is colored kermes (compounded from the dried bodies
of female ants that die bright red).
The covers of jewels and gold are gone from the Book,
stolen for a while from the Kells
Monastery in County Meath
and then found, some of its gorgeous pages cut apart
and the whole stuffed beneath the sod.
These designs were all gestures of the bold minds of monks—
their devils still whirring about their ears while angels
blasted their inner eyes with colors not in any
spectrum, and moaning, primitive Celtic gods still cast
up out of their hermetic interior lives strange figures
which we can all recognize as
fragments of our inhuman dreams:
all this is emblazoned here in the unimagined
and musical colors of a medieval church.
Ah, friend, look how this Book of Kells
pictures all our heavens, all our hells.

3
The Green

Up Grafton Street to Stephen's Green
(which young Dedalus thought his own)
I pass the street named Duke. There two of Joyce's favored
pubs still stand, and one of them holds
in a blank wall the red door of Leopold Bloom's home:
it bears the golden number eight
from the house razed on Eccles Street.
Bloom's and Joyce's friends still lift their glasses of stout.
Two doors down from the Green, Captain America's Inn
offers up burgers and cokes and
those Irish potatoes which once,
boiled, kept the families alive,
but here are prepared like the French.

At the entrance to Stephen's Green
an Irish musician keens
on his pipes that wail like a child,
and the beautiful Irish coins
designed by friends of Yeats (dolphins grace and unplayed harps
adorn) are tossed into his cap,
which matches exactly the scarlet tartan of his kilt.
Gray couples walk or rest on benches and some young men
lounge on the Green with girls who hitch up their skirts and sun
their thighs, while other silent men
go in and out of the latrine again and again.
Students listen to the red-and-gold clad band
play from the raised circular stand
and eat their lunch before heading back across the street
to school. Most go round the corner south to UCD
or back down Grafton Street where Trinity College waits,
but some still stroll across to Newman Hall
where Joyce followed Hopkins and Cardinal Newman too.
Gerard Manley Hopkins (who saw things through drops of blood)
agonized here in this garden
as Christ in his Gethsemane—
he tried to decide even to the eighth of a point
the marks for the students he loved.
(Without high grades the Catholics
could not go to school in England.)
I see him there, lean, at his lecture stand in the hall.
On the Green his and Joyce's and Newman's steps still fall.
They mingle with ours like voices
or like the shouts of the great God-in-the-streets that's Joyce's.

4
The Tower

I stand at the round parapet
of Joyce's Martello Tower.
I look over where the awkward, naked boys holler
and dive in the swimming place called "the forty-foot hole,"
since Joyce's time only for men, though now some militant has scrawled

in chalk at the entrance to the spot a woman's sign:
the Venus Mirror. I wonder
then: did *she* ever think of this?
Imagine Botticelli's figure (with her long, brown
strands) scrambling about those rocks amid angular kids.
How odd that sight. How odd this thought:
this tower was built in the fear of a French onslaught.
And this: Oliver St. John Gogarty paid the rent!
Certainly Joyce somehow did his share. The key's still there.
Huge, bronze, like the key of a king.
With it young Stephen unlocked the secrets of the heart,
but it was Joyce's hand the key
touched and taught. And there, down the long, curving iron stair
is Joyce's cane inside a glass case, and there's his watch,
his eyepatch, the memory of him—head in both hands—
struggling with the blindness of Homer. Or of Milton.
It is as if poets were forced to see inside themselves:
fall out of that insular tower of ignorance.
Tiresias, also blind, held up Venus' Mirror
and the Dart of Mars. Whatever man or woman dared
he did, he knew. There is no poet like that seer
as is Joyce, who was Molly and Leopold too. Jung
wrote him, "You know many things we psychologists don't—
especially about women."
Your cane, Joyce! Your key! The imprint of your foot on stone!
And your folded waistcoat fading there in a closed case.
On it in blue, brown the woven hounds chase the fox.
Or do those hounds that heaved when your body breathed, hunt deer?
I feel the chase inside my chest,
here. Joyce, I feel I wear your vest—
and like you am more than human.
I too have within my self the boy, man and woman.
But your clothes make my heart inflate,
for that is not 'more than human.'
Why, Diana had the hunter who desired her
transformed into a deer, his flesh rent by his own dogs.
How often has the woman punished the man in her?
Or the man the woman in him?

How often have both choked back as they became adult
the boy or girl who wept in them
(although its sight was not the less)?
Joyce, here in this tower with its enigmatic patch
for your omniscient eye, I
see better too. Women have taken up and used with strength
the chalk of men. And those boys have the teats of a girl.
Now, from your tower's top, let the pen-
nants of all our humankind unwind.

for Peter Logan—1977

ELEGY FOR DYLAN THOMAS

1

In the Welsh town of Laugharne across the way from the Brown
Inn your wife Caitlin lived (by half her life): she had brought
your body back from where you died—
the White Horse Tavern in New York.
The old pub at Brown's stays open
long as the patrons want, for Laugharne is a little town.
The people—even the barkeep—stay awake and drink
and talk of you (now famous in this place), and they tell
the tale of Caitlin on the way to the funeral:
she was late because she came across the street and cried
and drank the warm pints of bitter just as you had done.
The funeral procession weaved,
lurched up the street toward the Church.

2

In October, month of your birth,
my friend and I took the night train
from London's Paddington Station past the sleep-tossed towns
and the sheep nudging gently on the hills,
through Swansea town where you were born
and came to Laugharne—where you wrote your last and best
    poems—
to follow your funeral steps.
But first we looked where you had lived—
saw the Laugharne Castle ("brown as owls"),
your herons standing on one leg tentative as life
in the rich, reaching waters of the estuary,
black as funeral priests against
the sun, black as the crow-capped Sir John's Hill where we
    walked
with you up the thigh of childhood
toward the crown and vision of age you never reached—

although in poems you clowned how it would be to be old.
We stared through the glass in the small door of the house
where you wrote, imagining we could see manuscripts
strewn across the floor and the circular stains from beer
bottles interspersed, like abstract geometric spooks,
among the books you loved: Hardy, Hopkins and Traherne
and the pictures pinned to walls: Lawrence, Whitman, Blake,
and the few nudes you always had.
This shack where you worked seems precarious on the ledge
above the sea, like the boathouse
nearby at the end of its breakneck of rocks on stilts
where you lived with your wife and kids
and watched the tides lap at the house's stone foundations.
But these places are more durable than our life. They
are more durable than our life.

3

The bright cobbled streets wind briefly,
beautiful, up the leaf-strewn hills of Laugharne. (Trees tell truth.)
For such a tiny town, it is well supplied with pubs
for there are seven, and my friend
and I visit all of them (after you did, Dylan).
We sit at the very window table where you drank
in Brown's and we look through the lace
across the way to Caitlin's house.
We think, are we ready for the trip to Trinity Church?
We decide we are and set out.
But it is hard to feel the funeral, hear the dirge
this sun-filled day (once you wrote of "the core of the sun's
bush") as we pass the white, green, yellow neat Welsh houses
and the hall where again tonight
performers from Swansea will act
your final work, and your books are all on sale—
because it's Dylan Thomas Festival!
But as the Churchyard gate swings shut
I feel my heart stepped on like a stone in the Church walk.
Here there are centuries of dead, for the Church is old,

and the ghosts of funeral processions pass and pass
as the two of us near the little, white wooden cross
that marks your grave, Dylan Thomas.
Now we stand at its narrow foot.
We know your body is as close to us as we are
to each other. My friend begins silently to weep
for you, and for him and me, but suddenly I see
your image stand before us there
among the gray, half-leaning graves of the ancient dead,
all of them. Dylan, you are buried up to the waist
in the yellow leaves of autumn!
Should I say, perhaps buried *only* up to the waist,
for despite the melancholy in your eyes, your art,
which you worked beneath "singing light,"
will leave you more unburied yet?
No. That is a trick of the heart.
Beneath my living feet, I know
your heavy body rots,
and I shake like these drying aster stems among the tombs.
Why, even the gravestones tremble
at the touch of time. So I will touch my friend once more
for the solace of the living —
and for the solaces of art,
whose mysteries deepen in the grave,
I will read your poems again.

for Joseph Stroud — 1978

PAPA'S HOUSE, SON'S ROOM

1

In Key West, poinciana trees bloom flamboyant red
before the leaves begin, and here in Hemingway's yard
the bare Lenten tree soon will bloom
bright as the blood from Papa's head,
red as the bricks from the wall he built around the house—
carting them home from the torn trolley track on Duvall
Street. Red as the blast from the safe
after his death—where his wife found the undone ms.
of *Islands in the Stream*: the father, his friends and sons:
their unfinished relationships.

2

I see the little boys sit
(Gregory, the younger, I knew)
at a small table between the dining room
and the kitchen—its appliances raised six inches
from the floor so great Papa could clean and cook his catch.
Those little boys sat and heard their parents eat at what
a table!—Eighteenth-Century Spanish, with storage space
for the gentlemen's swords fixed at the back of the chairs!
And one of Pauline's beloved chandeliers above—
this one hand-blown Venetian glass.
Over the black Greek mantle, a mounted gnu, trophy
from that extraordinary father's first safari.
The small boys played around Pauline's crouching crystal cats,
which poise on a table in the parlor and squint down
at the strolling or lolling fifty Hemingway cats.
Still the descendants scud through, each with six inbred toes.

3

Picasso's gift ceramic cat
overlooks, from on top a tall mysteriously tiled cabinet,
the master bedroom with its stiff midwife's stool and birthing chair
positioned at opposite walls.
That labor chair Papa took down to Sloppy Joe's Bar
and bore stories inside his head,
while he sat with friends all afternoon and drank his beer.
His boys fished and swam at the tiny beach
the days Papa did not take them out on the boat.
His buddy, the bartender's son, said of him:
"Nobody could keep up with him—if you didn't get a strike,
you drank to change your luck. If you got that strike, you drank
to celebrate!"

4

Hemingway not only brought that chair,
he salvaged something from the bar:
he toted a cracked, old urinal home on his back!
He wanted to water the cats!
Pauline was shocked and mad a while,
then solved the problem with glued French tile!
Papa never went to the bar
until he'd worked all morning at home in his study—
after breakfast crossing from the upstairs veranda
on a frail bridge across the yard
to the loft of the rebuilt barn,
breathing sun-warmed tropical plants
he'd trucked and backpacked and sweated
to plant from all over the Keys
to make a garden for the muse.
(But to the boys it must have seemed he reared a jungle!)

5

Those weird chairs and the gifted cat
in the bedroom were made quite small
by the custom king-size bed, its broken-hinged headboard
fashioned from a mahogany gate he'd brought from Spain.
How did those young brothers feel in their plain room beside?
But now their small beds are broken down, and Gregory's
gnarled headboard leans against the larger one of the maid.

6

Gregory. His Catholic books
(there was only school through eighth grade)
are now in a glass case in his room, and the priest is dead.
The priest was an old friend of his Dad's, whose own cases
overgrow that childhood room, filled with pictures of *him*
and *his* friends, and souvenirs from all over the world.

7

Gregory. I knew some of his later history
when I was his teacher at a school in Maryland.
He was a smart and beautiful man.
We would have coffee after Mass,
talk of his restlessness with college and with himself.
He never spoke of his father
and, unlike his brother, did not become a hunter.
He didn't finish the term. I haven't seen him since.
It's thirty years, but today our lives breathe together
briefly as I stand in your parents' house and your room
and wait (Oh, it will happen again soon)
for the Lenten tree to bloom.

TRAVELING

In the little mountain town of Urbino
the air was raw for winter.
My teeth began to chatter
and I went to bed with fever.
The pensione we had reserved was closed,

but we found a place at last. Then you went out
for food and for a doctor.
Still it was you who healed me.
You had to learn to give me shots,
although the clinic gave us a prescription

and the girl at the hotel loaned us her pan
and syringe and wished the best.
So it was you who made me well.
Then we went off to hunt the work
of Raphael, for he was born in this town.

But we found that some Cardinal or other
had hauled his paintings off
to Rome to the Vatican.
The poet we went to meet
in Urbino simply never showed his head.

Why, only you were always there, my dear friend.
When in Rome we went to Mass
in the vast church with its black
baroque Bernini pillars,
but again we found the Sistine Chapel closed.

What would we have done if we had been alone?
But we had been together
since the day we left New York.
The rug in that terminal
was as red as the one Agamemnon trod

the day he died. What did this augur for us,
vulnerable professors
who cried we'd had enough of class
and fled for the holidays
to France, Italy and Greece: went first to Chartres

where you thought I prayed. I did, but first collapsed
from the beauty of the place.
The drive from France through the Alps
looming winter white at tops
was, well, I was about to say "breathtaking"

but this doesn't seem quite right, since in Paris
I'd begun to catch bronchitis!
But we were bound by beauty
on this trip. We were bereft
of friends at Christmas—happy with each other,

though, warmed beside the cold canals of Venice
after San Marco's marvel
and with good native pasta
and wine in us. There the Bridge
of Sighs beautifully leads to jail

where all of us will go somehow, exiled by
our color, race, creed or a style
that the world does not allow.
Well, I want to go with you.
For now we went to Florence! Found the David

which rises there like the masculine center
of the world, though cut from flawed
marble. We watched the vivid
grief of Michelangelo's
Palestrina Pietà, the stone figures

flowing together like wept water. Beauty
fountaining out of the rock
brought us nearer. Then inside
the convent of San Marco
The Annunciation of Fra Angelico

made us hear God's astounding song. The waiting
virgin leaning forward, just
so, to hear the melody:
the wings red, blue, gold and brown
quivering as the angel half-kneels before.

You were the one who inoculated me.
I conceived this song for you—
now of Ghiberti's golden doors
opening onto Paradise.
Next we climbed up the five hundred steps at Church

(third largest one), were awed by Brunelleschi's dome,
researched by him while he built—
architect and engineer,
a massive Renaissance man
as was Uccello, painter, geometer

developing the laws of perspective
and old Pollaiuolo,
engraver, unearthing bodies
to study the anatomy.
Together we carried away from Florence

memories of giants who intimidate
the powers of the teachers.
Silent from the Uffizi,
we crossed the Ponte Vecchio,
covered and earlier lined with goldsmith shops

that seemed to bulge with their wares over the edge.
I remember your blonde hair
blowing in the Florentine wind,
your eyes bright with the vision.
From what we'd found, we learned each other better.

From Italy we crossed to Greece by ferry.
It was January now
and yet the sun was vivid
and it ascended huge, hot
over the splendid blue Adriatic Sea.

Some passengers doffed their shirts and sunned
        themselves
in the very sight of snow-
capped mountains as on Ithaca
where it is said to this day
no horsemen ever go—or on Delos,

smallest island of the group, where Artemis
asked for Iphegenia's death
so her father Agamemnon
could sail on to Troy: later
to step on that royal rug of his own future.

But what did his death augur for us I asked.
Well, we got caught up in the myth
and could not sail from Athens.
After the Acropolis
mused and bloomed with ruins like a great garden

for half a day, it was closed for Epiphany.
Then God showed his awful hand
and the weather turned around.
We could not ship for Delos
or even travel by bus to the oracle

at Delphi. This we hated to miss:
for half our lives we had saved
up questions for it. The myth
kept us marooned in Athens.
We could not drive or sail back to Italy.

Suddenly, you and I found our holiday over,
and as soon as the weather
broke for us we took to the air
and before we could dream were
in New York again, younger, wiser, closer.

for Phyllis Thompson

BELIEVE IT

There is a two-headed goat, a four-winged chicken
and a sad lamb with seven legs
whose complicated little life was spent in Hopland,
California. I saw the man with doubled eyes
who seemed to watch in me my doubts about my spirit.
Will it snag upon this aging flesh?

There is a strawberry that grew
out of a carrot plant, a blade
of grass that lanced through a thick rock,
a cornstalk nineteen-feet-two-inches tall grown by George
Osborne of Silome, Arkansas.
There is something grotesque growing in me I cannot tell.

It has been waxing, burgeoning, for a long time.
It weighs me down like the chains of the man of Lahore
who began collecting links on his naked body
until he crawled around the town carrying the last
thirteen years of his life six-hundred-seventy pounds.
Each link or each lump in me is an offense against love.

I want my own lit candle lamp buried in my skull
like the Lighthouse Man of Chungking,
who could lead the travelers home.
Well, I am still a traveler and I don't know where
I live. If my home is here, inside my breast,
light it up! And I will invite you in as my first guest.

for Tina Logan
After visiting the Believe It or Not Museum
with her in San Francisco—1980

MANHATTAN MOVEMENTS

POEMS 1981–1987

I

.

THE TRANSFORMATION

Dissonant music of the night.
Two o'clock. The ancient dogs cry.
Seventeen-year-old Harry, homing from a party,
hauls a radio that sounds the harsh tones of the young.
Joseph, soughing, sighing on the couch, twists in his sleep.
Poor Joseph sleeps off who knows what.
But I am heedless, for tonight
I was warmed by my father's touch.
I want to tell you how it was.
After Bartók at the symphony
Renée and I found a good spot high in the sky and talked
out of our growing, friendly love
far above the buildings, shining attractive at night
in Waikiki: suddenly, a strangely dressed lady
(I can't tell you where she came from)
stopped at our small table and sought to take our picture.
Renée and I at first said no to her, then by some quirk
or other I ran after her.
We moved our black rattan chairs close together, smiled and
twice we let her flash our picture.
We had another drink, chatted,
and with a slight edge of expectation, we waited.
After an undetermined time
the mythical lady returned
and we were amazed to find quite fabulous photos!
Renée was radiant in a dress now trimmed with stars,
and as for me, I had lost weight
and showed the true bones of my face.
For the first time I knew I looked like my father's son.
I am fifty-eight. Let those dogs
of the moon bay again tonight,
the young stage their noisy parties
and Joseph sleep his obscure sleep.
I am pleased because I see I have my father's face.

Honolulu, March 23, 1981

THE WHATNOT

How many people have thought to keep a whatnot
today? Mine makes me old fashioned,
but I am fascinated by it.
Five shelves of bric-a-brac to dust,
backed with mirrors on each to clean.
There is the candy box with its boy with a blank face
weathered off above his pale jacket and black knickers.
I bought it in an antique shop
because it showed the way I felt
as a young runt hurrying about my paper route
in the winter weather. A straw man astride a straw horse
is a relic from Mexico
along with a cubed onyx face
(as of an old god) bought from an Indian peasant,
whose brightly dressed wife had huge breasts.
The black elephant, trunk raised, is a gift of my son.
The brown, wooden ducks, gifts of Dora who jilted me.
They sit beside a white, curved ceramic or bone fish.
I don't know where from. They're the saddest —
things of lost origin. What shores
are these shells from? What did I feel as I picked them up
at La Jolla, Hawaii, Assateague, La Push
or someplace else I found? What great hopes went through my mind?
The mind's trace of them is like that boy's white, empty face.
Pictures are another matter:
my father's austere young profile,
hair shorn back, intense ghostly eyes,
or the scary full front view of him in uniform.
If he had not returned, I would simply be unborn —
so would my brother who stands beside my grandmother,
me, younger, on her lap. There is the formal portrait
of my father, all stiff-suited,
and my beautiful, dead mother
in a buttoned dress and broad hat, hands filled with flowers.

I can't help wondering, did she ever suckle me
at her great breast? I always thought
not, since she died within the month.
But, God, perhaps a little bit?
Is it too much for a grown man to have wanted it?
Why, I am energized like the boy
holding the reins, scampering off on a rabbit's back
on this bright silver napkin ring—
my father's gift to my whatnot!

THE PIANO SCHOLAR

for Aunt Gladys Woods

1

My grandfather Remmers was a German immigrant
trained in classical piano,
and he gave instruction to the richer town ladies.
He would ride his rounds on horseback,
carry with him a horn baton
and rap on his pupils' knuckles
if they erred. Years later, when I carried village papers,
aging ladies lied they'd find for me
some pieces of his music in their rambling attics.
They cried to me how much they cared for him.
I carry carefully one memory of him,
sharp look under metal rimmed eyes,
but I was just an infant when he died.
Through my youth I wished he had tried to teach me art.

2

Why, when I was just a child I pretended to play
on the great open atlas stretched across my lap
as I listened to the ancient fading radio
in the corner of our parlor.

3

My aunt lifted up my fingers
and placed them one by one on the keyboard, naming notes.
It seemed such a tender thing to me.

4

But when she wasn't home, my fond, clement uncle
let me clatter away, seated at the ancient throne.

Later I convinced the grade school teacher I could play
like fat Junior Odell used to
when we kids laid our heads down on desks to take our naps,
but it was dreadfully bad when I began to clang
the piano, random and loud.
I was quickly, harshly removed from the spinning stool
and made to stay in after school.

5

One day after much long thought I begged a grown-up girl
who was on my paper route
to give me lessons and she coyly agreed but charged
a nickel each. Still I didn't care because I liked
to sit on the brown bench next to her and feel her long girl
fingers guiding my boy ones slowly over the keys.
I began to break into set pieces as if to speak.
I remember in my primer "The Happy Farmer."

6

In college I paid my good friend Stephen Barrister
who majored in piano and who was fond of boys
fifty cents to give me lessons at 7. A.M.
I was light-headed from lack of sleep and the lessons
seemed to make me high. Soon I
really loved the piano.
Once I played Debussy's "Submerged Cathedral,"
where the mythic sunken church slow-
ly emerges from underneath the water louder
and louder until you hear the chimes
like a full-scale chorale.
It's all chords repeated in the same hand positions,
but then I thought to myself,
"God, this is really beautiful!"

7

Having started late I specialized in slow movements—
never developed the agility for speed:
first movement of the "Moonlight Sonata" and second of
    the "Pathétique."
My friend and I climbed into the Carnegie Music
Collection in the basement of Barnes Hall and played Brahms
concertos in the dark middle
of the night, and I broke into the chapel to play
the Baldwin Grand whose beloved, dark black shapely skirt
I undressed slowly on the stage, and I can tell you
these were some of the plain happy days of my brash life.

8

Once when I broke in, Mary Beth Turacek, the school's
leading scholarship pianist,
was playing Debussy's "Isle of Joy"
and waves of sound broke over me, quite hidden away
in the darkened church. There are great climaxes of tone
and every one of the cells in my skin trembled
like its own little place of joy.

9

In my senior year at school I remember
my piano teacher, Miss Schram,
once played for me with swollen arthritic hands
a few thumbs-crossed-over notes of a Schumann Romance,
and I sensed that day I was peculiarly blest.
It was mainly for Miss Schram, with whom I fell in love,
I outdid myself in the school's final recital:
played the slow movement of the
F# Minor Piano Sonata Johannes Brahms
had written at twenty.
It is very rich and reads like an orchestral piece.
I was also only twenty and jealous of him—
no, that's not quite the word, for his music made me feel

I must somehow find a way to change my very life.
It's not an easy piece; even in the andante
there are seven notes on one hand.
Don't ask me how I did it,
but my fulfillment came when my beloved Miss Schram
moved back to the loges,
where the recitalists mingled,
and said to me, "Jack, that was simply gorgeous!"

Mt. Vernon, Washington, February 22, 1981

THE PRESENT

The huge purple elephant came out of my crayons,
and it took shape on the paper
as I wrote to my grandmother.
I was just six and I sent her my benign creature.
She would visit and bring presents
or mail us a box at Christmas.
It was good to sit together
in the living room—curtains with pumps or pails on them—
and then to open up the box
with its layers of presents wrapped
in red and blue and green tissue
and great-bowed Christmas wreathes scattered through the
        package. I
want to remember a toy,
but think only of a white horse
rocking on the walk, its neck broke.

MY REBEL GRANDMOTHER

What a furious grandmother
you were, I think, as I look at the bronze framed picture—
me, one-and-a-half, in a bright embroidered jumpsuit,
sitting on your lap, and my brother, three-and-a-half,
in a dark sailor's blouse beside.
You had mothered us since Mom had died when I was born—
quit your job at the calendar factory to boot!
(I remember the lovely colored inks streamed out there,
the gas jets of flame, too, beneath the presses.)
When my father remarried when I was two-years-old,
you kidnapped my brother and me
and smuggled us miles away to an obscure uncle's farm,
so the honeymoon couple would not find us at home.
You strung our little baby clothes
all about the house to intimidate the new wife!
(I remember a small purple cloisonné pitcher
with white dragons all over it
filled with rose petals from the wedding, preserved with cloves:
I was not allowed to lift the lid and smell, but I did.)
Grandma, you were quite a bandit.
Once when Dad was a small schoolboy,
his divorced father gave him a pony and saddle.
You were so enraged you arranged to have the small horse
stolen while my Dad was at school.
You would not go back to the calendar factory
with the new wife in town. You went
clear to California and, at age forty-five,
placed yourself in an old people's home, where you worked
and lived and died at age ninety,
having been at the place longer than anybody else.
But for awhile you came back at Christmastime and brought us
marvelous presents. I was your favorite boy.
(I remember a complicated bluish sand toy
and a yellow felt elephant.)
I grew up with the feeling
(I will carry it to my grave)
that all your fury was moved by love.

THE PAPERBOYS

1

In the thin cold town where I was born, I hauled and groaned
my red wooden wagon uphill, its wheels squeaking loud
in the still thickly blowing snow,
wound by my fond brother's long blue scarf clear up to here,
my nearsighted eyes peering out—
like the filmed Invisible Man—
I headed for Cozad's station, which wanted at six
o'clock (two miles out) the first newspaper on my route:
and I must have been quite a sight,
blind in my short pants and laced legs,
my corduroys open at the knees (which chilled my thighs)
and my blank face destroyed by snow
like the boy's bleak look on the antique candy box at home.

2

There was no place to get warm (Cozad's not open yet)
so I headed for the hotel, its pillars swept white.
First, I bought a jelly donut at the shop inside.
It was warm and good going down.
I was always spending my money here when they paid
for my papers in advance,
and then I was broke till next time.
It was nearly dawn in the long halls of the hotel;
it seemed everybody was asleep, husbands and wives
snoring together over the transoms and *breathing*!
and you could see the messed up beds
when the thick doors weren't tightly hitched
and had the chains on. Once at dawn
I carried my papers up there and I saw a woman
with big shadowy teats and only her nightgown on.
I saw somebody else also
under the covers. I wished they wouldn't leave their doors

open like that or that at least I wouldn't look in.
I was glad that my dead mother didn't sleep in bed,
her hair stringy like my step mom's
and I hoped she didn't see me
when I sat in that hidden corner of the hall on my
big bag and did it to myself.
My young cousin John and I had practiced in the barn—
we couldn't get it right at first
(I whirled it like a crank, but I was getting better).
I knew that I shouldn't do it, and I was afraid
my mother saw me from heaven.
I was ashamed the rest of the way around my route
and threw my handkerchief away before I got home.

3

Then once when I was grown I saw a young paperboy
going about his rounds near my home. He was thinly dressed
and I guessed he was shivering in the winter cold;
he pulled a red metal wagon behind and my mind
simply fled at once back to me.
I felt that this young boy was a double for myself.
I invited him (whose name was Jim, like my brother)
to come with me into my house
and get warmed up before he had to finish his route.
Jim came in, so I excused myself to make cocoa.
He sat on the brown couch and admired my pictures,
which are all by Northwest painters who are friends of mine.
I came back carrying the cups
and he was standing by my favorite work—a drawing
by Morris Graves: it is pencil on yellow paper
with the revision lines left in
lightly, so that the deer seems to leap out of its frame
beautifully. I felt quite moved by the boy named Jim
standing amid the pictures that I had loved so long,
and then quite simply I turned toward him and hugged him.
I was surprised when Jim hugged back:
I thought that perhaps in my eyes he had recognized

the boy whom I had for fifty years imagined dead
and I knew then that my young spirit lives on in me.
And I saw in Jim his vision of the man he'd be,
which made him seem so vulnerable to a father,
for he still must pass through pain and loss to know himself.
Our exchange of touch like art returned the world to us.

4

Pablo Neruda tells the tale of the boy next door,
a neighbor he had never seen:
one day the boy pushed a toy lamb (awkward on its wheels)
into the small hole in the wall.
Neruda took it in his hand
and ran into the house to find his prized old pine cone.
He placed it in the hole and saw the neighbor boy's hand
snatch it up quick and disappear behind the stone wall.
Neruda said poetry was like this: an exchange
between strangers, and when Jim left
he was warmed and asked to return
for a break from his hard, cold route.
I hoped that we could become friends,
the old and the young paperboys.
But with Jim's extreme youth it seemed
Neruda's wall stood between us.
So we'll grow and be satisfied in our chaste exchange.

MATINEE

So music is supposed to charm
the savage breast? Well, I'm still pissed.
You didn't show up for the concert—Shostakovitch,
Barber (Incidentally, you are barbarous to me,
for the word means "one exiled from hospitality.")
and Bruch's Violin Cocerto.
You told me you were studying
violin and I got seats up close—third row center
so you could see the performer.
Well, you'll be sorry to hear that she was fabulous:
Korean, long, black hair, she whirled
with heat in this most fiercely romantic of pieces;
a beautiful, mobile face, forehead and mouth, she moved
visibly to the music's beat
in between her own passages
when her shoulder would wed the chin to the violin
as in one sculptured instrument,
either serene or violent.
And she would wheel her black silk dress-
clad body toward the orchestra,
bow live but quiet at her side—
like some wand she wanted to raise
to conduct her own concerto.
Well, here I go. I knew I would.
I wanted you to guess what you missed.
Why, I even left a ticket for you at the door,
but you just never showed, you boor.
Yes, I confess I wanted you by my side—black curls
and young face linking the eternal melancholy
and the joy of youth to the performer on the stage
and contrasting to the gray-and-white and brave, drab dress
of the matinee audience.
Why, I am almost as old as these others are, and
I was nearly alone at the intermission bar.

I would certainly have enjoyed your company there.
And then afterwards you were meant to be the first guest
at my new apartment. Champagne
to light us into my new home!
A stereo not meant to be listened to alone.
You missed the round oak antique table, the rocking chair,
the wool tapestries hung instead of posters there,
and the large-sized couch that opens into a bed.
Wait, was that it? Were you afraid that I would try to
play musical chairs with the bed?
Oh, I probably would. You, no doubt, would have refused.
So, what's new? Perhaps only this:
I'm tired of being stood up by you. This is it.
I'll show you. I'll take an *old* friend to hear Horowitz.

CAMBRIDGE REVERIE

for Thomas O'Leary

The rust cat leaps through the gap in the screen:
We climb in the Saab and head for Stowe.
October leaves turn from green again
And we will haul the pungent apples home.

Tom and Ray and I share these rich skies.
It's not the first time. Once in Amherst
In October we swam together
Naked with Diane under the sun.

She cooked dinner for us all. We looked
Quite naked again at the table!
Guests saw us—played they didn't notice.
Tom's sandals gleamed against his bare feet.

For my part, glowing underneath my heart
I felt the deep wine warmth of friendship.
And you too might be ripened by this
As fall bugs scurry across the walks

And last flowers blaze in the dying grass.

FEBRUARY AWAKENING

for Michael and Mary Lou Rust

In the Skagit Valley, cherries
blossom quite unimagined.
It's so every spring. Still there's no remembering
of such blooming, as there is not
of each last rhythmic thrust of love.
And now the delicate blue and white striped crocus
trembles its yellow filament
when the flock of wild trumpeter swans climb to the air,
lumbering their great eight-foot wings
to leave the ground in formation with a giant "whoosh!"
as they part from the sweet roots of winter wheat they've poked
all day to fly to their nighttime keeps.

Mount Vernon, Washington, February 22, 1981

II

AVOCADO

for Robert Bly

It is a green globe like a vegetable light bulb
with a stem to meet either soil or small living tree;
it is mottled like an old man's face or is wizened
like the enormous head of a fetus. Now the stem
has come away from a navel.
It has the stolid heft of a stone. The smell seeps up
and leads the mind far away to the earth's ancient cave.
Its taste is also pungent dirt with a kind of bark
that is quite difficult to chew:
here is the small tomb of woman.
Mother smells its fresh soil even with her dead sense. She feels
its husk. Her body inside is the soft flesh of fruit,
and her heart this oval green core.
Her grief, her anger is that she
no longer has life, but the stuff of her breathes a res-
idue that has remained in earth
and in the minds of the children.
Oh, now I know her skin sighs green
as this fluted fruit: her spirit
is the taste of it, transmuted.

Honolulu, January 30, 1981

TWO POEMS OF GREECE

1   Impressions of Ydra

The scent of smoke from the oil of the Flying Dolphin
hydrofoil, moving us from Athens to Ydra.
The white turmoil of the wake itself at the ship's back,
the island of Aegina off
to the left. We dock on this quiet island (no cars)
which rises like a great amphitheater, a mesh
of cobbled streets and live white eighteenth-century homes,
waterfront cafes and gay shops.
The Mania Express, the Sironic Star, the Hermes,
the Pegasus lie at anchor,
while speed boats stream their blue-white wakes behind.
The purple bougainvillea bushes burst beside the road.
Since there are no cars, the natives
use donkeys to take you up to the monasteries;
two kids ride in a blue cart behind a donkey, too.
Very red poppies bloom on the hill beside cypress.
Water glistening on their backs,
the young Greeks dive high off the rocks,
moving among young girls sunning topless
and the very dark-tanned lounging Greeks.
We go to the second bar up—
Ydranetta, the Sunset Bar—
and the seeds from the strawberries
gather at the bottom of my glass as I watch the man
leaning forward on the bar, the hair furious black
beneath his armpit, but delicate
(feathered) on the white of his skin
where his bathing trunks separate from the dark of tan.
"Tonight Laura Live on Ydra!"
says the bright sign inside the bar.
(The fern in a pot and the candle drippings red, blue,

luminescent on the bottle.)
I wonder who Laura is and if she is a blonde,
as my friend photographs me in a black sailor's cap
fixed in space above the clear waters off Ydra.

Kalamata, Greece, June 11, 1982

2   Happening on Aegina

for Al and Daphne Poulin

The beach on Aegina is a bit tawdry, although
the island lies gorgeous beyond.
Rusted cans, a blue abandoned bic and overturned
boats, paint peeling, lying dead on the beach in the sun.
My small friend Al wades gingerly
among the rocks, legs half cut off
by water. His black socks look despairing in their shoes
left behind. What brings this scene alive is a sailboat
quite far out and glowing with a strange brightness in the light
and the goddess on the beach—Daphne, Al's fifteen-year-old
daughter lying in the sun
in a blue bikini, her luminescent body
oiled, narrow hips, narrow bosom.
Her slim body brings to mind the one pillar still standing
in the temple to Apollo
on this ancient isle of Aegina.
Except for long black hair and eyebrows, unmistakably
a girl's, she's androgynous. Suddenly, I feel she has been left behind
by that mysterious boat, its diaphanous sail
like wings just disappearing in the long twilight sun.

Aegina, Greece, June 22-23, 1983

HOMAGE TO JOHN MUIR

God himself always seems to be doing his best here, working like a man in a glow of enthusiasm.

Of all the sights in Yosemite
perhaps the first to hold our eyes
will be the Bridal Veil, a beautiful waterfall.
Its brow where it first leaps free from the cliff is about
nine-hundred sheer feet above us
and as it sways and swings in the wind, clad in the gauze
of sun-sifted spray, half-falling,
half-floating, it seems infinitely gentle and fine,
but the tones it sounds tell the solemn fateful power
hidden beneath its soft clothing.

One afternoon, John Muir, the ancient champion
of the Valley, waited at Yosemite Falls
for wind to move the column
of water so he might slip past
to look at the moon through the falls.
He was hammered hard against the rock
by the weight of falling water,
but he moved through the water and stood alone
and he watched the moon luminous and drenched
from behind the cascade of blue.

When the atmosphere is just right
on a clear and calm moonlit night,
one can see from the road a lunar rainbow in the falls,
and the gorgeous colors in it
bring to mind the landscape of another planet.
First a white arc of light and then,
as the moon rises, a shudder
of violet and reds at the edges.

(Every rock in the Valley's walls
seems to glow with life. Some lean back in royal repose.

Others, absolutely sheer or nearly so, thousands
of feet advanced beyond their companions in thoughtful
attitudes, giving welcome to storms and calms as well,
seemingly aware yet heedless of what goes on around.)

Awful in stern unmovable majesty, how softly
these rocks are adorned and how fine and reassuring
the company they keep—their feet
among amazing groves and fields,
their brows silent under the sky:
so El Capitan and Half Dome, the great monoliths,
hold heaven and earth in their span,
and the Three Brothers huddle hugely together.

"Yonder stands the South Dome, its crown
high above the camp," wrote John Muir,
"though its base is four-thousand feet
below us; a most noble rock
it seems full of thought, clothed with living light and no sense
of dead stone about it, all spiritualized,
neither heavy looking nor light,
quite steadfast in its serene strength like a very god."

A VISIT TO BILL MERWIN
AT HIS HAWAIIAN HOME

I never see red very well,
especially against a background of green and brown,
and Bill had to stop the blue, aging dusty pickup
and bring me a flower of the African tulip.
Then we bumped along the bad Maui road on our trip
to see the trees and plants. Merwin
was concerned to find the eucalyptus trees
crowding out along a low hill,
the stand of Formosan koa
which had just begun to flower,
the yellow blooms giving off a scent like mimosa,
sharp, filling up the morning air.
He was aghast at the bull-dozed
hala tree and gathered up a number of striped slips
to plant above the house with ironwoods against the wind.
We hauled the plants home. What a house!
Away from the road, it juts out
twenty-five feet over the slope
with a high-ceilinged dining room,
lanais on every side,
two studies, bedroom, kitchen and a tiny dōjo,
Japanese shrine, a Buddha with a round stone behind
and a stone incense bowl. We three
bowed, approached the Buddha, bowed again, our hands pointed,
and each lit a stick of incense
to the memory of James Wright
now dead a year this month of March.
The incense rose and billowed like the beloved white
birds of Wright over the oiled, brown eucalyptus floor.
Dana prepared a Thai dinner
of shrimp on a bed of sprouts, small delicious crab puffs,
and freshly baked blackberry cake
served on a long table from France

beautifully set for four (there was another guest)
with great ceramic plates and silver
gleaming in the big wine glasses
in the candle and lantern light.
After dinner, Bill sat in a huge reed peacock chair,
and we read poetry there, the natural light
playing fine shadows over our faces, which were rapt
with the beauty of the language,
and would you believe it: this new Hawaiin home
hummed with the tones of Rilke and the old French of Villon.

Honolulu, March 27, 1981

THE LONG SEARCH

It is a Presbyterian
old people's home. I am very
determined to find my mother.
I'm sure I see her—but lose her
at a nearby pleasant table.
I recognize her by her hair.
It shrouds her young face a wine red
or rich brown in this old neat home.
Why, everything is genial here,
and there is a room full of cakes!
The buildings are imposing, though
the chapel is a little small.
But I just heard a beautiful
chorus singing there. Now they've stopped.
All at once it is a huge church.
The room explodes suddenly
and is full of people where Mass
is being said. But not for me.
The priest averts his solemn gaze.
I'll never see my father's great eyes!
I fall to my knees at the rail
of the baroque Mary Chapel,
where bronze angels will not rise high:
"Mother," I cry. "Mother, hear me!"

HOMAGE TO JOHN THE BAPTIST

John the Baptist spoke in the great
dry desert of Judea, saying in a loud voice,
"Repent now, for the kingdom of heaven is at hand.
I am he who was prophesied in the ancient time.
I am the voice of one crying in the wilderness.
You see me dressed in camel's hair, which punishes the flesh,
and I am laced with animal hides. For my dinner,
I eat lean locusts and wild honey. I came to say,
all my life I have prepared for Him who is greater.
Why even in my aged mother Elizabeth's womb
I danced with joy when her cousin Mary visited,
big with child, with Him, and the two women placed their hands
on each other's swollen bellies.
My father, who had been made mute when I was conceived,
broke into speech again and praised God when I was born.
I speak to you to preach repentance before He comes."

Men and women, both old and young, from Jerusalem
and from all over Judea, too, came out to John
to hear his preaching and to be baptized at his hands
when they had each confessed their sins.
But when John saw many Saducees and Pharisees—
those hypocritical old priests—
coming to be baptized in the bright river, he cried,
"Oh, breed of snakes, who has taught you
to escape the great wrath ahead?
Do not expect that you can say,
'Old Abraham was our father,'
for the axe is already laid at the roots of trees,
and each tree that does not bring forth
good fruit is to be cut down and thrown into the fire."

John's beard shook out drops of baptismal water as he taught.
"I can baptize you with water for your repentance,

but He who comes after me is mightier than I,
and I am not worthy even to lace His sandals.
He will baptize with the Holy Spirit and with fire."
John's huge rolling eyes seem to glow fiery as he spoke.
"Jesus, for that is the Messiah's name, has His win-
nowing fan in His hand, and He will thoroughly cleanse
His threshing floor and will gather His wheat into the barn,
but all the chaff He will burn in an undying fire."

Then Jesus himself came down from Galilee to John
to be baptized by him, and John tried to prevent it,
catching a hold of Jesus' arm and saying to Him,
"Lord, it is I who ought to seek
baptism of Thee." Jesus said, "Now, all this is to
fulfill the letter of justice."
Then holding onto Him, John dipped the thin lord backwards
into the shivering water,
and when Jesus had been baptized,
He came up at once, body shining from the river.

Then suddenly the heavens with a loud sound opened,
and all the people gathered there
saw the Spirit of God, beautiful,
descend like a bird of many colors toward Him,
and a voice from heaven said,
"This is my beloved son, in whom I am well pleased."
Then Jesus went into the desert to be tempted
by the devil and to meet all those final horrors,
and the Baptist himself turned back
to the healing waters of the river for a time
before his awful trials at the hands of Herod
and his daughter Salome, trials ended only
when the woman, whose advances he had once rebuffed,
ordered that his martyred, severed head be brought to her
at the banquet table upon a dinner platter.

A MONTH OF SAINTS

for Daniela Gioseffi

1

Well, I am sorry to admit
I missed Mass on August fifteenth,
the Feast of the Virgin's Assumption into heaven.
Her body is here in the world
somewhere, or is that heaven home
outside our own world? In any case,
the bodies of Mary and Christ
both are still alive someplace that shall be known to us
at the center of the universe. Mary's body
suffered the anguish of adolescence and the first
menstrual flows that prepared her womb
for the fetus of Jesus planted by the angel's song.
He burgeoned in her and he swam
in her amniotic sea linked by the placenta
that pulsed with her red virgin's blood
and tied his life into woman's life as they still bind
together, man and woman's body somewhere around:
Christ, who lived his young childhood as a carpenter's aid
and underwent puberty like you and me, quite complete—
the upset of wet dreams in his fresh celibate life.
Ah, Christ, did you not suffer too,
even as you began to teach at twelve,
pains of the adolescent heart, agonies of self!
The bodies of Christ and Mary hurt and sweat as ours,
and it is our solace to know
their bodies beautifully changed
are together still, and they shine
on all relationships of men
and women, and the two of them
reflect in the androgynous

life we each of us live out, the man in the woman
and the woman inside the man.
Why, we are each of us blest by their permanent lives.

2

And I missed Mass on St. Augustine's Day, the twenty-eighth
of August: Augustine, whose lewd father leered at him
naked at his bath and battered
his wife, St. Monica, for he was an ignorant
and angry man. The young Augustine always loved to play,
and whether "nuts" or "birds" or bouts
of sin, he played the game to win.
He showed a literary streak early but hated Greek.
His mother didn't understand all his boyish pain,
although she wept and prayed hard that he would come to God.
The child also prayed in school, hoping to avoid that beating
which cuts a sensitive aesthete.
Their home was in the northern village of Tagaste where
many Roman roads crossed. The married saint was twenty-three,
the year she heard Augustine's loud complaint. She gave him
milk, but having learned to tipple
in her father's cellar as a young girl fetching wine,
she was afraid of drink, and so for all Augustine's
later sicknesses and chronic fears, Monica
only gave him tears. The saint's secret faith,
her creed, and solemn parts of Mass
she loved so well she was not allowed to tell, but when
the boy was young the sacred salt
was placed upon his tongue. It marked a claim upon him
but did not serve his need or salve her pain, and Austin's
pagan dad was little help. Monica told her son
of Christian love and asked the boy
becoming man to use his gifts for this and not for fun.
She spoke with saintly indignation of the evil
ways of fornication and begged him
not to break the laws of Christians.
He smiled at what he thought were simple words of women.

He took a mistress. Still he never could escape her
prayers no matter where he fled. She dreamed a shining youth
walked toward her, standing on a rule.
Augustine went to school where all the students danced
the Bacchic rite instead of Mass
and read the ribald book of a
native son, Apuleius' *Golden Ass*. College days
were spent in "Babylon," he later said. He watched the jigs
of courtesans around their fertile gods and saw, too,
the single-eyed or double-sexed or the missing-mouthed
mosaics preserved along the waterfront (as bright
as jars in sun) for the tourists' looks.
The Carthaginian shore also bore—too huge to have
a ticket sale—a monster reeking whale, and Austin
thought of that which carried Jonah
underneath the sea on that awful trip that alters
men sometimes and sets them free. A sea
of tears, a great fish of prayers which Monica sent her
son, bore him from his Carthaginian house of lust.
He fled from home and went to Italy. The cooling
tides of Christ reached him at Milan where St. Austin's life
and Monica's death began. As one in mystic vision,
they watched the formal lights of Christ
above the vast Ostian Sea.
"My dear God," St. Austin said, "Too late have I loved thee!"
and cried hereditary tears when his mother died.

3

Thinking of Mary's body and Austin's pagan youth,
I went to Mass on September fifteenth, the feast day
of Our Lady of Sorrows, who stood beside the tree
of Christ, pierced with the same keen sword.
The Letter to the Hebrews says on this day of Mass,
"In the time when Christ was in the flesh he offered prayers
and supplications with great cries
and tears to God who was able to rescue him from death."
This feast was a joyous time, for a young woman friend,

dressed in a suit of rust and blue,
made her first Communion at the age of twenty-two.
I learned in a bar, as we conversed the night before,
she had been baptized as a child
but had never walked to the altar rail for holy bread.
The young woman and three of her friends confessed at Mass,
and we all passed to the front of the Church through the nave
with this lovely-eyed, brown-haired girl,
an artist and so a handmaid of God's creation,
and took the host upon our tongues
and drank the holy blood from the plain brown cup of wood.
Graced and happy, then we all danced off in our small bunch
for a fine Sunday champagne brunch.
The table was top heavy with Sunday specialties —
Eggs Benedict and Florentine and freshly baked bread.
And at the table with us that good day were Austin,
Monica, and the radiant, broad
shades of the bright bodies of Mary and Christ our Lord.

III

GALLERY WALK
Fifteen Italian Drawings 1780–1890

1
Felice Giani: *Odysseus and the Greeks in the Caves of Polyphemus*

Two solemn soldiers helmeted
slosh quantities of wine into the lolling giant,
his cup held in his right hand
while his left clasps his shepherd's pipes.
The cave's stone floor is littered with empty wine flagons,
denuded armor and the cannibalized skull, rib
and limb remains of Odysseus' men.
In the middle ground, soldiers trim
the log whose point they will heat to pierce the single eye.
Polyphemus' sheep mill behind the wooden paling.
A solitary ewe on a hill in the background
overlooks the barren carnage.
The giant nearly dozes beside his massive club.
His scattered beard and hair outstart from his muddled wit.

2
Telemeco Signorini: *Study of a Nude Girl*

She has no feet but her legs are askew and her arms,
too, akimbo, like a Degas.
Her face is in profile with a disinterested smile
and her hairless young hips thrust forward their bizarre grin.

3
Vincente Cabianca: *Nuns at the Seashore*

The nuns stand with folded hands in groups of three or two.
One sits on a step of white stonework. The sea is dark,
lapis under a vivid blue sky

and overpowering sun. One casts a long shadow.
These sisters seem abstract in the light. They have great point-
ed white winged caps or coifs whose shapes suggest the gulls
that fly over in Cabianca's watercolor,
their flight caught up quick in the paint.

4

Giuseppe Cades: *The Rape of Lucretia*

His heavy metal sheath and helmet
crash on the floor before her bed.
His sword at her wrist, protectively raised, terrifies
the crying girl, her wild eyes and mouth:
it forces her face away, and her right arm pushes
at his huge muscular shoulder.
He lifts his finger to his lips,
but from the over-lush drapes
a half-hidden maid watches the rape.
Lucretia's bare breasts seem to heave
and her great navel is like another frightened eye.
Surely her still bed-garmented thighs,
the left leg already unclad,
must spread before his club-like knee.

5

Bartolomeo Pinelli: *Interior of a Roman Inn*

Beneath a frescoed basket of flowers on a wall,
with a hint of blue buds, a grinning faced and rayed sun,
and eternally crowing cock,
and a fat, naked Bacchus straddling a barrel of wine,
young life bursts at the Roman inn.
Two women and ten men flirt, argue and drink. But one's
passed out at the table, his head folded on his arms.
All ten men, even he, wear hats!
A man eyes a girl, her white blouse fat under her cloak
folded and dropped from her two hidden hands. She watches
two jaunty men, feet astride, in green and white pantaloons,

the buckle of one hung open at the knee, sleeves rolled up,
arms outflung, fingers pointing in a genial fight.
One, knees drawn up on the bench, sits alert with his pipe
contemplating the argument.
Red and brown cloaks over their shoulders, with their arms
thrown round each other, two young men
chat with a girl, her hand clapsed around a glass of wine.
Like their life her hair is hardly contained
in a blue-bowed bonnet. Her elbow on the table,
her left hand dangles quite beguiling toward her lap.
A final man sitting on this table, his left foot
drawn up on the bench, watches himself strum the guitar,
and he seems to catch us up in Pinelli's picture
to ask can this self-conscious art vie with vivid life?

6

Giancinto Gigante: *View of Lake Averno*

The olive trees reflect in the limpid lake. A man
lolls on the hill with a basket of wine and food,
and two strollers above the ruins of Apollo:
black chalk with white heightening on greenish blue paper.
But they say the vapors of this ideal pool
where now a small boat scuds across
used to kill every bird who dared to fly above it,
and the Romans tell it is the entrance to hell.

7

Giuseppe Cades: *Academic Male Nude*

The great swinging left leg is crossed in front
and the sketch has beautifully proportioned teats.
Cades ignored the modelling pole.
The profile hair is sculpted, and the marbled body
is pushed forward as in bas-relief
by the shaded, rubbed background: a paradox, the lyrical
rococo elegance of the style
and the strong neoclassic nude—

the heroic proportions of a Michelangelo
with some distortion in the left foot and the right hand.

8
Andrea Appiani: *Cartoon for Apollo and Daphne*

An erotic whirling vortex
of hinted drapery and trees.
Apollo's left foot tries to separate both of hers,
who has turned away, and his insistent hand fondles
the thinly veiled belly of Daphne.
But her hands! Her hands! Fearfully flung
over the figure of her head,
and ten fingers already burgeon,
broaden, into twigs, thick and blunt!

9
Andrea Appiani: *Tondo Portrait of Napoleon Bonaparte*

A youthful, sensitive Napoleon on circular
pink tinted paper. Straight hair to the shoulder partly
hides the black collar which frames the face,
its thoughtful mouth, its nostrils yet
unflared. The ingenuous eyes
gleam gently, their mind- and world-tearing dreams yet undreamt.

10
Vincenzo Camuccini: *Romulus and Remus*

Imagine the very moment
when the herdsman, who had discovered the two babies
floating in the River Tiber,
who did not know they were the children of Mars and who
had raised them on goats' milk as his own,
looks around a tree, staff in hand,
having just come home from the herds,
and finds the naked kids suckling the teats of a wolf!
What goes through his mind? Not, surely,

the glories of Rome the grown twins will found. Does he even see
the woodpecker, sacred to Mars, sitting in the tree?

11
Andrea Appiani: *Head of a Woman*

The luminous hair and, Leonardo-like, the soft
androgynous lines of the face.
The soul-haunting grace. In smoky
rubbed style, black and white chalk on greenish
blue paper, the mysterious Gioconda smile.

12
Antonio Canova: *Lady Reclining in a Chair*

At his death he was considered
the greatest contemporary sculptor in Europe.
Stendahl placed him among the ten
greatest men he had ever met.
Yet this giant sculptor's "Lady Reclining in a Chair"—
the elongate, abstract elegance of the grieving
woman clad in classical dress
as if from some funeral vase,
her face only suggested by three dots, her head nest-
ling into graceful, disappearing bent arms and hands
as in a dance, her fine figure
indelible as in a dream—
sears the mind with the exquisite delicacy of its ink.

13
Tomasso Minardi: *Academic Male Nude with a Staff*

The fierce expression of the man!
His black pupils rolled to the left corners of his eyes.
His right hand borne stiff above his head to hold the staff
pressed against the powerful right breast. His diaphragm
curved like the wing of an enormous bird. Belly flat.
His full pubic hair abounds, re-

peats the black chalk of the background.
His penis falls in a fecund
mature repose. From this strong man's
aggressive stance with his straight staff,
what generations might we guess that he can father!

14
Cesare Mariani: *Studies of a Reclining Female Nude*

There are three figures emerging from the blue paper
drawn from three differing angles.
All show profile head and tresses.
Two emerge as ghosts, one lying over the other.
There are a pair of disembodied feet, both well drawn,
and at the left, the hints of hands.
But only the third lower is complete,
the girl lying on her belly,
raised upon her arms which show most
of the left breast, the full buttocks,
feet crossed, her beautiful hair burgeoning down her back
in a lush and luminescent light.

15
Giuseppe Cammarano: *Amor and Psyche*

Because he warned her not to know,
they have been together only in the dark of night.
She, the soul who so wants to see the body of love,
comes to his bed at break of dawn:
she shines her lamp on him and draws
the veils of his winged limbs aside.
He raises his left arm to his sleep-filled eye, above
the muscled chest and uncovered thigh.
Why does she hold a knife in her hand?
It is the mystery of male love and female mind.

San Francisco, January 21, 1981

NIGHTHAWKS

after Hopper's Painting

A thick man with his back to us squats at the counter.
The blonde white-capped cook lingers by the complicated
aluminum coffee machine, and he does not look
at his three customers or us.
The hatted, hook-nosed man facing us
looks straight ahead, and the woman
next to him stares at what she eats.
Most of the cafe is empty.
It is garish under the neon light where details
abound: the sign for only five-cent Phillies cigars,
the glass salt and pepper shakers,
tie around the neck of the cook.
All folks seem utterly alone,
and yet the hands of the man and woman facing us
approach each other, almost touch.

SPIRIT OF THE DEAD WATCHING

after Gaugin

The body of the youthful bronze girl, her eyes fearful,
watches us, as if for escape.
She reclines on her belly, nearly half off the bed.
She is large and mysterious. Her legs are crossed,
and I can tell you she shall not be violated
although she lies quite naked here.
The mystery lies some place else.
There are three angels or devils, shooting spots of light,
hovering against the terrible purple (Gaugin
said he wanted to picture dread)
above her, and at the opposite edge of the bed
a black-coated and black-hooded
watchful figure of the living dead stands over her.
He (or she, an ominous crone?) leans against a pole.
In profile its eye oddly bright
looks straight ahead, not at us, nor
at her. The attractive girl's hair (The Spirit has none.)
lies in tresses on the pillow.
Ah, girl, must you always lie so,
half-off, half-on the bed, just as far as you can get
from the Spirit of the Dead who detracts from your youth.
Watch with me: suddenly its eye
flashes very white over you—
whose eyes are almond and afraid.

THE YELLOW CHRIST

after Gaugin

This light is the cold light of Brittany. The field holds
harmonies of green, red, yellow.
The trees, spread all through the painting,
are club shaped. They lie out of grace.
In the forefront of the painting,
The Yellow Christ hangs in mute misery from the cross.
His color shows the illness of the world he bears here.
He has no blood or bled it all
for the three peasants and the three
kids who scamper over the wall.
The kids don't care. They are off to paradigms of play.
Two peasant women of Breton
are faceless with grief at the foot
of the cross, while a third shows us a profile of peace.
So we must each of us give in
to enter the world of Gaugin
by one of four moods: grief, misery, peace, or child's play.
We are not able to ignore,
for Gaugin's art sweeps us in too sure.

THE DREAM
A Reflection on Morris Graves's Paintings

The wan enormous head bowed beside the hollow tree.
I cannot describe the bird that hovered by that head.
What was the luminescence sprung suddenly from earth
that seemed to arc between the bird's beak and the tree's root?
It echoed (or was echoed by) the eyes in the head
which led my own self into them as they slowly closed.

IV

MANHATTAN MOVEMENTS

1

My friend Daniela met us in her Subaru
after we had found our way through a crowd or two
at legendary LaGuardia,
and Tom and I went off on a prearranged sojourn
to Mother Cabrini's tomb in Fort Tryon Park—
one hundred and ninetieth street,
way out the line on the A train.
We visited her bones in their black habit with wax mask,
her skeleton which for certain will rise up again,
for that is what it means to be a saint. We knelt,
and I prayed for my family
and the new found friendship with Tom,
who is Christ's age at thirty-three.
Then we touched each other's fingers
with the holy water and walked off into the park
in the October sun. I felt young
and smiled at the aging faces
of couples sunning themselves on benches on the walks.
I am fifty-eight, but this day
was a respite from my age.
Tom and I stood by the wall and watched the passing ships
like those visions of Fellini
on the gorgeous blue-black Hudson.
We didn't talk much, both of us wrapped up in our thoughts
as we approached the Cloisters, medieval branch
of the Metropolitan Museum, monastery
carted over stone by stone from Spain
and then reconstructed around a small central court.
It is easy to be overwhelmed here where they store
what is thought to be the true chalice of Jesus Christ,
where the polychromed and gilded
wood Pietà strikes to the heart with its anguished
faces of the pierced Christ and the grieving Virgin and friends,

and where the melancholy white unicorn is penned
in a field of bright flowers bleeding from a neck wound,
its beard and tail both majestically curved, heroic.
And the crazed, craven faces of the hunters, their dogs
yelping and nipping from the threads of the tapestries.
One thanks God for the Gregorian chant which sounds there
so beautifully filling the air of the Cloisters.
Tom and I left, caught the subway,
and descended into the frenetic city again.

2

On the next day, we went to the Light Gallery
to look at the photographs of Harry Callahan.
The naked picture of his wife
Eleanor holding the hand of their small nude daughter
particularly struck me with its beauty. The two
are stepping up onto a sill
fully into the sunlight, the child just visible,
and the wife's thigh and torso are quite handsomely turned.
This photograph is the amazing color of flesh!
And who would believe the ten brilliant red tomatoes
ripening there in another scene on a blue sill?
But this frame has black behind it.
What puts the tomatoes and the nudes both on a sill
but the genius camera eye and hand of Callahan?
And the mannequin—her long forefinger gesturing
beneath her chin! Then in *Venice*
1957 an old man strides in a single
flash of light in a dark chasm
of buildings and blackened canals.
"I wish," writes Callahan, "that more people felt as I:
Photography is an adventure, the same as life."
We left the gallery and went on to drink champagne
in the loft of the rich boyfriend
of a lovely member of our party. He was gone
to L.A. and turned the loft over to us for the day.
What a scene: two floors of paintings reached by a spiral

staircase, a greenhouse and an open porch looking out
over lower Manhattan—Wall Street, World Trade Centers,
the East River and the Lady—
all drenched by sun, as the bright edge
of the Brooklyn Bridge whose cables hummed in the afternoon.
There was much pleasant talk, some of it inane,
as we friends sipped champagne and began to reel a bit,
so that some of us flopped onto the twenty-foot couch.
Tom and I went off to dinner
at Daniela's in Brooklyn Heights
where we had stayed the night before.
I remembered the time well, because I woke up once
to find I had flung my left arm over his belly
in our sleep, and as he breathed, his diaphragm rose and
fell with the young life he keeps so well.
Tom played on the piano his song, "Mannequin's Dream."
Then after fettucine, wine, and gook talk, we were off
to listen to the astounding musical statue
and all his gifted friends in Mozart's *Don Giovanni*
our last night in the city.

Buffalo, October 21, 1981

STAYING AWAKE

But we are old, our fields are running wild:
Till Christ again turn wanderer and child.

—Robert Lowell

You see, I did not want to leave,
so I kept the young couple up.
It was the reverse of the scene when Robert Lowell
read at St. John's College the year I turned twenty-eight.
I wanted to follow him wherever he would go.
I knew he was headed off to Iowa to teach,
but I had a wife and three kids.
(While she did dishes, I bathed the kids and put them to bed.
I loved their infantile white flesh and their touseled heads.)
I was teaching. I was not free to go, but I held
Lord Weary's Castle in my hand
as I hurried from class to class,
and the evening Lowell read I got high on rhyme
and his fierce family vision,
oracles that move through his verse.
I knew he was master then,
and so I wanted to apprentice myself to him.
Well, they say that I'm a master now, but on this night
when I was reading Lowell's poems with a pupil,
it grew late: I still wanted to take what the student
had to share. I am sixty, and I'm tired of giving.
So I overstayed and kept the couple up, I said,
away from their conjugal bed.

A FEAST OF FRIENDS

for Tom Lucas

Tom is a man who yearns to have his friends about him.
He moved into our part of town
last week and at once began to plan a dinner.
Tom is thin and slight and giving.
You'd like him—the shock of light brown hair and blue eyes.
He's been through Vietnam and was grazed by mortar fire.
He has a ten-year-old son Jeremy, whom he loves.
He made a rich feast of turkey—
which was light and moist—with dressing,
fresh green beans and mashed potatoes,
cooked with a special ingredient that he'd not reveal.
Tom used to run a restaurant
and so he knows what he's about.
The dinner with four friends was hilariously rich
with camaraderie and wine.
After eating, we turned more serious and read lines
of poetry to each other,
blending our loud, separate voices into one grand piece.
I told of the drinks and dinners
the Chinese writers used to celebrate together,
and there was a new Chinese rug on the floor, its threads
of blue and red and gold woven together like the ties
of friendship we all felt that night
because of Tom and because of the lordly poem.

THE ASSESSMENT

for Tom Lucas

Beloved student, what makes you think I can still teach?
You came to me the first time five
years ago. Then I was younger.
Now I'm nearly sixty years old.
My memory grows short, though my enthusiasm
is none the less. I could not teach number theory
anymore or Greek, biology, metaphysics,
as I did in my younger times—
and all of these are in my poetry, as you know.
You have been to Vietnam and you have studied Jung.
Sometimes I feel you are ahead
in what you write. You do not need
any academic weight to improve your smooth lines.
You have met Rilke, the greatest
of the twentienth century. I can't teach you him.
I can tell you to read Roethke—
that's one thing—and some Cavafy,
not for heft and greater literacy, but for soul.
And I can repeat over the two cardinal rules:
First, that poetry comes from that
part of the personality that binds two in one,
the part that loves, no matter what
the militancy of the subject matter may be.
Poetry's form always brings a temporary peace,
brings a natural form of grace.
Second, that poetry is a ballet for the ear.
Without the dance of language,
the music and rhythm, nobody believes the vision.
I've said these things to you over and over again.
Maybe in these years you can train
in the regimen of these rules,
and I'll be glad, glad again that you've come back to school.

SPRING REVELATIONS

We had begun to think the winter would never end,
but today, it was seventy. Right in the middle of April!
It was spring. Not the first.
April had fallen into snows and disap-
pointed us time and time again.
Sitting on the still brown lawn,
my friend took off his shoes and shirt.
I was surprised he had a layer of fat
above his belt. I had thought he was an athlete.
I know he loves to swim and ski.
My roommate walked inside and shaved
his beard which had disguised him the long and strict winter.
He reappeared with acne scars,
looking fresh-faced for the summer.
I sat on a case of Rolling Rock beer and talked to them,
roommate and friend, celebrating the coming of spring,
though the trees were not yet green.
Beside the porch steps crocuses—
purple and yellow—blossomed bravely, one with a bee
sniffing hopefully inside, and they reminded me
that winter never fully stays.

MY DAUGHTER'S WEDDING

It began with light lute music
in the high parlor of an old Victorian house
in Santa Cruz, Alice dressed in luminescent white,
carrying a bouquet of carnations and roses,
a garland of baby's breath in her flowing brown hair;
Marcus dressed in blue corduroy.
Then Alice's sister, Tessa, sang a capella
a lovely and simple folksong.
The minister began to read the ceremony
which Alice and Marcus helped write.
It declared how they had lived together for four years
and learned to love and trust and now wanted to make public
their vows of loyalty so they could receive support
and be free to raise a family.
They exchanged gold rings, symbolic of unending love,
and then they kissed long and deeply.
At the end, the audience sang a Bob Dylan song,
and everyone turned to champagne
and to congratulating them, the new bride and groom.
Photos were taken in every conceivable
grouping of the two families.
After feasting on hot tamale pie and salad
with their friends, Alice and Marcus
changed and came downstairs to walk through a shower of rice.
Smiling happily, they moved to their car which was dressed
with shaving cream letters and taped bouquets of flowers,
and I smiled with the deep satisfaction of fathers.

LETTER TO MY SON

Now I have no notion whether I will be able
to conjure up music and rhythm for this letter,
my well beloved son, Peter.
My senses of taste and smell are made waste by disease.
Too, I am afraid I have lost my intuitive
assay of association through sound and memory
out of which there fountains up the gift of poetry.
Peter, I feel closer to you
because you are a second son,
as I am. Second sons do not have their fathers' names
and the womb where they frame themselves
already has been entered into. Nothing is new.
But I have wanted to write you,
my fond son, for over a year,
since receiving your long letter,
a loving, articulate tribute to my own work
and my role in fostering your care for literature.
You said that I was one of your favorite writers!
Such a breath of air like lilacs
and what the French call *orange pressée*
went through my head! — and these are tastes
and odors that I have dreamed of
(which have only faint remembrance in my now dead head).
"I taste the bones of my enormous skull," Lorca said.
This has been my feeling through this eerie lack of sense.
I have been saying to myself,
"I have a *sore* on my pocket!" — so surreal it seems.
But when I reread your statement in your letter, Peter,
I seem to breathe and taste better.
Mother and I gave life to you,
and now you give life back to me.

I can't begin to tell you what it has meant to know
you chose to follow in my steps

I not only refer to the teaching of writing and literature
you may undertake and your own creation of art,
but think of your taking up drums
after I had mastered that instrument. Why, I had
learned the two sets of snare drum rudiments (thirteen each!),
the ratamacue, the triple flamacue, single
stroke roll, five stroke roll, playing them faster and faster,
then slow, and I performed at a national contest
on a blue mother-of-pearl snare
(which my teacher had on test from an instrument house)
a piece called "The Siege of Paris"
that I was told was played in the French Revolution
to guide troops in regular march.
Oh, yes, I battered great blasts from that mother-of-pearl.

I watched you on TV in Buffalo with the Youth
Orchestra of Oakland—your wild, long, blonde hair blowing
and bending in the pulse of drums.
I knew and loved that you followed me—the absent one,
the father who (for reasons I will not go into
in this letter) left the young needy family and,
with help from you and the other beautiful kids, packed
the mahogany and walnut table and the green
fluted glass and brass study lamp and the stereo
into the long, light brown DeSoto station wagon
to move alone into a tiny square, black-and-white
studio as new as me. I remember saying
out loud, in that single room with a shelf divider,
"This is just between you and me. I must get to work
on my piece, 'The House That Jack Built'"—
which I think, Peter, is a favorite of yours.
I'll never forget how that began—one Easter Day
when the entire family had its picture taken
outside the gaunt brick Sacred Heart Church at Notre Dame
and I, of course, stood the highest over all the children.
It was at that moment I decided to write down
everything that I could remember about my own
childhood, and structure the piece by association.

I think, in some way, I was jealous of my kids.
Not that my own childhood had been so happy either—
but like the poet Stephen Crane says of his bitter
heart upon biting into it—
I like it because it is mine.

To stray for a moment to that story which you like,
I wrote down everything that I could remember from
my childhood—my earliest memory of turning
a corner in a wagon on moving day with some
unknown thing beside me (I thought it was my brother
or else a laundry bag)—from then
until age thirteen or fourteen,
when the world changes because of sex
and you begin to wonder, at least in retrospect,
if there is something wrong with you if you haven't fucked yet.
Hence, the end of the piece, "One shoe off and one shoe on./
Diddle diddle dumpling my son John."
I remember with shame poking fun at you one time,
saying, "Peter doesn't know the meaning of the word
fuck." I was cruel. It was my duty to teach you.
John was the only one of all my six sons I taught.
It was on his tenth birthday, and I can remember
we were walking down Lincoln Way West toward downtown.
He said the good nuns had told him
his dick could only carry waste, and I set him straight.
We went to the only football game at Notre Dame
I ever saw—(I always thought
I would go, if they had bull fights!)
Strange thing about that game, Peter:
it was played against Navy, who were the better team,
and they were colorful in blue and gold jerseys
(Notre Dame played in their drab green.)
Confused by blue and green, I did not know till later,
the losing team was Notre Dame!

John and I went to one baseball game in Chicago,
and I wrote a piece about it,
feeling some shame for doing so.

But then a part of the occupational hazard
of the writer is that he's not sure what has happened
to him till he's written it down.
I recall taking you, Peter,
to a baseball game in that damn cold Candlestick Park.
I'm afraid I remember the hotdogs and beer best.
I've always had trouble with sports.
I have imagined that it was because I never
wanted to compete with my brother
who, like my father as a boy, was gifted at sports,
even though he had bad eyes and had to wear a mask
to protect corrective glasses.
So, as I said in a poem,
I was in the marching band instead.
I just couldn't follow the games.
(Perhaps my eyesight was bad—perhaps
I didn't watch.) I did love playing the marches, though.
It got so bad I would come home
from a game and, after washing out my socks downstairs
as was required by my mom,
I would try to sneak past their room
without my father asking me
in a loud censorious voice,
"Jack, who won?"—and I didn't know.
But I knew that we'd played Sousa's "El Capitan March"
with the drum solo! That was *my* game.
I remember having to go to the baseball games
with my father and my brother
and looking out the back of the stands with green envy
at the kids whirling by in the wild carnival rides.

Fishing! That was another matter. I didn't care
much for that either, except once,
when I was alone with my brother
and we fished and swam together naked in the river.
I think it was the nakedness
I liked most, not the ugly bullheads and the catfish.
But you, Peter, you were a fisher. You won the test

among the kids in the summer
at Necedah. Why, I think you caught 21 fish,
which is the same number of pancakes I ate to win
the contest at the summer camp when I was a kid.
We ran out of real syrup and had to use jelly!
That was the summer we named Junior Johnson "Doctor,"
because he cut up a frog he caught.
He also broke up when we sang
"When I grow too old for dreams," because his young voice cracked,
and he pissed on the unzipped tent
we were lying on. As it dried,
we slept under the open stars.
I found those naked stars over the lake as fresh as
the first shimmering lights of Hawaii we sighted
after many days and nights at sea...
To get back to your fishing prowess, my dear Peter,
I remember you dragged a pike
down the main street of the town to weigh it on the scales.
My son, you were a small Jonah. It was your big whale.

Then, when you followed me to Buffalo, I was touched.
I know you decided on that school partly because
I was there. You and I had a fine trip to New York,
stayed at the Chelsea Hotel and visited my friend,
Isabella Gardner, whom I always remember
in a green silk dress invading
you nine kids at the Oak Street house
in South Bend. We made an aborted try to visit
the grave of Melville, your namesake—
(He is your mother's ancestor.)—
we started out too late: it takes
an hour to get out to Woodlawn Cemetery
on the Lexington Line. Well, another time, we said.
The train ride back to Buffalo was fun and noisy.
I drank beer and pondered the scene.
In Buffalo, I knew you wanted to live with me,
but I was too selfish—too jealous of my lifestyle
which included a lot of drinking and other men.

I remember the new apartment on Linden Street
where you found a small space you thought you might fit into
along the ugly brown tufted rug. But I said no
and took on an easy, familiar roommate. You went
to a single room some distance
from school and trudged there through the terrible winter snow,
stopping at our friend Angela's
for the breakfast I did not offer. I remember
taking you to dinner once or twice
—always with others, not alone—where we might have talked.
I can see you grizzled with snow
in your navy peacoat, having walked the several blocks
to my Linden Street place to improvise piano jazz,
music you so loved. I offered
money (stingily I am afraid), but you said no,
"Just take me to dinner once in a while." I was a
real shit, I confess, not much help,
even when you suffered the agonies of the draft,
writing your tough conscientious objector statement
on my desk. I could have helped. You got sick at that time
and you coughed all night without sleep in your single room
filled with your stereo, your legacy from Berkeley.
I visited you in the school infirmary once,
and I knew that your problems went far beyond a cold.
You took a job in a liquor store delivering
bottles to places that you had to find on a map,
then some way find your way home in that endless winter
to write short stories for John Barth.

I would give anything now if I could change that time
and be a help to you, my son.
I feel I always disappointed you and I know
once you dreamed I died. Was that when
the coleus you raised from a seedling and gave me
at Christmas time tumbled over in its pot in the rain
and washed away? I should have taken better care of it.
Oh, I should have taken better care of you, my son!
I remember only once I bought you anything—

a pair of corduroys on Telegraph Avenue
at Christmas time, and I swear I felt
that I was Santa Claus himself!
And now in your adulthood you are a beautiful
young man. Your small moustache, which I quarreled with at first
because it hid part of your face,
I now like. I remember when I grew a moustache,
my mom said she would not kiss me
unless I shaved it off. I tell you, I left it on.
I like your wife Cathy, but for some reason could not
remember her name for a time.
I've admired your fine, tenacious home-making gifts—
watched you rework the windows in termite-proof metal
and scour the fireplace until the square, ceramic tiles
emerged, and some were beautiful.
You and Cathy made a lovely house—Paul stripped the floors.
You nurtured a lively garden, too,
and I especially admired the strawberries, which
I had never been able to grow at home. I tire
of hoeing but I love the harvest. Now I believe
that you love both and planted a tree in the front yard.
You were full of hope. I am full of hope for you now.
Why, you may choose to follow me
in the writing and the teaching of literature.

I yearn to share my knowledge and my love of books with
you. I want to tell you: Derek Traversi is my
favorite commentator on Shakespeare, except
for that remarkable book of Ernest Jones on Freud
and *Hamlet*—and that Norwegian,
whose name I forget, on *Hamlet*
and the Orestes myth. Eric Fromm is exciting
on the Sophoclean Trilogy—the mystery
of the maternal and the paternal tug of war.
But it was I who discovered
that the drama *Antigone* is really about
the struggle between the masculine
and the feminine element

inside the self. I found this out
because seminars were always
evenly divided between the men and women
as to who the hero is—Antigone or Creon—
this and Creon's statement, that if he gave in to her
and allowed her brother to be buried, he would then
be giving in to the woman's part of himself.
I much preferred Euripides'
version of the *Hippolytus* to Racine's *Phèdre*,
because Racine introduces a girlfriend for him,
and Hippolytus' choice is not between women,
but between his boyhood, with his horses and his bows,
and the mature world of sexuality and women.
And what about Jocasta's word
to Oedipus that many a man had dreamed as much—
that he had married his mother?
If that is the manifest content of the dream,
what, then, is the latent content?
I believe it is the desire
to remain long in the infant high chair, so to speak,
to keep one's dependency on the mother figure.
Oh, what a horror it must have been for Oedipus
to realize this, when he believed he was the king!
And Oedipus had to leave Thebes
to make his news available to the rest of Greece,
so he was assumed into heaven at Colonus,
as Jesus was assumed—or is the term assumpted?
And didn't Hamlet die for us
so that we would not have to undergo his torment?
My son, I would share with you these mysteries art probes
and the intricacies of Joyce,
whom we both love: Bloom is heart, Molly flesh, Stephen mind,
and the three together make up the man Ulysses.
So I would teach and have you listen, my beloved son.

San Francisco, February 3, 1985

THE GIFT

Your gift to me was like a girl
dressed in white (beautiful!) bringing
me a glass of cold fresh water from the lucid spring.
Your gift was like the quick vision
of a pair of swift roan ponies
galloping together along a wild, white sand beach.
Like the sight of two young people
making love with tenderness in a field of flowers,
whose blossoms are of a deep rich indigo and wine.
Your gift was like a small pillar
covered with lapis lazuli.
A girl shaking out her long hair.
Like the naked back of a man
washing, the view caught just as he bends to the bronze pan.
Like the taut neck of a guitar
trembling with the music it gives.
The hand of a friend extended.
I felt it was the green burst of light after the sun
goes down so slowly out at sea.
Your present was of the flesh and so much more beside.
All that I will give back again.
This is my testament of love.

John Logan was born in Red Oak, Iowa, in 1923. He received a B.A. in Biology from Coe College (1943), an M.A. in Language and Literature from the State University of Iowa (1949), and he did graduate work in Philosophy at Georgetown University and at the University of Notre Dame. A master teacher—many of whose students have become distinguished American poets— John Logan taught Creative Writing and Literature at St. John's College (1947-1951), the University of Notre Dame (1951-1963), the University of Washington (where he succeeded Theodore Roethke in 1965), San Francisco State University (1965-1966), and the University of Hawaii (1975-1976). From 1966 until his retirement in 1985, he was Professor of English at the State University of New York at Buffalo.

In addition to publishing several major volumes of poetry, a fictionalized autobiography, and a collection of critical essays, John Logan also served as Poetry Editor for *The Nation* and *The Critic*. Moreover, with the internationally re-knowned American photographer, Aaron Siskind, he was Founding Co-Editor of *Choice*, a journal of poetry and graphics.

For his last two books published simultaneously in 1981, *Only the Dreamer Can Change the Dream: Selected Poems* (The Ecco Press) and *The Bridge of Change: Poems 1974-1979* (BOA Editions, Ltd.), John Logan was awarded both The William Carlos Williams Award for Poetry by The Poetry Society of America and The Lenore Marshall Prize for Poetry by the New Hope Foundation and *The Nation* magazine. Logan's other awards and distinctions for his poetry included a Writing Grant from The John D. Rockefeller Foundation (1969), Summer Writing Fellowships from The Research Foundation of the State University of New York (1970 and 1979), The Morton Dauwen Zabel Award for Poetry from The American Academy and Institute of Arts and Letters (1973), a Fellowship from the John Simon Guggenheim Memorial Foundation (1979-1980), a Creative Writing Fellowship in Poetry from the National Endowment for the Arts (1981), and the Robert and Hazel Ferguson Memorial Award for Poetry from The Chicago Foundation for Literature (1982).

John Logan died on November 6, 1987, in San Francisco, California, survived by Guenevere Logan and their nine children, John, Tessa, Tina, Peter, Stephen, Alice, Mark, David, and Paul.

BOA EDITIONS, LTD.
AMERICAN POETS CONTINUUM SERIES